THE
PLAYWRIGHT'S
TOOLBOX

THE PLAYWRIGHT'S TOOLBOX

Exercises from 56 Contemporary Dramatists
on Designing, Building,
and Refurbishing Your Plays

JUSTIN MAXWELL

APPLAUSE
THEATRE & CINEMA BOOKS

Essex, Connecticut

APPLAUSE
THEATRE & CINEMA BOOKS

An imprint of Globe Pequot, the trade division of
The Rowman & Littlefield Publishing Group, Inc.
4501 Forbes Blvd., Ste. 200
Lanham, MD 20706
www.rowman.com

Distributed by NATIONAL BOOK NETWORK

Library of Congress Cataloging-in-Publication Data

Names: Maxwell, Justin (Professor), author.
Title: The playwright's toolbox : exercises from 56 contemporary
    dramatists on designing, building, and refurbishing your plays / Justin
    Maxwell.
Description: Essex, Connecticut : Applause, [2024] | Summary: "A
    stimulating and wide-ranging resource for both beginning and
    experienced dramatists, comprising invigorating, provocative, and
    irreverent exercises contributed by nearly 60 contemporary English-
    language playwrights, covering all stages of the writing process" —
    Provided by publisher.
Identifiers: LCCN 2023049997 (print) | LCCN 2023049998 (ebook) |
    ISBN 9781493077823 (paperback) | ISBN 9781493077830 (epub)
Subjects: LCSH: Playwriting. | Drama—Technique.
Classification: LCC PN1661 .M328 2024 (print) | LCC PN1661 (ebook) |
    DDC 808.2—dc23/eng/20240214
LC record available at https://lccn.loc.gov/2023049997
LC ebook record available at https://lccn.loc.gov/2023049998

∞™ The paper used in this publication meets the minimum requirements
of American National Standard for Information Sciences—Permanence of
Paper for Printed Library Materials, ANSI/NISO Z39.48-1992

CONTENTS

Preface: The Duck Anecdote   vii

1   *How to Use This Book*   1

2   *Prewriting*   43

3   *Drafting*   97

4   *Revision*   149

5   *Techniques and Tactics*   231

Appendix: Dramatic Format   253

About the Contributors   257

PREFACE

THE DUCK ANECDOTE

Like many self-serious young men, I wanted to be a poet. I liked poetry's layered emotions and abstraction, but I was in it for my ego. Back then, I had no interest in playwriting because I didn't want my precious words getting mixed up with all the other things of theatre—actors and the like. Most of the theatre I saw as a child was terrible. Growing up in rural, western New York between pockets of Rust Belt dereliction meant that the theatre I was exposed to was museum somber or surface flashy. Plus, the sets were obviously sets, and the actors were obviously actors. I wasn't interested.

By grad school, I dealt with the worst of my ego and was merely difficult instead of unbearable. I was hungry to learn instead of just talk. Somewhere in that process, I had the epiphany that genre was just another tool writers had to make art. I was an artist working in language, and I could move between genres to use whichever one served the art best—thank you for putting up with me, Mary Francois Rockcastle, Roseann Lloyd, Sheila O'Connor, and Deborah Keenan.

Simultaneously with the realization about genre, I encountered the work of Eugène Ionesco, who embraced the heady and the ridiculous. His work, then about a half-century old, showed me that most of my conceptions of theatre were misconceptions. I am deeply grateful to have been so wrong. Ionesco did breathtaking things with those obviously fake sets and talky actors. His work never asked for my willful suspension of disbelief; an actor in a costume saying words was an actor in a costume saying words. When I found out that Ionesco was within a tradition, I got an opportunity to read voraciously, which I really loved. I could read back in time to his predecessors, like Gertrude Stein, Tristan Tzara, and Alfred Jarry, and then forward to people like Adrienne Kennedy, Richard Foreman, and María Irene Fornés.

Fortunately, I could do more than read because I was surrounded by the vibrant theatre community of the Twin Cities—thank you, Playwrights' Center—and I could see theatre that was profound, vibrant, and substantive. When I actually took a playwriting class—thank you, Patricia Weaver Francisco—it held a new epiphany every week.

I never thought, "I'll be a playwright," but I saw how all the other artists in theatre heightened the immediacy of the art. My poems were almost exclusively persona poems, really just odd monologues wherein a character narrates the text. My fiction was dialogue driven with sparse narration, which was a lot like stage directions. Without ever intending to, all my work turned into drama. Plus, my dramatic writing was producing better drafts from less work. The one-act play I wrote in that first class became my first production—thank you, Greg Giles.

Pushing further into this exciting genre, I worked with John Fenn, an elder statesman of the Twin Cities theatre community. In our first meeting, I talked about the deeply weird stuff I wanted to write. He handed me a playwriting how-to book and said, "Read this so you'll know all the rules you'll be breaking." I never looked back—thank you, John Fenn!

In the decades since, I've read lots of writing books and made my students read them, too. They're valuable. As I write this preface, there's a stack of them on my desk, surrounded by still-ungraded student manuscripts and drafts of this book. If those books did what this book does, I'd be working on my next play instead. I wanted to make this book because of all the people I met who heard my odd, difficult, challenging, or stupid ideas and responded by saying, "Theatre has space for that." It was an expansive and welcoming experience. I got to write whatever I wanted to write because theatre could contain it.

When that freedom on the page was coupled with the evocative addition of real people and physical objects, I found an opportunity to make art out of language and move it to an immediate physical reality. At some point in grad school, I and another writer were joking about why we were falling in love with this genre, and there was an epiphany: If a fiction writer wanted to have Che Guevara walk into a room wearing a prom dress and carrying a duck, then that writer would have to spend pages of prose to get their reader to believe that moment. But, when Che Guevara walks onstage wearing a prom dress and carrying a duck, the audience just thinks, "What's he gonna do with that duck?" They don't have to believe it because they see it. I had come a long way and owed a debt to big-hearted writers whom I can never repay.

I learned a lot from textbooks and personal essays about writing and sitting through every artist talk I could attend. The Twin Cities were (and are) a big community of supportive allies who helped me mature into an artist without ever telling me drama is made in just one way. Consequently, I wanted a book that didn't tell people how to write or what to write. *The Playwright's Toolbox* comes from the notion that there's no one way to make a play and more than enough room for everybody. There's a near-infinite variety of actions that can be theatre. There are many excellent playwriting books out there. However, they tend to fall into two categories: either (1) an author articulating what they do and making it universal or (2) a collection of essays that are deeply abstract. While I'm guilty of such sins in chapter 1, hopefully my overt guilt makes it a venal sin. This book is designed to be concrete and practical at every turn, thus the toolbox metaphor. It's important to know how the tools work because with that knowledge somebody can build what they want to build.

There are countless people to thank in the team sport of theatre. Thank you to Lisa D'Amour and Caridad Svich for supporting this book from the beginning; to Sara Farrington, whose experience making *The Lost Conversation* was invaluable at the start of this journey (anyone this far into the preface really needs to read it); to Reginald Edmund and the *Black Lives, Black Words* collection and the bravery it carries into the world; to Leanna Keyes and *The Methuen Drama Book of Trans Plays* for the voices it brings to the foreground; to Farrah Cukor at United Talent and Lynde Rosario at the Playwrights' Center for being so willing to engage and connect; to previous Playwrights' Center leaders who sustained that sustaining institution, including P. Carl, Hayley Finn, and Jeremy Cohen; to Chris Chappell at Applause for patience, trust, and freedom while I made this super-complicated book and wrestled with long COVID; to Ross Peter Nelson, T. L. Jacobson, Season Ellison, and Ashley Hemm, who offered invaluable feedback on drafts; to Liz Hutter, who helped when I was sick and scared; to the Twin Cities theatre community, who was always glad to see me; to the great theatre makers in New Orleans, who welcomed me when I washed up on their muddy shore; to the long list of amazing writers who cheered on this manuscript even though they couldn't contribute. Also, my apologies to the handful of writers who got crazy emails from me before I realized what long-COVID brain fog was and to the folks who got crazy emails after I realized it. A final thank-you to the Creative Writing Workshop at the University of New Orleans. I'm blessed to have colleagues who unflaggingly buoy me up and dedicated students whose classroom experiences were the rough drafts of this book.

May *The Playwright's Toolbox* help your writing be a little easier.

1

HOW TO USE THIS BOOK

WHAT IT IS

The Playwright's Toolbox is a practical, hands-on guide to improving dramatic-writing skills. This book helps playwrights make the scripts that they want to make in order to build the theatre they want to see in the world. We need a panoply of voices in the contemporary theatre, thus the diverse contributors to this collection. The *Toolbox* is an attempt at making space for many voices to help readers gain mastery over their own!

As with high-quality carpentry, playwriting requires a host of complex, interconnected skills. This chapter lays out the structure of the book and the main ways it can be used to help make better plays more efficiently. It expands on the toolbox metaphor of the title and provides an overview of the writing process itself. Some of these tools are applicable to the writing process overall, and some have more particular applications. Because every craftsperson has strengths and weaknesses, this book is designed to help writers with the various components and skills of writing.

The *Toolbox* takes a fundamentally different approach to the process of playwriting. Conventional writing books almost invariably steer their readers toward the approach of their author or offer collections of personal essays. Some subjectivity is inevitable, including my little manifesto later in this chapter. For new writers, copying a single author's personal approach can feel desirable because the more established writer has accomplished the things the beginning writer aspires to. However, this approach can pass biases and assumptions from one generation to the next and conflates cultural and individual preferences with maxims and absolutes. Instead of an individual's singular approach, this book presents a host of master craftspeople offering their insights into the use of various tools. Imagine walking into a hardware store and having Norm Abram there to explain his insights into a table saw or entering a music store and having Jimi Hendrix offer his thoughts about selecting guitar strings. They're not telling us how to build a desk or play a song but how to improve so we can go back and build the furniture we want or play the music inside us. After all, good carpenters don't simply unbox a new router and make a masterful cabinet. Instead, they learn the tools of their craft individually and collectively. They learn how to use that router with more complex bits and more involved cuts. Then they make that cabinet.

Later, that carpenter might want to make a drawer, so they go from using the router for detail work and shaping to cutting a rabbet joint. They'll want to diversify their skills. Consequently, after this chapter, the *Toolbox* is nonlinear. It can be used like a literal toolbox, the contents of which the reader can pick and choose from. A beginning writer might start at the beginning of the next chapter with Azure D. Osborne-Lee's "Feed Your Obsession" and move straight through the book to Erik Abbott's "Last Things First (Sort Of)" in chapter 4. A more experienced writer, though, might come to the book and select a specific device they want to hone. For example, a writer who wants to develop better characters might jump to something like Deborah Yarchun's "Character and Language" or L M Feldman's "Said and Unsaid." However, this same writer might return to Yarchun's exercise when they're a few drafts into a play and find themselves struggling, just like the carpenter who's able to shape wood for a chair might need to return to improve other skills before building their first drawer.

HOW IT WORKS

This chapter offers an overview of the writing process called "The Writing Wheel." The wheel isn't a breakdown of how we make "good" plays but of the order of operations for effective writing. It's about what tool to use when—or at least my take on it. The wheel breaks down into four broad segments: prewriting, drafting, revision, and proofreading. After all, whether a carpenter is building a desk or a chair, they make blueprints first and stain last. While one could stain wood first, it's a colossal waste of resources. So the purpose of the wheel is to help writers consciously structure their time and energy to be of maximum service to the writing. It also provides a useful structure for the book, keeping the various tools easy to find.

In the later chapters of this book, the book follows the wheel, and individual playwrights' contributions are organized by where they're most likely to be useful in the writing process. Of course, many contributions could go in several sections, and many could go in other sections with only minor changes. Use the exercises in whatever way is practical for you. For example, Gary Garrison's "Uniquely You" is in the "Revision" chapter because it helps develop characters who already exist in the script; however, because Garrison's contribution ties to dialogue, it might help a few writers in drafting, too. There's no reason a particularly exciting exercise can't be useful to an individual writer at some other point of the writing process.

The next chapter is "Prewriting," with exercises designed to help begin the process of writing a new play: what we do before we write a draft and why. Then comes "Drafting," with skills that help to get a crude first draft down on the page. These are the things that help us make the vaguely ordered pile of words that we later shape into art. After "Drafting" is "Revision," where we labor to shape the words from drafting into an evocative text. This is where the serious work of writing gets done, as we consciously focus on the major elements of craft. Eventually, the writing process finishes with proofreading, where we make a manuscript polished and professional. The writing contributions to the book conclude with the chapter "Techniques and Tactics," which contains valuable ideas that don't fit comfortably into any of the previous chapters. Biographies of the contributors are collected at the end of the book, so readers can explore the art made by these contemporary master craftspeople. Their writing is a resource in and of itself. After all, their practices are valuable, and their works are the manifestation of those approaches or the perspectives that generated them. (One of the things this book can't do is make writers read a lot of plays and see a lot of theatre. The *Toolbox* makes up for that by introducing a lot of writers who are worth exploring.) Finally, an appendix lays out conventional dramatic formatting to show how a play should generally appear on the page.

WHY IT WORKS LIKE THIS

This book works like it does for some important reasons that all lead back to the pragmatic reality that there's no absolute right or wrong way to write a play. At least, that's my opinion on the matter. The writing process is simply the application of tools and imagination. Those applications vary from writer to writer and from project to project. Consequently, if a writer thinks about writing as something with a singular right way, then they end up writing only in that way, which doesn't necessarily work from one script to the next. A woodworker building a utilitarian tool shed does things differently than when they make a hand-carved grandfather clock. As writers take on new challenges or encounter unexpected obstacles in new drafts, they can come back to the relevant exercises of the book and apply the tools to help resolve those obstacles.

Sometimes frustrated or new writers will ask a question like "Why not just tell me how to write a play?" Sometimes they'll do it with an exclamation point after the question mark. The problem is that two assumptions are buried in the subtext of the question: that there's one right way to write a play and that there's only one aesthetic outcome possible. This book denies those assumptions, which are often unconscious and come from a place of surreptitious cultural bias. Leaving them unacknowledged makes the work of writing harder and less fulfilling.

There's a breathtaking range of material that constitutes a "good" play. Anyone looking at the work of the contributors to this book will see how writers can differ radically from one another; plays by Young Jean Lee look different from plays by Lavinia Roberts. There can be wide aesthetic variation within the individual oeuvres of our more prolific contributors, like Caridad Svich and Adam Szymkowicz. For a carpenter looking to make bookshelves, there are vast differences between an IKEA showroom and the library at Trinity College—yet both have their place. If one can't imagine both outcomes or the infinite variety in between, then they're limited in what they can build. Knowing what the tools can do increases what we can imagine.

Moreover, *good* is a slippery word. I can say, "This is a good jelly donut," and "Mother Teresa was a good person," but if I say, "This jelly donut is as good as Mother Teresa," then I've said a serious non sequitur. However, writers can fall into the psychological trap of saying they want to make a good play without realizing that's not a viable path to make art. We need to do something else instead.

We need to make the art we want to see in the world. It's an aphorism that floats through the writing community, and it's valuable. Assumptions about a "good" play can deeply limit our work as artists. Some of the most powerful and moving things I've seen in the theatre have stood in direct aesthetic contrast to one another. The fact that such contradictions are even possible shows how arbitrary the term *good* really is. Personally, I go to the theatre looking for things I've never seen before and emotional landscapes I've never imagined. If I were going in with a preconceived notion of *good*, then I'd never find them. Worse, I'd dismiss innovative work, which by definition can't play by preestablished rules. If we make art that fits someone else's definition of *good*, then we hinder ourselves. If we try and make art through someone else's process, then we struggle to fulfill our own needs. There are several contributions to help with that fulfillment, including Rachel Lynett's "The Worst Play (a.k.a. Get Out of Your Own Way)." As the architect Frank Lloyd Wright famously said, "If the roof doesn't leak, the architect hasn't been creative enough."

Similarly, "good" is often shorthand for cultural biases. The dominant culture often defines *good* by ticket sales or critical reviews, which is deeply problematic for us as artists. If one isn't served by the dominant culture and its most popular modes, then one probably wants to make work that interrogates, parodies, or ignores them. In a masterwork like August Wilson's *Fences*, he appears to tell a conventional narrative wherein a protagonist's desires drive the plot of the story through rising and falling action. Yet Wilson denies that convention by killing his protagonist well before the end of the show. Had Wilson taken the path of tradition, his masterpiece would probably still have won a Pulitzer Prize, but it probably wouldn't have been one of the best narrative works of the twentieth century. Wilson is such a master of storytelling that his narrative continues to have high stakes after the protagonist's death.

The writers in this collection don't tell us what we must do. Instead, they're telling us how tools can be applied. In some contributions, we might discern some things about their own process, or they might reveal themselves when we use the exercise, but these moments illustrate practical applications or unique interpretations. Sometimes we want a hand-carved newel post; other times, we need a 4" × 4" post bolted down so our stairs pass the safety inspection.

In contrast to worrying about good writing, assuming a draft is irredeemably bad is the other side of the same coin. There are no bad drafts, just drafts in need of more revision. After all, we're building something with these tools. Fortunately, unlike woodworkers, it's much easier for language workers to change blueprints or recut the material or keep working on the project until it does what we want.

An intuitive notion of good writing is often intimately related to the idea of how a story works, but such ideas can create problems for writers. While Joseph Campbell saw universality in the monomyth, or hero's journey, there's a lot of selection bias in that intellectual trope. The relationship between how members of a culture understand story is something for the theorists and the anthropologists. As craftspeople, we need to be aware that there are many ways to make art out of language, and whether we're within the bounds of cultural convention or outside them, we need to make that choice consciously. After all, if we follow the cultural rules or if we defy them, we should do so as a choice, not by following a subconscious impulse toward the "good."

The cultural idea of good writing often gets conflated with a sense of universality, and this confusion can be a tough hurdle to clear for some writers or some projects. Contributions like Liz Duffy Adams's "The Bad Play" and Sara Farrington's "The Most Boring Play in the World" are helpful for writers struggling with the idea of "good" writing. Fortunately, this universality is a mistaken perspective coming from a dominant cultural mode that simply looks ubiquitous. What seems natural is merely dominant. We can see this illusion with a quick overview of the two main literary modes that dominated Western art making in the twentieth century. When Romanticism reached its peak in the late nineteenth century, it seemed like the way that art should be made. Of course, artists resisted this hegemony and split into two general approaches: the representational and the nonrepresentational. While there are hundreds of schools, styles, camps, and modes of art making and libraries of ingenious criticism and insight, this simple dichotomy provides a solid starting point. Anyone wanting to explore further can find works about the rise of modernism and its replacement by, or maybe reemergence as, postmodernism, which can keep an obsessive reader busy with many doctoral dissertations' worth of ideas. Personally, I think such reading is deeply valuable, but to get into using the tools of playwriting only requires openness, passion, and curiosity.

Both representational and nonrepresentational work are reactions to the "good" art of the Romantic writers like Goethe, Hugo, Wordsworth, and Shelley. One broad aesthetic wanted artists to represent the world accurately, which gave rise to the realistic writers, like Chekhov and Ibsen, whose influence dominated the early twentieth century. The other broad aesthetic wanted to push deeper into the subconscious and the abstract, which gave rise to nonrepresentational movements like Dadaism and Surrealism and writers like Gertrude Stein and theatre makers like Tristan Tzara. Then the world wars and influenza pandemic shattered Western culture in a way that's hard to even comprehend. While I've lost their name to the mists of memory, I once heard a historian say that because of technological and cultural changes over the last century, the year 1900 is more like the year 1600 than 2000, and I have yet to see evidence against this idea. Reacting to this global social upheaval, some artists wanted a more representational theatre, like Eugene O'Neill, while others wanted more abstraction, like Eugène Ionesco. And a few moved between these modes, like Tennessee Williams. These traditions carry on into the contemporary moment, with powerful work being made with both approaches. The writers contributing to this collection come from multiple aesthetics across the contemporary landscape. Whatever the carpenters build, they all use the tools.

Psychological realism, with a narrative that follows a traditional dramatic arc, might feel natural, like the real world, but it's simply the cultural mainstream. While artists may want to write realistically for a complex host of valuable reasons, realism, like any other tool in the box, is one that should be picked up consciously. Different groups and identities all have different ways of experiencing the world and different things they want to say about it—thus the need to make different kinds of theatre. This book is designed to support that need with skills and training in this quick exploration of unconscious bias and conscious choices.

If you're a writer worried about stepping on cultural toes, then good. With centuries of cultural misappropriation as the norm for mainstream Western society, stopping to think of the well-being of others and making a point not to harm those with less cultural power is an invaluable step forward. Writers struggling with this moment of cultural growth will find books like *The Anti-Racist Writing Workshop* by Felicia Rose Chavez are excellent starting points. When such steps are taken, writers have space to make art that engages, explores, and challenges instead of simply serving the self.

DIVERSITY OF VOICES

To try to honor a multiplicity of voices, the *Toolbox* lets contributors speak for themselves. It does not speak for them. The contributors were given a general template and a sample, which they could use, ignore, repurpose, or subvert as they saw fit. After all, an inclusive book—one that starts by saying there isn't one way to write—can't turn around and make all its contributors do things one way. The contributors are using the tools, too. Some contributing writers have major awards, Obie wins, and Pulitzer nominations. Some have hundreds of productions. Some are only recently out of grad school. They cover a panoply of sexualities and genders and a spectrum of racial and cultural identities. In the contemporary moment, our ancient craft is practiced by a truly complex cadre of people, and all those perspectives add to the pragmatic application of these exercises. These differences are a strength and increase the overall accessibility of the material. Reginald Edmund says it concisely as he concludes his contribution, "Major Dramatic Question," with the simple call to action: "Write your revolution!"

TWO PATHS

As mentioned at the start of this chapter, there are two general ways to move through this book. First, a writer who is stuck or struggling with part of a play can leap to specific skills, allowing them to improve particular elements of the craft to target their weak spots or get unstuck. For example, a writer who can't make crisp dialogue even though they have compelling characters might skip ahead to Jon Elston's "The Michelangelo." If the dialogue doesn't sound authentic, head to Carmin Wong's "Toolbox for the Theatrical Lyricist: Our Language." If the new protagonist lacks depth, then there are many options, including Sheri Wilner's "Real Estate" and Alice Tuan's "Building from Viscera." If the plot is missing something, then Becky Retz's "The Organization Arc" or Lisa D'Amour's "Expanding the Matter of Your Play" are both worth a look. Because writing is never the same experience twice, writers who want to grow, explore, or take on evocative new ways of presenting a text should look at Kristina Wong's "The World's Longest Preshow Metadisclaimer." A writer who made representational plays but now wants to try something nonrepresentational could find Ruth Margraff's "Painting the Voice" or Rinde Eckert's "Toward a More Polysemous Theater" wildly epiphanic.

Alternatively, a writer who has not yet started can move through the entire creative process and build a complete script. An aspiring playwright can start at the beginning of the book, work through to the end, and have a manuscript. Someone who has never built a bookshelf can start with the desire to get books off their floor and end up with useful and beautiful furniture. The best way to build a play directly is simply to read the whole book, return to the contributions that produce the most excitement, and do them sequentially. Everyone who comes to the following chapters will probably want a different sequence for each project, so there's no universal best way.

PLAYWRITING AS A MEDIATED GENRE: A LITTLE MANIFESTO ON EKPHRASTIC PLAYWRITING

The Toolbox is designed to support writers with as much artistic freedom as possible, but I do want to step in with a brief manifesto. This section is an epiphany that helped me as a writer and consistently helps my students. It's offered as its own section to be easily skippable. If a reader doesn't want advice outside of the tools in later chapters, then it's easy to move on to the next section. That said, even this section isn't so much advice on what a play should be but more on thinking about what scripts do.

Playwriting is a mediated genre. Our art form is something brought about by an intervening medium. To flirt with algebra a bit, we can think of the formula for moving a finished play to the stage as "S affects C, which in turn affects A," with S being the script, C being the creative production team, and A being the audience. We may write to make the art we want to see in the world, and we should, but the first people who will see that work outside of friends, supporters, and the people involved in the writing process are the theatre artists who mediate it from the page onto the stage.

Being a mediated work makes playwriting unique among the language arts. Other writers have a much more direct relationship between their text and their audience. A published poem looks much like what the poet sent to their editor and what the reader reads. The differences are primarily cosmetic, with changes in trivial things like font and point size. That's not true with theatre, and we're lucky for it!

The upside of our mediated genre is that a script can get multiple productions and live with a vibrancy unavailable to other genres. After all, look at the dynamic life of a Shakespeare play in relationship to his equally excellent poetry. Odds are there's a Shakespeare play done in every major theatre market every year. How often does a poet get up at a reading and present one of Shakespeare's sonnets? In the hundreds of poetry readings I've been to, I've never seen it happen. I suspect most poets would find it laughable to start their reading that way, but few theatre makers would be surprised to hear an actor perform a Shakespeare monologue in an audition.

The downside of our mediated genre is the reality that we compete for stage time and resources with the surviving scripts from across history. My own shows have been immediately followed by productions of *Antigone* and *Macbeth*. The theatres that have staged my work also have staged plays written in 441 BC and 1601 AD. That's serious depth of competition.

As writers, we need to consciously celebrate and make the most of our mediated genre by inspiring the mediators, all the other artists who actually stage our work. However, it's wise to simply keep this need in mind as a goal we work toward. Because these other artists are going to be shaping and informing our work, we want to make sure our scripts inspire them to stage it, like we were inspired to write it. Think of this as ekphrastic playwriting.

Ekphrastic poetry is poetry written in response to or inspired by another powerful work of art. An inspired artist is excited and motivated to practice their craft. If other theatre artists can engage with the soul of the script, then their vision is evocatively linked to the playwright's vision. It shouldn't be too hard to imagine an artwork so powerful that it inspires others to make poetry. It's easy to see this power in the real world: a leisurely day in a popular art museum will provide surreptitious glimpses of scattered people scribbling contentedly in notebooks.

The plays we generate should inspire all the other theatre artists. Actors should want to dig deeper into the dialogue. Costume designers should want those actors to look just right. The sound designer should want to fill the space with effects to heighten the moment. The lighting designer should want to add light and shadow to support the tone. The director should want to go over a scene again and again, connecting everyone involved in the staging. A producer should want to pay for it all and shout about the show to anyone who'll listen. We need to make scripts that inspire all these other artists to practice their craft in response to our art. We do this by fueling the imagination of the reader and inspiring action. That's easy advice to give, but it takes months or years of work to accomplish.

Along these lines, don't mistake playwriting for screenwriting. The genres are mirror images of each other. Plays are generally driven by dialogue, and screenplays, by physical action. This difference is even visible in their layout on the page, where play format foregrounds dialogue, and screen format foregrounds action. However, I suspect that our heavy exposure to cinema and television causes lots of writers to imagine filmic devices, like zooms and pans, unless consciously thinking of the stage. A quality director, inspired by an evocative play, will be able to move the eyes and mental focus of the audience, allowing for plenty of room for surprise and action. Trust them. Zander Brietzke's *American Drama in the Age of Film* explores this difference with academic rigor. Scripts work best when they inspire.

The reality of theatre's mediation is that we have two audiences: the house and the production team. The house is the folks we think of when we think of audience, the people watching a play who (hopefully) stand up and clap. The production team is the whole complex group of artists and administrators who actually work to manifest the play on the stage. For a solo show, this team could be one person with a smart phone and sleep deprivation. For a large theatre, it could be dozens and dozens of people, many with advanced artistic degrees.

While it's not necessarily a conscious choice, a theatre company needs to be profoundly moved by a script to make the investment necessary to stage a work. Part of that profundity is that they want to stage it; part of it is that they can imagine it in their space or care about it enough that they dismiss any problems as solvable. And all plays have problems. Part of the artistic fulfillment of making theatre is solving those problems. A script must make a production team care, or an audience will never see it. Even that aforementioned solo show with a team of one still needs an intense passion for the material, perhaps even more so than the large theatre, because that one hypothetical workaholic is doing everything. We need to write scripts that inspire action and avoid scripts that order or demand.

Similarly, we need to trust the artists. The company producing a play is engaging in a huge act of trust. They trust they can manifest the script on the stage in a powerful and evocative way. They trust their investment of money into making the show will be rewarded. They trust their investment of time with the material will be fulfilling. They trust the audience will stand up and clap. There are probably a few folks at that theatre company who earn their livelihood from it, so they invest their economic well-being, too. It's our obligation as playwrights to make work worthy of that trust. If a script can't be trusted to produce the results we want to see, then it's not a script ready to go out in the world. A writer stuck in that moment could find Liz Appel's "Starry Night" or Sophie Sagan-Gutherz's "How to Fall Back in Love with Your Play" quite useful.

We're manifesting emotions in both our audiences. We want them to feel and think because that's part of what good art does. If we can make the members of the production team have a big emotional response, then they'll work to mediate it onto the stage. In some ways, all the tools in this book are about getting a script to create such a response. A few even do it overtly, like my "Inspirational Stage Directions"; and others, covertly, like Gab Reisman's "Five Becomes Three." So how we try to manifest emotions matters. If we're trying to make a work that feels forlorn and we write, "blue light," because blue feels forlorn in our imagination but the uninspired lighting designer gives us a vibrant, lascivious blue, then we don't get the emotions we want. Instead, we need to write a scene that feels so forlorn that all the other artists manifest it.

Avoid unnecessary absolutes in the blocking and mise-en-scène. Writing that a couch is gray, has been partially shredded by a cat, and has a strange stain isn't as useful as describing it as a "sketchy couch," unless the show is going to return to the idea of the cat or the stain. *Sketchy* is the emotional quality that's trying to be manifested. A "red dress" doesn't carry the same emotional response as an "embarrassing dress" or an "empowering dress," unless the color is used specifically elsewhere.

While phrases like *actor crosses to downstage left* may help get a vision from the imagination to the page, it's not an inspiring moment. Published plays that have such details are usually an accounting of the Broadway premiere or another major production instead of the writer's intent. Those directions often record action from a production; playwrights inspire imagination for production. Making problems instead of inspiration on the page can keep a producer from considering a show in the first place. Pragmatically, imagine if the production venue has a bad sight line and crossing to downstage left is counterproductive. Not only does the production team struggle to make overly particular direction happen, the audience will be trying to see instead of getting to feel. Similarly, as we imagine a play, the living room where the action happens might connect to the garage where offstage action happens through a stage-left door, but this is uninspiring. Saying "the door to the garage" is much clearer and allows potential producers to imagine the work in their space. If they can't put a stage-left door on their stage, then it gets harder for them to imagine the script.

The playwright Mac Wellman has sage advice on this topic. I don't know when he first said it, but he's been repeating it over the course of a long, influential career. He first said it to me back in 2005, when I interviewed him in the *Rain Taxi Review of Books*: "Most visual scenarios in stage directions are written from the north side of the human soul—if it says door up right, there should be a door up right, that sort of thing—but my experience with these sorts of stage directions is that people always get them wrong. Whereas if I write something like 'something strange happens,' they always get that right." *Strange* is ekphratic.

Many years ago, a director and I were moving a script from the end of development into production, and we had an epiphany, which I've come to call the "Ten Hour Rule." We realized that about ten hours of work went into each line of dialogue in the play. If I had a character say, "Your dog is so friendly," then it would take about ten hours of time out of the human experience. Actors would memorize; the director would block; the lighting designer, sound designer, and costume designer would all be laboring away. That ten hours is time that all those mediating artists couldn't rest or socialize, couldn't enjoy their families or lovers or hobbies. So it was crucial to make every line matter because dedicated people gave up real things for it. The art we make as playwrights has an economic cost, but it has a human one, too. We cover the human expense through inspiration, through ekphrasis.

THE WRITING WHEEL

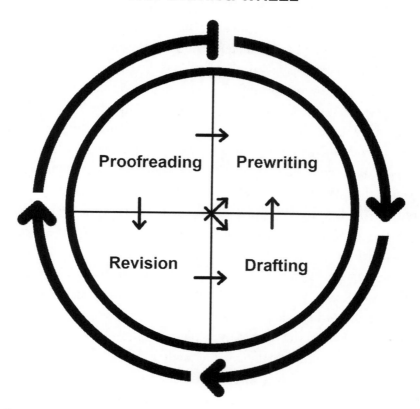

Overview

To expand the toolbox metaphor of the title, the Writing Wheel is the box itself. All the tools offered by the contributing writers can fit somewhere in the box. So along with holding a pragmatic approach to the writing process, the wheel is the rhetorical frame that holds the contents of the book. This frame means exercises that help writers at the beginning of the writing process are toward the front, in chapter 2, and exercises that help with the end of the process are toward the end, in chapter 4. So a struggling writer who knows where they are in the writing process can come to the appropriate section of the book and find the advice to help them. In the simplest sense, the wheel is a pragmatic and flexible graph of the writing process. Having an awareness of what to do and when to do it makes the work of writing streamlined and efficient without compromising moments of inspiration or idiosyncratic needs.

Because we write from inside real brains and real bodies in the actual world, we need to manage that process. The wheel offers a way to manage time. It provides us with focus by helping us think about what to do and when. It makes sense for some parts of the work of writing to generally happen before or after other parts. It helps us prioritize. Working to make a joke in dialogue absolutely perfect only to then go back and delete the scene wastes time. Being sure that the scene is necessary before polishing the nuance of the joke is a wise priority.

Writing can often feel mystical or trancelike, and a few exercises, including Rachel Jendrzejewski's "Problem as Point," develop that. However, the wheel also offers some concrete steps to keep us moving forward when the Muses aren't talking. It also helps us to channel inspiration, to make the most of it when the Muses start talking. The wheel acknowledges that writing is a thing that's made, and it gives us a general order of operations to take on tasks in a useful sequence.

The wheel is subjective and flexible. It won't be used the same way by different authors, and it won't be used the same way by the same writer from one project to the next. It's a general procedural layout to make the abstractions of writing something a little more manageable. After writing one or two plays, these steps become unconscious and integrated.

Consequently, the four quadrants of the wheel don't always take up the same amount of time in terms of getting a play written. For example, an author writing a play based on a historical figure might well spend more time in prewriting as they research contextual information; if so, Duncan Pflaster's "Background Timeline" could be invaluable. For someone like me who struggles with dyslexia, I know I'll have a much harder time with proofreading and polishing a final draft; thus I need to plan to spend more time further along the wheel. With experience, the wheel is something that quickly becomes sublimated and personal. Of course, under stress or with a particularly complicated project, having the basics there to fall back on helps the writer move forward when there's adversity.

As a side note, the wheel works for any genre of writing: poetry, fiction, nonfiction, and screenwriting. While this book focuses exclusively on playwriting, the procedures can be applied to any other mode of making text. A friend of mine uses it for writing computer code. X-rays of Da Vinci paintings show a visual artist meticulously revising, so it works even when we don't use language. Some genres might spend more time in different quadrants of the wheel. For example, academic writing generally requires far more time in prewriting and less in revision because of the research required and a focus on cogent thinking instead of beautiful writing, whereas novelists might spend a lot more time in revision because the final product needs to be emotionally compelling over so many pages of prose.

As artists making art out of language, it's easy to get caught up in the inspiration and the excitement of the moment. After all, there are a lot of endorphins produced by the experience. Excitement in the early stages of creation can cause us to forget the practical side of the experience. The Muses don't give us art on demand, and even when the words flow, they often course wildly or puddle up. Relying on inspiration alone isn't effective. Instead, we can build a place for that inspiration to happen, and we must work with the material produced in those moments of inspiration to shape the watercourse we want. A writer struggling with inspiration should check out Sharon Bridgforth's "Stirring da Roux" or Matthew Freeman's "You Are What You Love," both of which offer profoundly different ways to get started using personal experience. All the tools in this book can help channel our excitement.

How to Use the Wheel

The writing wheel starts in the upper-right quadrant and moves clockwise. Of course, there are exceptions to this sequence because the writing process can be profoundly nonlinear, and this process is easily and frequently deviated from. For clarity on the page, the wheel is divided up evenly into its four main components: prewriting, drafting, revising, and proofreading. Modifying the process based on personal needs and the demands of any given project is part of the wheel's value.

By moving around the wheel, we prioritize the sequence of work with the most foundational thing done first. We start in prewriting, then move to drafting, as that's generally the order. We need to go from dreaming, thinking, and inspiration into a crude first draft. There are always exceptions. If one sees a typo in that crude first draft, then it's better to fix it than ignore it; however, it's unwise to go hunting for typos early in the writing process. The time to hunt for such cosmetic errors is in proofreading. Similarly, if we're outlining a scene and the Muses reward us with dialogue as the characters forming in the imagination suddenly start talking, then it's prudent to organically slide into drafting and write down what they're saying. After all, we can go back and continue work on that outline after the gush of inspiration passes.

Plus, we can return to the wheel under stress. When overwhelmed by too many loose ends, confusion, or external pressure, returning to a concrete overview can help focus on the work of the moment. Knowing each problem will get taken care of in time can reduce stress, freeing up mental and emotional space so creativity can flourish. The wheel also helps with time management. Because we live in the real world with real demands, time is a deeply limited resource. I don't think I've ever met a writer who had enough time. Consequently, using time well is invaluable. By being aware of the order of operations, we can keep from mismanaging a precious resource.

Prewriting

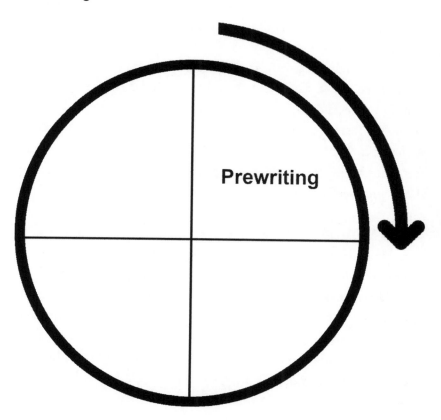

In the liner notes to the Tom Waits collection *Used Songs 1973–1980*, the musician Charles Schwab writes, "Back [t]hen . . . we were all trying to make ourselves attractive places for songs to land." That's a wonderful way to think about prewriting. We're making space in our minds, hearts, and lives to start making art. Prewriting is all the work we do at the beginning of the writing process. We often encounter this kind of work in basic writing classes in high school and college. However, it behooves writers to come back to these basics and think about how they can serve our artistic practice. Plus, with so many ways to begin, sorting out the infinite and getting started can be demanding; Caridad Svich's "The Object Lesson" can help with that. Prewriting involves activities that are creative and intellectual, but these all happen in the context of our real lives. Being aware of our dynamic, physical lives allows us to make the most of our resources while minimizing the things that hinder us.

There's a long list of conscious things we can do at the start of the writing process. Things like brainstorming, freewriting, daydreaming, and research generally top the list. They all make appearances in the next chapter. Variations on the ways that people can generate and record their thoughts are vast. Anything that involves thinking about what we want to write, why, and how falls into this category. Molly Rice's "The Five Whys" can help make sense of it all. If we're writing narrative, then we'll need dramatic tension to hold the audience. That requires plot and character. There are a lot of things to help with plot and character in this book. For anyone making a representational drama, they're the heart of the matter, so there are lots of approaches to dealing with them. If we're writing nonrepresentational theatre, where we won't have plot and character in a substantive way, then we need to ask ourselves, "What holds the audience?" There are good exercises to help answer it, including Ed Bok Lee's "Sensibility, Marginalization, and the Lingering Umami of Your Play World" and Paige Goodwin's "Subtext as Relief."

Along with the conscious things are the unconscious devices to help us start the writing process. Things like meditation, introspective walks, and engaging with other art always make the list. Plenty of contributions help with this, including Gary Winter's "What Haunts You?" and Greg Vovos's "Character Creation Exercise." All the different ways we can tap into our subconscious or connect with the Muses or get to that trancelike, often mystical experience of creativity are part of the process.

Writers dedicated enough to be reading this book are probably fairly adept with the basics of artistic and intellectual work. However, after teaching writing for twenty years, I consistently see a disconnect between the work of writing and the real world we inhabit. I was guilty of it as a student, but I didn't realize how pervasive the mental separation was between the living of life and the work of writing. Let me illustrate with a quick anecdote.

When I was in college, I would get up, have breakfast, and walk to the library. But I lived off campus, and it was a solid mile from my apartment. It was also by Lake Erie, so it was snowy, and I lived on a rise above a creek that separated my side of town from the campus, so it was also uphill both ways. The walk seemed like no big deal. I was young, and I had a warm hat and headphones. I'd get to the library; search out the books I needed; gather the books; and then organize my reading, research, or notes. Then I'd get hungry. Then I'd get distractedly hungry. So I'd pop over to the campus center for a quick lunch. Because it was a small campus, I'd invariably encounter friends, and lunch would be long. And I'm an introvert, so friends (while wonderful) also took a lot out of me. I'd eventually stumble back to the library—ill prepared to think or write. Plus, a lot of my time was wasted when an efficacious meal became a social event.

When I started to account for my real life and simply packed a sandwich and an apple, I became much more productive. Eating quietly in my study cubicle made me a much better writer. I wish someone suggested it before I figured it out the hard way. I had all the tools I needed to succeed at the level of sophomore college student, but I hadn't thought about how to use those tools in the context of the real world. This is perhaps why extension cords come with a note about not running them through water; we're thinking about the need the tool is supposed to address but not the real word in which we use it.

Part of effectively writing in the real world is regularity and structure. The more consistently we write, the more we can get done. However, it's easy to confuse *consistent* with *idyllic*. We can imagine a writer at their desk, gleefully typing out a masterpiece, but feel like we can't write because we're not in that mode. Such fantasy is a disservice. Instead, we need to make time for writing in the context of our real lives. An hour before work is better than nothing. Notes scribbled in a notebook through the day are better than ideas that wake us up at night but fade like apparitions by the morning. We're well served to make the most time possible for writing and to be well prepared for it within the context of our lives.

We need to know what our bodies need. If we're introverts, then maybe we need to write before dealing with people. If we're extroverts, then maybe we need to write after engaging with people. If we're easily distracted but only have time to write on the bus to work, then a pair of earplugs or noise-canceling headphones might be invaluable. If we get ideas while driving, then a full tank of gas and the ability to effectively use our phone's voice-to-text feature can make a world of difference. If we've got a little ADHD, a crowded coffee shop might be perfect. If we can only write after a 9-to-5 job, then a premade dinner might be the way to go. When we're hungry during our writing time, it's harder to write. When we're exhausted, it's harder to write. When we're craving a cigarette, it's harder to write. Our bodies have real needs. Fortunately, these needs are predictable, and we can plan for them.

Like our bodies, our lives make predictable demands that can keep us from writing. If the kids get off the school bus at 3:45 every day and we can't write after that, then we have a fixed moment in time that we can predict and work around. If the dog always goes out at 6:15 a.m., then make sure it won't interrupt you. If the battery in the woodworker's power tool only lasts an hour, then they're foolish to plan for two hours of use. We're better off understanding our real-world needs and then planning for them instead of ignoring them or trying to resolve them through magical thinking.

Such planning doesn't shut the door on inspiration. If anything, it opens it wider. An idea scribbled in a notebook at a stoplight can be returned to when safely at the desk. An idea that wakes us out of a deep sleep might mean that morning writing time starts a little early today. When we turn our focus away from a project, our subconscious often keeps trundling with the idea, so inspiration can show up unexpectedly. We can set up our real world to accommodate that. For example, as an introvert, I can't easily write after seeing people all day. This means, whenever possible, I need to write before I do anything else. I get up and write before I talk to anybody. As a night owl, I'd rather write at night, but indulging that combination of introversion and late-night activity makes real-life scheduling impossible, so I write in the morning.

Similarly, moments of inspiration often arrive when our subconscious has time to ruminate while our conscious mind takes on mundane activities. For me, a moment of inspiration that solves the morning's writing problem often happens when I'm in the shower, transitioning from one part of my life to the other. For many years, this meant an idea lost or an idea recorded after stumbling and dripping to the nearest notepad, a less-than-productive system. When I got some bathtub crayons, the kind toddlers scribble in the tub with, I had a viable solution. I knew I got ideas in the shower from time to time, and while I couldn't plan when or if they came, I knew they did, and I could prepare for them.

Consciously thinking about the conditions that we have to actually write in helps us make the best use of the space and time we really have for writing. We don't write in a contextual vacuum or in an ideal world, so we must plan. Obviously, random events and miscellaneous chaos will affect our best plans, but knowing what we need and when we need it allows us to make the most of what we have. Imagine a carpenter setting up a little woodworking shop. They want to build a crib to celebrate the imminent birth of their new grandchild. If they buy a drill, a jigsaw, some boards, and paint without a place to build or blueprints to work with, then that crib might not be done before their nine-month deadline.

Where can we write? Almost anywhere. Trying a few different places to see what works well for you is invaluable. A space dedicated to the task seems almost ubiquitously valuable. Consider the carpenter building the crib. They could build it in a garage or an attic or a basement or a backyard. Each place will have its own challenges. Weather, temperature, electrical outlets, lighting, sawdust management, and noise can all be issues. Maybe we write on the bus or at a public computer in the library or at a kitchen table. Each has advantages and disadvantages that we can accommodate. Without good blueprints, that carpenter is guessing at the supplies they need. It's faster and cheaper to design on paper or an app than to buy a bunch of boards and try stuff. Of course, they might try something they designed and need to redesign it later, but that's what revision is for.

When can we write? Almost anytime. While it's usually easier when our minds are fresh first thing in the morning, if personal, familial, or professional obligations take our attention, then maybe we write after they're sufficiently resolved. To return to that carpenter, they could build the crib at any point, but if they're new to wood working, then it's better to start early. Nobody wants to put a baby in a crib that stinks of polyurethane. Planning out steps matters. If the spindles get glued and clamped and need twenty-four hours to dry, then that's probably the end of the time that can be invested in the project on that day, or at least that part of the project.

Formatting

A simple way to save time and increase efficiency in playwriting is by being conscious of dramatic format at the beginning of the process. Plays are generally written in a standard format, with a lot of tolerance for variations. At some point, a conventional play needs to be in a standard form. Plays that break or eschew standard form need to do so for a reason. There are many effective descriptions of the standard form scattered across the internet and various kinds of software that will automatically format plays. However, formatting can be done easily in any common word processing software. The Dramatists Guild's webpage has a clear, visual explanation of various professional formats, and a basic layout is included in the appendix at the back of this book.

Sloppy formatting is one of the clearest indications of an unfinished or unprofessional manuscript. This is particularly tricky in theatre. Our cousins working on screenplays have tighter expectations on the format for their genre, while our cousins in poetry have almost none. We are painfully in between. This problem is compounded because conventional theatre is written in one format and published in others, so an author can't look at the publication of their favorite play and copy its formatting. Plays are written to be easily used by all those mediating artists, as the format provides a sense of run time, with a page of dialogue usually running about a minute onstage. Plays are published in formats that maximize profit margins, and paper is expensive.

Writer's Block

Writer's block can happen at any point in the writing process, but the transitional moment between prewriting and drafting is when it's most likely. The transition from the first to the second part of the wheel is a movement from thinking and dreaming to making the real thing. It's easy to hold the false belief that the stakes have risen. It's easy to think about the next stage of the writing process as a real start, even though it's the organic progression of what we've been doing. This transition feels significant because we move to doing.

While writer's block is a real phenomenon, it is eminently manageable. We thought (or worried) ourselves into this moment, and we can work ourselves out of it. Writer's block happens. After all, we want to make art, and we want it to be quality art. We arrive at drafting, and suddenly we're trying to make something impressive instead of progressing from the previous step. The desire to write something good then makes it impossible just to write *something*.

There are a few ways to manage writer's block and get our brains to relax into the work, to unmake our anxiety. Often, a simple return to prewriting can solve the problem. Maybe the vision in our head isn't fleshed out enough. If freewriting was producing quality results in prewriting, then more freewriting might be a great solution. After all, many pages of freewriting typed up can work for a first draft that is then expanded or contracted. Similarly, if outlining was productive, then consider a more detailed outline that develops until points in the outline become dialogue and direction on the page. Freewriting and outlining help us generate text, and that big block of words is all that we're making here.

Generally, we don't simply write quality plays; we revise drafts until the play fulfills our vision. Maybe that takes hours, or maybe it takes decades. Whatever the length of time, it doesn't happen at this stage in the process. The carpenter building the crib might love the soothing repetition of hand sanding, but this is the stage of measurements, repeated measurements, and rough cuts. The poet William Stafford's advice about writer's block is "Just lower your standards and keep writing." It's great advice. An internet search shows a long list of writers suggesting the same. Like the woodworker's adage "Measure twice; cut once," writers repeat, "Lower your standards." It's easy advice to give but hard to apply.

Unfortunately, our internal editor gets in the way of our work as writers and often contributes to writer's block. The internal editor is the critical voice in our heads that all too often says, "This isn't right," or "We're not good enough," or something else that impedes writing. For many of us, the editor often sounds like the voice of reason. Mine is duplicitous and sounds like the practical voice that says practical things: "Pants, then shoes," or "Don't forget the grocery list." The excited imagination that got us started suddenly moves in the wrong direction, imagining catastrophe based on the fate or merit of the as-yet-unwritten play. At this point in the writing process, the internal editor can make us neurotically explore endless rabbit warrens of research in response to the anxious idea that we could make a quality first draft if we only knew more. Or the editor can wipe our minds blank because we can't see the script in our imagination materializing on the page, and that blank page can be tyrannical.

While the internal editor is not the voice of reason, it does have value. Later in the writing process, that editor becomes an ally. The more we can do to set aside that voice until we need it, the easier the work becomes. Of course, stuck is stuck, regardless of our skills or experience. Consequently, chapter 3 on drafting starts with several exercises that deal with writer's block, either directly or indirectly.

Drafting

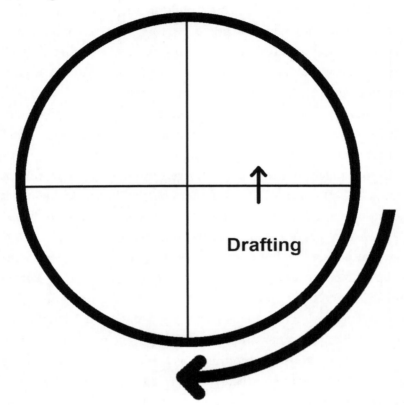

Drafting

The purpose of the first draft is simply to get words on the page. We're taking the materials we gathered in prewriting and are now measuring, marking, and making rough cuts. The work here isn't an end product and will in all likelihood change substantially in later steps. This quadrant of the wheel isn't about making a quality play; even thinking about quality can exacerbate writer's block.

In the essay "Shitty First Drafts" from her book *Bird by Bird: Some Instructions on Writing and Life*, the novelist Anne Lamott writes, "[S]hitty first drafts. All good writers write them. This is how they end up with good second drafts and terrific third drafts." Her advice about shitty first drafts is a masterful way of understanding the problem and making peace with the quality of the material generated at this step in the process. Lamott says, "Very few writers really know what they are doing until they've done it. Nor do they go about their business feeling dewy and thrilled." Understanding that this foray from idea to page is the beginning of the next step can make it a much easier step to take.

Perhaps we get to this step by trimming down freewriting or by building up from an outline, like in Rachel Rubin Ladutke's "Mapping the Story." Perhaps we're recording various images as though we're recording a dream or tone poem for the stage, like Sam Hamashima's "Describe the Elephant." Perhaps we're simply letting characters lead us as they fight for what they want, perhaps something else altogether, like Lindsay Carpenter's "List of Twenty." The ways one gets from idea to text are as boundless as anything else in the writing process. Drafting gets us from our artistic inspiration to substantive words on the page.

One of the best reasons to embrace a low-quality draft and ignore the internal editor is that this major transition from thinking to writing often requires a return to prewriting. Drafting can inspire new or better ideas. It can reveal missing elements of our artistic vision that need more thinking, like plot holes that need outlining or characters that need research. It's not uncommon for writers telling narrative stories to realize that what they thought was a complete one-act play was actually the first or second act of a longer work, so they go back to prewriting to outline and develop this epiphany. Perhaps the second-most useful thing about the wheel (after its order of operations) is that we can move backward to a previous step whenever we need to. The carpenter who realizes the spindles on the side of the crib are too far apart can redraw the blueprints and then turn a few more on the lathe.

We try to ignore the internal editor in the drafting process because refining work to a high level of quality is counterproductive. Too much of the first draft will change in the steps to come. Investing an hour getting a character's dialogue to be "perfect" on the page only to realize the character is redundant and needs to be cut from the script means an hour wasted. Letting the first draft of that character stand with clunky and awkward dialogue is just doing the work necessary to earn the epiphany that the character needs to be cut.

Eventually, the crude version of our artistic vision is laid out on the page. This shitty first draft is not a text to brag about nor a text to share. If we put it in a drawer and forget about it for five years, then it probably won't make much sense when we come back to it. This writing won't be engaging for an audience, but it gets us the cut and measured wood we need to do our work. It gives us the draft we can shape; it gets us to where the central work of writing happens.

Revision

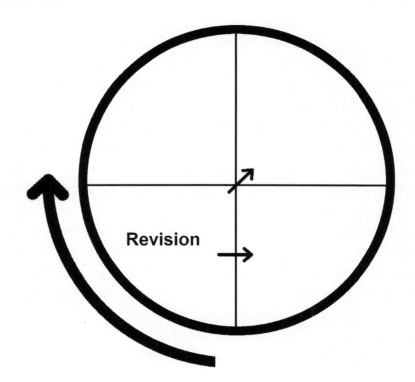

Revision is where most writers spend most of their time. During revision, plays undergo the demanding transformation from shitty first drafts to compelling manifestations of our vision. A wise writer with a limited amount of time should budget most of it for this part of the wheel.

Because a draft is already generated, the transition from drafting to revision doesn't usually generate writer's block; however, for some writers, revision can feel like a slog. If so, then there are exercises to help with that, including Timothy Braun's "Writing Isn't Writing; Writing Is Rewriting; or, Making It Look Like You Knew What You Were Doing All Along" and Erin Courtney's "Revision through Writing a Dramatic Question and Mapping." If the raw creation and dreaming of the previous two steps were particularly emotionally invigorating, then coming to the serious work of revision can feel grinding. It's fun to imagine the beautiful crib and the happy folks around it, but turning dowel after dowel after dowel with a gouge and a lathe can feel tedious. Part of serious writing is finding the joy and beauty in the labor itself. A true craftsperson at their bench can find contentment in the repeated success of each perfectly turned dowel.

In practice, revision focuses on major changes. The plot develops, the characters deepen, the language expands, and the actions become evocative. We come to our script and continue to shape it until the words on the page inspire all those mediating artists to accurately manifest the play in our heads. The revision process often starts by simply reading through the play and shaping the words on the page with an eye toward perpetual improvement. The stakes become higher, like in Trista Baldwin's "Predator and Prey: An Exercise in Tone and Pacing"; or the language, more evocative, like in Timothy Braun's "The Metaphor Is the Road to the Simile; or, Aren't We All Trying to Make Metaphor-Jazz Work?"; or the outcomes, more pronounced, like in Charissa Menefee's "Does It Have to End

This Way?" The time frame for this process can vary wildly from writer to writer and project to project. By taking on big things like characters and plot points in narrative or tone and image in nonrepresentational work, we're keeping our order of operations effective. We're shaping its structure, generally moving from bigger to smaller things.

In revision, we're shaping the play on the page to manifest the play in our head as best we can. Unfortunately, this process leads to a complex dichotomy. A subtle problem forms as we revise: the text on the page starts to blur with the text in our head. Effectively, the text on the page becomes a mnemonic device—something that ties us to a memory. We stop seeing what's really on the page and start seeing what's in our imagination. The words on the page simply lead us through our imagination. The reality is that the contents of our head are forever trapped there. As we revise more and more, we get closer and closer to the material and struggle to know what's succeeding and what needs more attention. We have a play that lives in our head, and we have a play that lives on the page.

The phenomenon of the text on the page becoming mnemonic is easy to see. We can probably all recall a moment when something we wrote was "done," polished, as good as we could make it. Yet when we took a few steps and picked it up from the printer's output bin, we immediately saw a glaring typo. In the minutes or seconds it takes to go from the computer screen to the printer tray, we break the mnemonic thread and can see the printed page for what it is. The glaring typo or obvious mistake suddenly pops out because we're no longer looking at a mnemonic device representing the contents of our head. So as we push deeper into revision, the work of revision gets harder to do because it gets harder to separate the page in the world from the page in our imagination.

Fortunately, other people never have access to the play in our head, only to the play on the page. Their lack of access serves us in revision. We can hand a text off to people we trust, have them read it, and tell us where they got lost or bored or where their minds wandered. We can ask them questions about the text, and their response tells us how they understand the play on the page. If the play in their head sounds a lot like the play in our head, then we're probably going in the right direction.

Similarly, we can gather a few folks and read the work aloud, with various people taking various parts. When they say our words aloud, do they sound like the characters in our heads? Do people laugh at the jokes? Do they gasp at the drama? When they describe the choices they would make in staging the text, does it sound conceptually right? What in the script inspired these choices?

A brief note on bad actors. Personally, I've come to believe that new works and neophyte writers are well served by having a few private readings with performers who aren't skilled actors or who aren't natural fits for a role. A good actor can make terrible text sound okay; a bad actor or one inappropriately cast can't hide the warts. There's a reason for the sentence *I could listen to them read the phone book*. After all, the phone book is so iconically boring that its reputation for being dry survives in the era of cell phones, long after the ubiquity of the books themselves. No writer wants to make a phone book. A bad actor can't hide the boring, can't sell a poor joke, and can't evoke emotion where none exists on the page. Consequently, I believe that as we transition away from those shitty first drafts, a few bad actors help keep us honest with ourselves about the quality of our material. Keep in mind that these private readings are different than the public readings that constitute an important element of professional development. Such readings are invaluable but should happen after a script has gone through the wheel and is as polished as possible. Public readings regularly send the most finished-seeming scripts back to the wheel. To help make the most of audience responses, look at Saviana Stanescu's "How to Process Feedback from Workshops/Readings/Discussions."

Eventually, all the structural, conceptual, and artistic elements in our script work. At this point in the writing wheel, we return to the internal editor. Finishing revision means all the parts of the play remaining in the manuscript are important and contribute something valuable. Here, the internal editor becomes our ally. Because the big things in the play are staying (at least for the foreseeable future), we can afford to listen to the little voice that whispers, "Something's wrong here." If that internal editor says something is wrong with a character's dialogue at this point, and we know we're going to keep the character largely unchanged, and we know we need all the scenes they're in, then we can come back and see if there's a reason it's raising a subconscious warning flag. My "Targeted Revisions" and Matthew Paul Olmos's "Honing'in on Dialogue" can help with such flags.

Unlike earlier in the process, thoroughness at this point is a wise use of our time. Maybe the character is doing redundant work and we have to go back to prewriting and imagine the play without them. Maybe the character sounds a little too much like another character and we have to make them distinct, so we keep revising. Maybe they have an epiphany offstage that the audience needs to see, so we go back to draft and revise that scene. There are innumerable reasons for the editor to whisper to us, but now we listen. In these final steps of revision, we organically move from revision, where we resolve the substantive issues, to proofreading, where we address the cosmetic ones.

Proofreading

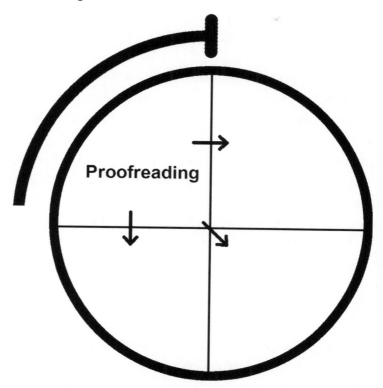

In proofreading, we take on the small, cosmetic issues that impede our manuscript from communicating the play in our head to the mediating artists staging it. Lots of small things happen at this point in the writing process. However, these are labors of cleanup, like a carpenter sweeping sawdust or a battery placed on a charger. Because of the mundane nature of this finishing up, there aren't creative, pragmatic exercises for it. There's no gain in watching Amy Devers with a broom and dustpan. The important thing is knowing we should sweep up.

The one exercise I have for proofreading, "Know What You Don't Know (Targeted Proofreading)," can be tucked into revision easily enough. Beyond the few notes in this chapter, the creative element of proofreading is that it can lead us back to the other points on the wheel. Because we're still working with a script in a perfunctory fashion, late-arriving feedback, fresh epiphanies, or other insights can lead us back to the previous parts of the wheel, and epiphanies at this stage of the process should be honored, as they were hard earned through the investment of time made in our script. Here we're finishing the process or at least making a document that can stand on its own as a respectable work in progress.

This final stage is when we seriously use the checks of our word-processing software. Spell-check, grammar check, and the assorted other features of various forms of word-processing software are valuable tools. Like any other tool in the box, they have their limitations. Don't trust the checks, but don't dismiss them. Don't assume the machine is right. After all, *can't* and *cant* are both spelled correctly. Also, because we're making art, the conventional rules of writing can impede the work. Any rule of syntax can and should be ignored, broken, or violated as needed. Our obligation as writers is to break the rules intentionally, to violate them for a reason. If those mediating artists understand why they're seeing something unconventional (or suspect its value will be revealed), then they're going to be far more likely to embrace our art and enthusiastically manifest our vision.

At this point in the process, it's often a good idea to double-check format. While it's probably easier for most writers to write in a traditional format most of the time, the Muses can be difficult. It's easy to abandon format for a host of reasons in the writing process, but now is the time to double-check and make sure it's serving us as artists. Much like syntax, our choices can be deeply conventional or wildly experimental, but we need to be in control of them. When we abandon conventions, we should do so for a reason.

Another wise choice is to go on a brief inconsistency scavenger hunt. In the writing process, many things can change, and it's a good idea to give a quick search for substantial, surface-level changes. If the character of Cop 1 slowly turned into Billy during the revision process, then it's probably wise to make sure that they're only ever called Billy. If a new character appears, are they on the character list? If we shifted the time period when we moved from drafting into revision, is all our slang definitely from the right era?

While proofreading is the end of the writing wheel, playwriting is never truly done. If you're building a crib, eventually that crib is done, but because of those mediating artists, theatre is uniquely vibrant, and the more open we are to that artistic reality, the more success we bring to our art. While I've seen plenty inventive restagings of plays from antiquity, along with icons like Shakespeare or Ibsen, I've also seen different versions of plays by contributors to this volume. When I saw Caridad Svich's *House of the Spirits* at Repertorio Español in New York, it was different from when I saw it later at Mixed Blood Theatre in Minneapolis. Similarly, my undergraduate students were shocked when the published version of Lisa D'Amour's *Detroit*, which they read in class, was different from the version they saw at Southern Rep Theatre in New Orleans. I saw Liz Duffy Adams's *Born with Teeth* at the Alley Theatre in Houston and then at the Guthrie Theater in Minneapolis, and I had noticeably different experiences, even though the show featured the same cast and the same director. We are wise to stay flexible and think of our scripts as living documents. So even after a work is "finished," don't hesitate to slide back into the exercises of this book to improve a play's vibrancy in a dynamic and changing world.

Techniques and Tactics

While every contribution to this book can go into one of the four parts of the writing wheel, a few exercises warrant a stand-alone chapter. These contributions step outside directly making a draft. Instead, they help build a skill or resee a core concept of writing.

These entries are wild and vast. These are the moments when the woodworker explores the nature of joinery and how to cut wood so that the pieces interlock. These exercises expand how the tools are understood; they are deep exploration. Don't dismiss them. Pragmatically, these contributions can be used at any point in the writing process. If a draft feels flat, then Braun's exploration on the nature of metaphor might fix that. If there's a desire to make work that goes in a new direction, then start with Margraff. If there's a need for profound immediacy, then Kristina Wong can make that happen. If that comedy isn't funny, then my contribution can help you get serious about how humor works. When you think, "I just don't know what to do," come to this chapter.

Starting

At this point, it's time to start construction. With the wheel as a conceptual framework, we can open the box and take out the tools. Remember, we can move through this book from the beginning to the end, making a play as we go, or we can use the tools to improve drafts that aren't working. Whether building or repairing, it's time to begin. All the contributing writers offer something from their practice or teaching or both. These writers don't necessarily agree with each other, and they don't make art in the same ways, but their differences strengthen the whole.

Engage with what's useful now and come back to the rest later—odds are, it'll will be useful eventually. As someone who loves lists, I'm inclined toward the contributors who offer listing exercises when I need to solve a problem in a manuscript. As someone who hates freewriting (but obviously sees its value), a book that only had freewriting approaches to any given problem wouldn't be particularly helpful to me. Of course, when I get out of my comfort zone and explore the resource of freewriting, I'm consistently humbled by the quality of the outcome. Thus, there are multiple approaches to the most common struggles: plot, character, and dialogue. Come to the skill-building exercises in the following chapters with an awareness that not every contribution will serve every reader every time, but as a whole, the contributions represent a wide spectrum of writerly proficiencies.

After all, we're each making our own art, so these exercises can serve to inspire, as well as to build and to fix. They're far more useful than merely following a formula, like the one in my manifesto. As several contributors suggest, when the writing gets tough, and it does, focus on the word *play* in *playwriting*, and build what you love. If we don't love what we build, then we can set it aside or keep revising until we do. If it hasn't happened yet, then now is the time to fall in love with the work of writing.

2
PREWRITING

Exercises in this chapter:

"Feed Your Obsession" by Azure D. Osborne-Lee.
Using your curiosity to get started.   *45*

"Toward a More Polysemous Theatre" by Rinde Eckert.
Using the body and the image to make unconventional
theatre.   *46*

"You Are What You Love" by Matthew Freeman.
Developing your voice by letting other writers inspire
you.   *49*

"Inspirational Images" by Bella Poynton.
Using a stockpile of images to create dramatic starting
points.   *52*

"The Five Whys" by Molly Rice.
Thinking thoroughly about theme.   *55*

"What Haunts You?" by Gary Winter.
Using personal experience to build tone, story,
and world.   *58*

"Stirring da Roux" by Sharon Bridgforth.
Using difficult memories and experiences to
inspire creativity.   *59*

"The Object Lesson" by Caridad Svich.
Building a world, scene, or character from a single image.   *61*

"Building from Viscera" by Alice Tuan.
Developing characters through guided imagination
and freewriting.   *63*

"Character Creation Exercise" by Greg Vovos.
A low-pressure approach to developing layered characters
quickly.   *65*

"Real Estate" by Sheri Wilner. Developing characters
through the setting.   *68*

"The Wallet Exercise" by Justin Maxwell.
A thought experiment to better understand a character.   *72*

"Get a Spine" by Katherine Gwynn.
Using action verbs to develop characters.   *74*

"Daily Schedule" by Sheri Wilner.
Going outside the plot to develop characters.   *76*

"Eavesdropped Conversation" by Gab Reisman.
A little snooping to start dialogue and begin conflict.   *80*

"Useless Superhero Power" by Justin Maxwell.
Getting a character and a conflict to start a plot.   *82*

"Mapping the Story" by Rachel Rubin Ladutke.
Drawing character relationships to develop the narrative.   *84*

"Background Timeline" by Duncan Pflaster.
Repurposing history to make rounder characters.   *88*

"Moment Mapping" by j.chavez.
Building an emotional structure.   *91*

"The Why of Where and When" by Justin Maxwell.
Developing a set and setting.   *93*

FEED YOUR OBSESSION

Azure D. Osborne-Lee

Category: Spark, world building

Overview: This exercise will help you get started, get past writer's block, deepen your writing, and fall back in love with writing.

Participants: Individual but could also work for groups.
Time to complete: 1–2 hours.
Planning time: 0–15 minutes.
Planning requirements: Make time and space to vibe and write. Make sure you're free from distractions. I've done this at home alone and in a crowded coffee shop with my laptop and headphones.
Other needs or considerations:

- *In a group:* You should have research materials (e.g., a computer with internet access and/or some books and magazines), a place to write down ideas (e.g., a computer, a flipchart, a white board, or good old-fashioned pen and paper), and perhaps a way to listen to music.
- *On your own:* You should have a notebook and a pen and a way to listen to music. Access to the internet is also helpful.

Instructions: Many of my plays have grown from a single image, sound, or question. What's the difference between rabbits and hares? How does one make prize-winning biscuits? What do the woods sound like on a summer night in Georgia?

I may not know where I'm going, but I build from that feeling inside me that says, "Yes, I could think about this for an hour." In this exercise, you are going to feed your obsession. Find a place where you can concentrate, and do a deep dive into whatever interests you. Research. Take notes. Don't try to make it into dialogue or anything resembling a play at this point. Just write down anything that seems interesting to you.

Don't be afraid to be really obsessive. Is there a song or sound that connects to your research interest? Play it on repeat. Keep scratching that itch until you feel satisfied. You may find that you want to draw pictures or charts. Do that. Or maybe you want to start a blog about the topic. Sure, why not? Want to pinpoint the exact moment your character was born? Go for it!

Is there a place you can visit related to this special interest? A museum or a bakery? Go ahead and go there. The point here is to capture your inspiration, so take pictures, take notes, or put on a costume or a special outfit if it helps.

I often like to find an artifact that reminds me of this point of inspiration. When I get deeper into the writing process, crafting plot and refining dialogue, I like to pick up that artifact and remind myself of the seed the work grew from.

Doing this at least once or twice at the beginning of a new project will give you tons of source material to look back on later!

Notes: None.

TOWARD A MORE POLYSEMOUS THEATRE

Rinde Eckert

Category: Generating content, structured physical improvisation, non-narrative writing prompts

Overview: This exercise will help you learn to see like dancers, sculptors, and musicians as a means of transcending the conventions of narrative and dialogue on the assumption that the poetics of these points of view will lend your work greater depth and breadth.

Participants: On your own or with a group of no less than 5 people and no more than 15.
Time to complete: 2 hours at least.

Planning time: A few minutes to take in the character of whatever room you are using.
Planning requirements: None.
Other needs or considerations: None.

Instructions:

In a group:

1. Give everyone a writing prompt of three to five sentences maybe. Ask them to include a color; a number; some feature of a larger environment (weather, volume, mass, topography); a physical feeling (warm, cold, sharp, dull, etc.); and a question. Don't give them too much time to write this. Read them out loud. Discuss them. Set aside the most evocative for use later.

2. Ask participants to bring in an object that they believe has intrinsic depth. Don't explain to them what you mean by *intrinsic depth*. Put them together on a table or on the floor. Walk around this collection. Ask questions about the objects (weight, shape, size, color, history, uses to which they can be put). Ask each individual why they brought in the object. Remove various objects from the pile, and note the difference it makes. Isolate two or three objects. Contemplate the arrangements, asking what happens to them in various combinations. How does our feeling about them change? Now take these objects and put them in different parts of the room. Does it change the way you feel about the object? Does it change the way you see the particular part of the room in which the object has been placed? Are there any shared features between the object and the room (color, shape, proportion, line)? What happens when someone is holding the object and telling a story or reading a text (try the texts they just wrote) in a particular part of the room?

3. Put on some music, and have everyone start dancing. Then ask them to dance badly. Solo the worst of the dances. Instruct the soloist to exaggerate the movements they are doing. When the movement has become sufficiently outlandish, systematically reduce it in increments of 10 percent. Watch each stage carefully. At some point, the reduction will produce something resembling movement integrity, a moment when the dancer's idea and the character of the movement seem of a piece. Pair different bad dancers, and repeat the reduction exercise. Discuss the results. Discuss this concept of the balance of idea and physical manifestation. Add a narrator using one of the evocative texts. Change the music to something radically different, and ask the dancer to continue the same dance with this very different accompaniment. If you have time, generate music as a group (rhythmic clapping, tapping on things, humming, whistling) to accompany the dancer or dancers. You can also think about the room as offering a variety of sounds that might be orchestrated, particularly evocative percussive resonance, interesting noises, and things that have pitch when struck. Take the time to consider what sound does to one's perceptions of text and movement.

On your own:
1. As in the group exercise, pick out some objects you believe have intrinsic depth. In a large enough space so you can put some distance between yourself and the objects, do the same examinations as in the group exercise, asking yourself the same questions. Hold each object, letting it work on you, assuming it has something to tell you, that there is a reason you picked it that you haven't discovered.
2. Put on some music, and dance badly. Reduce the size of your movements systematically. Try to assess for yourself when

you feel the integrity of the movement, when there is a sense of emotional balance: the music and movement in a kind of harmony.

Notes: I find that the simplest differences, differences that we think are obvious and not worth mentioning, are important to mention, to declare. The statements *This is red*, *This is heavy*, *This is soft*, *This is a toy*, *This is a tool* have surprising consequences. If we say, "Red" (rather than tacitly assuming), then our subconscious is alerted that red might be important. A whole set of neurons will fire. The result may be some provocative associations, both conscious and unconscious. This is what the practitioners of Zen might call "beginner's mind."

YOU ARE WHAT YOU LOVE

Matthew Freeman

Category: Voice

Overview: This exercise will develop your voice.

Participants: Single.
Time to complete: 30–45 minutes.
Planning time: Time reading your favorite writer.
Planning requirements: All you need is a blank sheet of paper or document.
Other needs or considerations:
- *In a group:* If you do this in a group setting, then be plain about whom you're imitating or paying homage to. Talk about why you love a particular writer and what qualities you hope to absorb. Then discuss the results as a group.
- *On your own:* Time and space to generate.

Instructions: Choose a writer you love. Then, write a scene in the voice of that writer. It doesn't have to be a complete one-act play, but it should be a complete thought: a scene with a beginning, middle, and end. Do your best to directly imitate, shamelessly, the voice of that writer or inspiration.

Before you begin, think about what you want to emulate in that writer's voice—not just the form, but the content. Pinter has a famous pause, but what's the function of the pause? Meaning and often menace. Pinter isn't

MAUDE: How are you today, Janet? It's a lovely day.
JANET: I'm fine. (Pause.) How are you?

Pinter is more

MAUDE: I was told you had a nice day today, Janet. Funny you should call a day like today nice. Of all days. (Pause.) How are you today, Janet? (Pause.) Janet? Have you had a nice day?
JANET: Yes.

The menace is as much a part of Pinter, the destabilization, as the pause itself.

Beckett, for example, is called existentialist and about "nothing." But of course, Beckett is funny, often drawing contrasts to poke fun at the whole experience. Beckett isn't

MONTROSE: Nothing at all, nothing, nothing, nothing . . . there is nothing . . . no, nothing, nothing, nothing. What is the point? I am alone, there is nothing, I do nothing, nothing, no, nothing.

Beckett is more

MONTROSE: There was nothing, then there was something, an awful something, a sandwich, terrible for the digestion, thank God there was nothing after that, a relief from the something.

In brief, think about the content as much as the form. If your inspiration is not another playwright but instead a novelist, poet, or screenwriter, imagine they are writing a play, and use their voice for the medium of theatre.

Notes: You are what you eat. What do you love to eat?

As writers, we struggle with voice. We're encouraged to find our voice and develop our style so it is distinctive and unique. In fact, most great artists come from a lineage and sit at the foot of masters. Writers and artists are often fans of each other and emulate their heroes. Some of the most renowned artists wear their influences on their sleeves, embody or imitate or pay tribute to the artists they love. Bob Dylan sounded like Woody Guthrie, then the beat poets, then Johnny Cash because he loved those artists. Samuel Beckett loved Joyce and Dante and Buster Keaton. If you know where an artist comes from, then you can see how their voices are the children of artist parents.

In this exercise, you free yourself from the fear that someone might discover whom you're imitating but fully embracing the voices you admire. My experience is that our voices are present even as we pay homage, that there's no way to remove oneself from what we write. So metabolize and embrace your heroes; interact with how they make words and make phrases; and in doing so, discover what about your voice indelibly remains within the margins of your forgery.

In my own work, I've used this to give myself a voice framework as opposed to just a dramatic structure: "That's my Paul Auster play." "That's my Shakespeare play." "This one has a lot of Ionesco in it." "Here's the John Guare of it all." Inevitably, those plays sound like me—my voice and intentions and turns of phrase show up regardless—but they also live in my fandom, taste, and history. They give me access to many voices, not just fealty to one. It also guarantees I'm making plays I would like to watch because they're lineally tied to the same voices that inspired me to write in the first place.

One might think of it as cooking: This is my spin on an Italian classic. You know this dish but never the way I've cooked it up!

INSPIRATIONAL IMAGES

Bella Poynton

Category: Prewriting, character development, setting and conflict exploration.

Overview: This exercise is intended to help writers at the beginning of their process. The exercise uses a stockpile of collected images to pinpoint the sort of ideas, conflicts, and characters the playwright is interested in exploring. Sometimes, when asked to write a scene with no parameters, playwrights can become overwhelmed and spend a great deal of time coming up with a scenario or concept before putting pen to paper or fingers to keys. This exercise is intended to help playwrights discover several potential starting points, characters, settings, and conflicts through the process of collecting a stockpile of images. After choosing, playwrights will slowly narrow their collections to reveal the images that are most evocative or have the most influence on each individual writer.

This method allows for playwrights to connect visually with images instead of being given potentially limiting exercises that require certain phrases, concepts, or character types. Playwrights will only be writing about the images they choose, and the nuance of how a writer approaches writing about an image is up to them. For example, if a playwright chooses an image of a table at a birthday party with balloons, gifts, and cake, then it may be only the gifts that have sparked their imagination. When the playwright then goes to write their play or scene, they may only be writing about a gift given from one character to another, and the rest of the party goes unmentioned. Not all aspects of the image need to be used. Each writer needs only to use the aspects of the image that speak to them. This exercise is good for anyone struggling with getting started, finding evocative imagery, or coming up with a setting or conflict.

Participants: 1–100.

Time to complete: 45–60 minutes.

Planning time: 5 minutes.

Planning requirements: This exercise works best if writers create an account with an online image bank, such as Pexels (www.pexels .com), or any other stock image website before the exercise begins.

Other needs or considerations:

- *In a group:* A laptop or tablet, a group leader/instructor to keep the time.
- *On your own:* A laptop or tablet.

Instructions: First, go to a stock image website like Pexels, and create an account. Any online stock-image bank should work for this. After creating an account, return to the homepage and begin scrolling through the images. Generally, these sites supply an endless cascade of imagery from many different categories, including landscapes, space, food, technology, art, nature, abstracts, photography, portraits, adventure, and lifestyles. In large groups, give anywhere from fifteen to thirty minutes for writers to begin stockpiling their images into a digital folder. With an account, participants should have some sort of "favorites" bank, and their images will be saved; without an account, participants will need to download each image into their own desktop folder.

Encourage participants to choose images that strike them in some way—images that elicit curiosity or wonder—or that they find exciting, beautiful, odd, unusual, haunting, moving, memorable, suggestive, alluring, or thought provoking. Collect images as quickly as possible! Tell participants not to think too much about why they are choosing particular images; if they have a reaction to it, then they should put it in their collection.

After everyone has collected fifty images, participants should go back and remind themselves silently why they've chosen each image. This can be as simple as "This one has a beautiful sunset"; "This one has a bookcase, and I love books"; or "This one has a vibrant shade of blue." Then, tell the participants that they must narrow down their image collection by half. Yes, *half*! There will likely be some hemming and hawing, but this is the point. Writers need to make serious decisions about which images have inspirational value and which don't.

Through this process, participants are pressed to think about images that they want to spend their time writing about and which images offer enough content for exploration. Tell participants to trust their instincts as they narrow their collections; they likely already have some intuition about which should stay and which should go. After they have narrowed their collection to twenty-five, continue the process three more times, halving the collection each time, from twenty-five to twelve, from twelve to six, and then finally from six to three.

With these three final images, the writers have selected the raw material with which to start writing their short play or scene. Objects from the image can become plot points, people can become characters, and locations can become settings. At least one aspect from each image should be used within the play or scene. Participants are then given time to begin writing with ideas and inspiration from their images.

Notes: Playwrights can always alter this exercise in whatever way serves their needs. For example, a playwright can challenge themselves by incorporating more or less than three images into their scene or play. An advanced version of this exercise might ask participants to use only one image—or ten! Playwrights can also invert the exercise by picking three images that elicit strong *negative* reactions. What sort of play or scene would emerge if the writer had to incorporate images that were frightening or off-putting or generated feelings of sadness or discomfort? Invent further parameters and categories as you see fit. Have fun!

THE FIVE WHYS

Molly Rice

Category: Clarifying themes; answering the question, "What is this play really about?"

Overview: Created as a problem-solving tool in the 1930s by Sakichi Toyoda, the Japanese industrialist, inventor, and founder of Toyota Industries, the Five Whys (or 5Y) became an acting and directing exercise in the hands of Bob Moss, the founder of Playwrights' Horizons. It was first shared with me by producer/director Rusty Thelin, from whom I adapted it for playwriting.

You can use this exercise to get clear on all kinds of issues in playwriting, from aligning characters with their actions to testing plot points for logic and believability. But I've also found it to work weirdly well when used by playwrights seeking to gain clarity on underlying themes, looking for the answer to the question, "What is my play *about* really?"—because if a play lacks a strong thematic spine, then it can often feel more like a mere collection of scenes or just a "story about a guy," failing to resonate beyond the plot.

The trick to doing the "Five Whys" is to balance your answers to each why between your first thought (which often contains much wisdom but may need a little refinement) and deep consideration, without overthinking too much. The process can feel a little unmooring, and you might have moments when you ask yourself if you're doing it right. Don't worry. Stick with it, feel around for the next answer, throw it out there, and you may find that your themes will magically emerge through the mist.

Participants: You can do this alone or with a partner.

Time to complete: 10–15 minutes.

Planning time: You'll need a few minutes to identify the artistic choice you're going to interrogate and to make sure it's central to your play.

Planning requirements: This exercise, as I outline it here, is for when you're midprocess on a play. There's no specific preparation required, but it works best once you've done some writing and are looking to clarify the deeper themes in your piece.

Other needs or considerations:

- *In a group:* This is best done in pairs. If in a group, split into pairs and ask each other the five whys, one by one.
- *On your own:* Ask yourself each why, and write down or audio-record your answer.

Instructions: First, make a statement about a central artistic choice you have made in your play, one that you may not be sure about. It can be a structural choice, a pivotal action a character takes, or a choice of scene location or environment—anything that you may be questioning or that others have questioned about your piece. I'll use one of my own plays as an example.

My artistic choice: There are no scenes between the songs in my cabaret musical *Angelmakers: Songs for Female Serial Killers*.

Ask yourself the *first why*: Why are there no scenes between the songs?

Because the songs contain all the information you need to know.

Proceed to the *second why*: Why do the songs contain all the information you need to know?

Because it's a concert.

Ask the *third why*: Why is it a concert?

Because a concert allows people a chance to sing, be seen, and be heard—which they deserve.

Fourth why: Why does everyone deserves a chance to sing, be seen, and be heard?

Because everyone's voice has value, no matter who they are or what they've done.

Fifth why: Why does everyone's voice have value, no matter who they are or what they've done?

Because to ascribe value to some people's lives and not others leads to injustice, rage, despair, and nearly all the other types of suffering in the world.

And guess what, guys? Turns out that was exactly what was at the root of my play and my impulse to write it. The tagline of *Angelmakers* became "Everyone deserves one song." And the structure and staging has come to support and recapitulate that theme.

During your process, you've most likely been hard at work crafting individual moments and scenes of a piece, which is of course incredibly vital, but making a connection between your artistic choices and their thematic underpinnings can allow you to continue with that basic thematic nugget in the back of your mind, a lodestar to guide your writing into the realm of the universal. And if the answers to your whys suggest your artistic choice isn't grounded in something meaningful to you, then you can change that choice and try a different course.

Notes: If the answer to that fifth why is not something you feel strongly about, then reconsider where your play is going. In my opinion, it's impossible to write a truly great play about something you don't care about, and the last thing the world needs is another drop in the sea of lukewarm material out there. Your time is worth saving for the ideas that light you on fire.

WHAT HAUNTS YOU?

Gary Winter

Category: Approach, tone, delicacy, mystery

Overview: Use your personal mysteries to prompt the beginnings of a play. This is a chance to use the energy of an event in your life that has always haunted you. You may have assumed the event was too insignificant to write a play about, and that's fine. The energy of the mystery has meaning and can prompt a drama.

For example, in my play *Barge*, I was thinking about a childhood friend who died of a drug overdose. That seemed to me to lend itself to an overly dramatic, uninteresting play. However, even many years after the incident, it haunted me, so I simply allowed two characters to talk about it and see where it went, without any preconceived idea or message. By following my characters, it turned out they did have something surprising to say.

Participants: Individual.
Time to complete: As long as you like.
Planning time: None.
Other needs or considerations: None.

Instructions: When you think back to the thing that haunts you, begin by having your characters talk about the event in the simplest terms, faithful to the facts. This might not feel interesting, but think of it as a source of energy. This energy begins the process of an unfolding. Focus on staying in the moment—try not to care too much. Trust that the talking is dramatic enough and is integral to the unfolding process. Trust that not having an agenda or idea will reveal things about your characters. You are always writing through yourself, and your voice will come through. Trust that you'll figure out what your play is about after you write it.

A guiding idea or image while you write is delicacy or lightness. Your body should feel light. That doesn't mean your subject matter won't be heavy. I find the feeling of lightness allows me to listen to my characters better. Stay in the moment, and be humble toward your characters. You don't know more than your characters. I find when I don't control my characters, when I follow them, let them lead me to unexpected and strange places, my writing is at its most dynamic.

Be in a quiet space. I think your physical state of mind affects your writing. Do some sort of warm-ups, gentle stretches, yoga, tai chi, whatever relaxes you. When you sit down to write, be as relaxed as possible. Visualize the scene and characters, and if that changes, go with it. If the scene and characters change in the middle of your writing, just go with it. Does she become a he? Does the space go from a living room to the laundry room to an abstract, nonspecific space? Revelations might be microscopic, but they are meaningful. Don't worry about entertaining your audience. This can also apply to the structure, scenario, costume, sound, lighting, and so on.

Imagine your characters in a space beyond the scope of your play. All of the above applies, but a switch of location could be useful because it might give you some distance from the event that sparked the writing. A new setting, tone, temperature, or mood might add a different energy to the play.

Notes: None.

STIRRING DA ROUX

Sharon Bridgforth

Category: Writing prompts to unearth buried stories, unblocking creativity

Overview: This exercise will help you deepen your ability to fully embody and manifest your artistic vision by doing the work of unearthing, examining, and articulating the stories that might be buried and blocking your creativity.

Participants: Alone or in a group.
Time to complete: Varies.
Planning time: Time to lean into support systems (therapy, friendships, spiritual practices, etc.).
Planning requirements: Be mindful in giving yourself enough time and space to fully respond to and feel what emerges. Write down and tend to what emerges for seven days after you complete the process of responding to the prompts included here.
Other needs or considerations:

- *In a group:* Focus on your own journey, insights, questions, creative responses, feelings, and knowings. Share the writing that emerges. Talk about your discoveries and experiences. This is *not* therapy, though personal issues might rise to the surface.
- *On your own:* Along the way, ask yourself, "What am I feeling? What is that feeling about? How does that feeling affect how I live my life? What does that have to do with how I make work?" Notice what is getting stirred, what is being asked internally of you, what wants to happen. There is no right or wrong. The point is the journey. Follow your gut, intuition, passion, curiosities, and knowings. Be courageous. Don't go where you can't safely return from. Care for yourselves in the process. Support yourself in whatever ways feel whole and right, especially now with so much isolation, horror, and openings all over the world.

Instructions: Write in response to the following prompts: What is the oldest story that is running your life in an unhealthy way? How old were you when this story first surfaced in your life? What is the story of that? Where does that story live in your body? Breathing into the part of your body holding that story, what does your body tell you? What would you like to say to that part of your body? What would you like to say to your younger self? What can you release that might just save, shift, or realign your life? What is the story of that?

Sitting with joy, curiosity, and passion and using as few words as possible, write what that story is about. Gather research (books, films, music, conversations, etc.) that supports your knowing about the story. Write. Write. Write. When you are ready, share what you have written with someone (or a group) whom you trust. Ask questions that you might have about the writing, and invite them to ask you questions. Then write, write, and write some more. And repeat the sharing process.

Notes: None.

THE OBJECT LESSON

Caridad Svich

Category: Focus, tone, spatiality, scene work, associative and observational skill-building

Overview: The purpose of this exercise is to focus on what is seen in the mind's eye, rooting it and allowing it to take shape. Think of this exercise as one that will move from portraiture to the frame of the portrait.

Participants: Alone or in a group.
Time to complete: 5–20 minutes.
Planning time: 3-minute dance, sing, or move; 3-minute freewrite.
Planning requirements: Dance, sing, or move in some way before doing this exercise.

Other needs or considerations:

- *In a group:* If you are in a group, set aside about three minutes to dance, sing, or move to some music and then about three minutes to freewrite before launching into this exercise.
- *On your own:* Same as in a group.

Instructions: focus on a still point in the distance in your mind. this could be a place from childhood, a specific object in memory, or a person seen from afar.

start drawing the portrait of what you visualize. render it in both line drawing and in word. try to capture what you see in your mind's eye as vividly as possible. make sure what you see is from the outside. try not to focus on what it feels like but on what and how it is or how the person is rather than what they feel. make the portrait as full as possible.

add elements of color, light, and shadow to the composition of the portrait. consider the rhythm and tempo of the portrait.

now set the portrait in motion in your mind. observe how the place, object, or person you have chosen moves through time and space.

make a new line drawing, this time with no words, maybe just with sounds and shapes. then start working on a scene that features this place, object, or person in a situation. the scene could be for a play, libretto, spoken-word piece, or film. try not to dictate the form of it yet. just focus on making the scene come alive.

incorporate the following line of text: "I could be here forever or just one hour." incorporate the following image: a gathering at sundown, a farewell to another day or time.

write the scene. let it flow.

midway through, change the tenor of the scene's temperature. maybe turn it upside down or simply relocate its physical dimensions or parameters. as you work, keep the tone of the work alive and present. stay anchored and focused.

Notes: None.

BUILDING FROM VISCERA

Alice Tuan

Category: Fresh-mind writing

Overview: In an overlanguaged world, it is difficult to write from a fresh mind. This exercise is a chance to visit with your natural core of expression and see what's under that kinetic distraction of social twitting language.

This exercise requires that you write before engaging with any device—this may be the most difficult part of the exercise. The head that you wake up with is your fresh mind.

The first day that I committed to fresh-mind writing, it took me thirty minutes to get out of bed and go directly to the writing table—thirty minutes—because I was mindlessly reaching for the device but then also wanted a new way into my language brain. The thing is to get yourself to your writing space and just sit there. Allow yourself to sit there. Blank. Still. Sit for five minutes. If you feel you can't do it, then try. If you still can't do it, then wait for that day when everything is off, your writing is shit, and nothing matters. Promise yourself the next day you will do whatever it takes to wake and go straight to your writing space, even if you have to get up thirty minutes earlier. Commit to the discomfort of breaking a habit or pattern and knocking open new doors. Start carving a space for fresh-mind writing and all the patience with and befriending of yourself that you need.

You are ready to start the light exercise. This is a scene with two characters. It is built with light. Light is power. Whoever has the light shining on them has the power in the scene. Write from intuition or deepen an existing character. Underneath it all is a reversal.

Participants: Individual/group.
Time to complete: 40 minutes.
Planning time: None.
Planning requirements: Pen and paper; ideally, one person administers/keeps time so that the writers are free.

Instructions: Think of a character. They may be out of air, from this moment, or an existing character in your play. Write the name of this character.

Close your eyes. Imagine light shining down on your character. Feel the light's warmth, the rays beaming on your/your character's surface. Keep feeling the light, how it gives strength and potency to your character, those associations with brightness, with heat, with expansion, with sun. As responses arise, open your eyes and write a monologue for your character in this light.

Write for ten minutes. If you get stuck, close your eyes and feel the light shining. Keep feeling the light shining until something arises. If nothing comes, keep feeling the light shining until something does. Continue to bask and write the monologue, when suddenly—

A knock on the door. Stop the monologue midsentence with a dash (—).

Close your eyes. Imagine your character going to the door. They turn the knob. They open the door. Write the name of the first person who comes to mind when the door opens. This is your second character.

Start a dialogue between your initial character and the second character. The initial character still has light, warmth, and brightness shining down on them. They have the power in the scene. They dominate the scene. Write this dialogue for ten minutes.

Wherever the dialogue ends after ten minutes, place a dash (—) and then write, "(pause)."

Close your eyes. Imagine the shift of light from the initial character to the second character. Feel the warmth, the brightness, the heat shifting over to the second character. The second character is gaining power and strength, and when the light is fully beaming on them, they then have the power in the scene. The second character dominates the scene. Write for ten minutes.

At the end of ten minutes, there is darkness—blackout. A new color slowly fades up and illuminates the two characters. Write for five more minutes. Finish.

Notes: None.

CHARACTER CREATION EXERCISE

Greg Vovos

Category: Free-form character building, intuitive exploration

Overview: The purpose of this exercise is to both strengthen your intuitive writing and help you build interesting and layered characters quickly and honestly. I use this exercise often because it's a nonpressure, quick, and easy way to create characters who surprise me. It's helpful when I'm beginning a new play, when I'm stuck or blocked on a scene, or even when I'm just searching for new ideas. Finally, I use this exercise when I just want to write and I'm feeling resistant or at a loss for ideas. The fun and ease of it helps me show up and write.

Participants: You alone but can also be done with a group of writers.
Time to complete: 10–15 minutes, but it can vary depending on the length of the responses. It's up to the writer, really.
Planning time: Zero planning time.
Planning requirements: Just find a place to write where you won't be interrupted, and have something you can write freely on. Though

you can start with this exercise, it's often helpful to do a short journaling or freewriting exercise just before to get deeper into your intuitive mind.

Other needs or considerations:

- *In a group:* It can be useful to have one person read all the questions at the beginning as the participants just listen, and then they can write to whatever questions strike them.
- *On your own:* Peace. Solitude. Writing utensils. I find it most helpful to just move from one question to the next, answering each one.

Instructions: The following are a series of questions. Just answer each one, and when you reach the end, you will have a character of considerable depth who might be of service to you in future plays. Feel free to swap out questions, add your own, or follow a question with other questions that might arise as you're creating the characters. This is a great template, but like all things in writing, sometimes off-roading is where we find the treasure.

Have fun and happy writing!

Think of someone:

- How old are they?
- What's their name?
- What is something they're crazy about or know way too much about?
- What will immediately get their attention?
- How happy are they right now?
- Do they have everything they want?
- What's bothering them today?
- In a perfect world, what would be happening today?
- What are their dreams?
- What is keeping them from their dreams: something internal, external, both?

- What is their biggest regret in life?
- What would they change if they could?
- Are they in love?
- Are they full of anger and hate? If so, why?
- Are they plotting something dastardly?
- What is the worst thing they've ever witnessed?
- Is there someone they want to connect with desperately? If so, who and why?
- What do they want today, in this moment?
- What do they want?
- What is keeping them from it?
- What. Do. They. Want?

Notes: The key to this exercise is to not think and to really channel and listen to your intuitive mind. Different writers work differently. Some of us are more conceptual, where we like to plan each thing out, outline, plot it, and so on. And some of us are more intuitive, where we just start writing and have no idea where we're going but are happy to find out. Obviously, both mindsets can be beneficial to us writers.

This exercise is a great way to strengthen your intuitive writing muscle, especially for the writers out there who are more conceptual. So for this exercise, do not think or impose answers that you might like. Simply trust your first instinct, write the answer, and move on to the next question. Enjoy the discovery process. Try not to stop writing, and don't allow this to take too long. The beauty of this exercise is that it asks very little of us in terms of time commitment but rewards us greatly for our intuitive focus.

This has been more fertile ground for me when it comes to writing drama, but with some fun and simple tweaks, it can be valuable for writing comedic characters, as well. Also, this exercise can be used to create new characters or to help you deepen characters you've already been working with.

REAL ESTATE

Sheri Wilner

Category: Character development, setting, conflict, physical action

Overview: This exercise helps writers deepen their understanding about their character(s) not only by identifying very specific information about the homes and rooms they occupy and the possessions they own but also by discovering the active ways they use these spaces. Often we set our plays in vague or generic locations (a bar, a suburban living room) that merely serves as a backdrop for the play's action rather than identifying ways setting can *affect* the play's action.

Being able to visualize our characters inside a very specific room, containing very specific items, in a very specific home, in a very specific town, and in a very specific part of the country helps to create detailed, three-dimensional characters and allows us to identify such things as their economic class; what items they treasure and value; their aesthetic tastes; the degree to which their environment positively or negatively affects them; and the ways they distract, deflect, communicate, or avoid through physical activity. So much about our characters' inner lives, psychology, and given circumstances are revealed through their homes, possessions, physical actions, and environment, and this exercise gives us countless possibilities for such methods of portraying and developing character.

Participants: Individual or group
Time to complete: 30 minutes individually or, for a group, 60–180 minutes, depending on class size.
Planning time: None.
Planning requirements: Internet access.
Other needs or considerations:

- *In a group:* Individuals in a group are given fifteen to twenty minutes of time to search the internet for images of their character's homes, rooms, and workplaces. Alternatively, they can be assigned the image search as a take-home exercise and present their found images in class. After each individual shares their images, the other participants brainstorm and pitch potential scenes, moments, physical actions, or conflicts that exploit of the specifics of each setting.
- *On your own:* This exercise can take anywhere between fifteen and sixty minutes, depending on the number of characters and locations in your play. You'll need internet access and some familiarity with how to find images online.

Instructions:

1. Choose a character in your play (preferably your main character, but eventually you should complete this exercise for all characters), and then make a list of all the locations in your play. If the play does not depict your characters in their homes, you should nevertheless add the exterior and interior images of their homes to your list.
2. Identify the city, town, and state where the play takes place, as well as the time period.
3. Go to such real estate and/or apartment- and home-finder websites as Zillow, Realtor.com, Craigslist, and so on, and enter the zip code of where you believe your characters live. If you have set your play in a fictional location, decide on an actual place that most closely resembles your play's setting. Alternatively, instead of using these websites, you can do a general internet image search using such phrases as *Midwestern kitchen 1950s* or *modern urban workspaces*.
4. Look at the results of your search, clicking on individual properties for exterior and interior views, and identify the property

that most seems like where your character would live. You do not need to limit yourself to one property. For example, you can use the exterior of one property but the interior of others. Feel free to mix and match!

5. If they do not live in a familiar location, also find a map that shows where their city or town is located so that you get a sense of how densely populated the area is, how far they need to travel to shop, how close or far their nearest neighbor is, and so on.

6. Regardless of where your play is set (e.g., a restaurant or office), make sure you find images of the exterior and interior of their homes, making sure to include their bedroom, kitchen, living room, and/or other important rooms or outdoor spaces (e.g., a garden, a crafting room). Also find images of the neighborhood where their home is located.

7. If the play is not set in their home, find images of where each scene is set, such as their workplace, a restaurant, playground, beach, or hair salon.

8. Once you have found images for all the most important locations, look closely at all the decor, furniture, doors, windows, and items in each room, taking note of such things as condition, value, and style.

9. Imagine your character(s) in each space, and make a list of all the items they can physically interact with. You can also list items that are not found in your image but you think the character would own. The important thing isn't your fidelity to your images but rather to have an actual and vivid representation of where your scenes are set or where your characters live. Feel free to add or subtract any items that do not match your conception.

10. (Optional) Write a scene (or revise one that already exists) in which you depict your character(s) engaged in a physical

action in one of the rooms you have found. Try to have them use as many items of furniture and props as possible. See how long you can sustain your characters performing the action(s) and using the items while keeping their dialogue tightly focused on the action and their emotional needs and objectives in the *subtext* of the dialogue. For example, for a scene in your character's kitchen, decide what they are cooking, baking, or cleaning; what items they are using to do so; and how the physical action can contain subtext and be used as a strategy for them to fulfill their objective.

11. (Optional) As examples of how playwrights make full use of their settings, read *A Streetcar Named Desire* or *Long Day's Journey into Night*, and note all the props that are used and reused and how every square inch of the plays' settings are exploited. In *Streetcar*, such items include a light bulb, a paper lantern, a radio, liquor, food, Blanche's trunk, the contents of the trunk (letters from the Grey boy, documents about Belle Reve, jewelry, gowns, furs), the kitchen/poker table, the bathroom and bathtub, the bed, and the lace curtains. Consider how Williams always kept his characters engaged in physical action and how the play's conflicts and escalation in conflicts arose from the characters' use of props and setting. Track, for instance, how the radio is used as a source of escape and entertainment for Blanche, thrown out the window by Stanley, and then later repaired by Stanley as a way to reconcile with Stella.

12. (Optional) Choose a prop or props in one of the play's locations, and try to identify ways the characters' usage of this prop can chart their journey and arc in the play. Can the prop have a different value, and/or can our characters' relationship to it change every time it is used? An excellent example of this is the school bell in *My Children! My Africa!* by Athol Fugard. Read the play, and note, how every time the school bell is

rung, it charts an escalation of the play's conflict. How might the items in your images be used to the same effect?

13. Whenever you work on your play, keep the images you've found of all the play's settings in front of you, always imagining your characters in these locations; using all the props and furniture in each location; and considering such environmental factors as sounds (traffic, sirens), weather (rain, sunshine), time of day and year (morning, winter), and smells. Try to identify how all five of your characters' senses are engaged by these factors.

Notes: None.

THE WALLET EXERCISE

Justin Maxwell

Category: Character

Overview: There's an anecdote in the writing world that an author can look at a menu and know what each of their characters would order. They know what the characters would order because they know the characters. The implication is that a writer who doesn't know what their characters would order hasn't fully developed their characters yet. While this exercise doesn't inherently lead to generating new text, it does create an opportunity for further character development.

Participants: Individual or in a group.
Time to complete: About 15 minutes.
Planning time: None.
Planning requirements: None.
Other needs or considerations: None.

Instructions:

1. Make a list of all the objects in your wallet right now. What do they reveal about you? What do they fail to reveal about you?
2. Think about your protagonist or any character that you're developing. Generate a list of their traits. Set it aside.
3. Without thinking about it (as quickly as possible), generate a list of things they have in their wallet.
4. What does the list reveal about them? What does it conceal about them?
5. Select a trait of the character that directly ties into the play's central conflict.
6. Consciously make a list of three to five objects in the character's wallet that reveal the selected trait in step 5.
7. If this is done in a group, have the participants read their lists from step 6. Can others in the group identify the trait that was chosen?
8. If the character reveals the contents of their wallet, what will the audience know about them? What happens to the stakes if that reveal happens at the beginning of the show? The middle? The end?

Variation: While this exercise is designed to have the writer use objects to reveal abstract traits, the character can unknowingly reveal traits to the audience.

1. Quickly generate a brief list of random objects, or pull a few nouns from the dictionary.
2. Pick one thing from the list that your character from the first exercise wouldn't be deeply familiar with. Be careful not to pick something completely alien to the character, but select something that they wouldn't have a technical knowledge of. For example, a character who watches a lot of police procedurals on TV has seen a lot of guns, but when they pick up a

handgun for the first time, they're going to have *something* to say about it.

3. Write a brief block of text wherein the character describes the object.

4. What does the character reveal about themselves in the description? What would an audience learn if they heard that description? After all, a character who picks up that handgun and says, "It's so heavy," is very different from the one who says, "The hour of blood begins," and different yet again from the one who says, "Are you as turned on as I am?"

5. Write another small block of text where the character describes the object for another character. How does the character change their description when they are being observed? What does that reveal about them?

Notes: This exercise and its variant are about letting concrete objects reveal abstract character. Remember that people are complex and paradoxical. Characters often should be, too.

GET A SPINE

Katherine Gwynn

Category: Character

Overview: The purpose of this exercise is to build strong and dynamic characters, and get to the core of what makes them tick. How do they move through the world? What is their spine built of?

Participants: Alone or in a group.
Time to complete: 15–30 minutes.
Planning time: None (don't overthink it).
Planning requirements: Paper, pen, or a laptop—however you prefer to write—and at least the idea of a character and what your play is about.

Other needs or considerations:
- *In a group:* You can jump right in.
- *On your own:* The same deal.

Instructions: (If doing this in a group, read or say the following paragraph.) I first developed this method when I was writing my first full-length play, and I was trying to figure out what drove my characters at their core—what I always needed to keep in mind with every piece of dialogue I wrote for them. For example, in my *Merely Players*, which starts in the middle of the epilogue of Shakespeare's *As You Like It* (*AYLI*), Rosalind and Phoebe play a game of cat and mouse throughout. I wanted to differentiate my interpretation of the characters without throwing out what had made them tick in *AYLI*. I realized I wanted to know how they would be choreographed around one another, as characters. I wanted more than a want—I wanted an *action*.

For each character in your play, you are going to attempt to build their spine—an infinitive verb that activates and propels all their choices and movements in your play. Choose a character of yours. Then generate a list of verbs that correspond to that character; fill at least a page. Once you've done that, pick a few that feel strongest to you, and then make each of your selected verbs an infinitive phrase. For example, maybe you've chosen *flay*, *stab*, and *run* as your verbs. Make these into *to flay*, *to stab*, and *to run*. Write this next to whatever character description you already have for your character and their name.

Consider each thoughtfully. What does it mean if this character's purpose is to flay? To stab? To run? If you've written a piece of a dialogue for the character, consider how that dialogue is changed by the undercurrents of these new verb phrases. Do they exist in the dialogue? Can they exist in the dialogue? Should they exist in the dialogue? And if you haven't written dialogue yet for them, try to write just a line for a scene yet unwritten with these undercurrents in mind. If this character has a moment where they confront their father, how do they say hello while trying to flay, while trying to stab, or while trying to run?

Once you find infinitive verb phrase that feels truest or most exciting, that's your spine. Place it next to your character description while you write the rest of the play, and if you ever feel lost about what that character should do, refer to the spine.

Notes: Don't overthink it. This is supposed to be fun and helpful, not drudgery.

DAILY SCHEDULE

Sheri Wilner

Category: Character development, plot ideas, physical action

Overview: This exercise helps writers deepen their understanding of their characters by discovering how they live their lives and spend their days during those times we are *not* depicting them onstage. By identifying what *else* they do; who *else* they see; where *else* they go; and what *other* activities, relationships, and conflicts they engage in besides and between the moments our play depicts, we not only develop a fuller understanding of our characters but also become able to identify scene by scene where they have physically come from and what has occurred the moment before they enter the scenes of our plays.

The more we replace the practice of writing puppetlike characters who exist and live only during the scenes or our plays, the more they become three-dimensional, complex individuals who have a variety of other experiences, activities, conflicts, stresses, and relationships outside the action of our play, which can all inform their behavior *in* our play. For example, a character who must sit in heavy traffic for an hour or more en route to work each morning will arrive there in a much different emotional state than the one who meditates for an hour before a casual ten-minute stroll to their job. Such details make our characters more interesting and lifelike to our audiences while also helping us discover ways to escalate the conflicts and tensions in the play.

The exercise also helps us to identify how our characters might continue the action of our play between the scenes we have written, helping us to sustain and escalate the emotional arc of their journey. When they exit our scenes, where do they go and what do they do? Do their anger, fear, and desperation rise? Do they take any actions to fulfill their emotional needs and achieve their objectives? What events can transpire after they exit a scene that cause them to enter the next scene in a different, more escalated emotional state?

Additionally, this exercise helps us to identify other settings, locations, events, actions, and characters that might inspire new scenes in our plays, specifically ones that involve physical action and more dynamic settings. It also shows us what our characters might value or enjoy (e.g., hobbies, physical exercise, cultural events, volunteering) in addition to what we depict them doing.

Participants: Individual or group (though the group should have familiarity with each other's plays).
Time to complete: 60–180 minutes for a group, depending on its size; 20–60 minutes for an individual, depending on their familiarity with their characters).
Planning time: None.
Planning requirements: Paper and pencil or laptop.
Other needs or considerations:
- *In a group:* Individuals in a group are given fifteen to twenty minutes of writing time to create as much of a daily schedule for their chosen character as possible. After the individual

writing time has concluded, everyone reads their work. The other members of the group provide feedback about possible scenes, events, settings, or characters that would serve the writer's story. The presenting writer benefits by hearing their cohort's opinions. The other writers are served by hearing the numerous possibilities members of their class conceived.

- *On your own:* Individual writers can do this exercise in one sitting or continually contribute to it through multiple sittings. The goal is to account for every minute of their characters' daily lives and to discover weekly, monthly, or annual events.

Instructions:

1. Choose a character in your play, preferably your main character, but eventually you should complete this exercise for all your characters.

2. Starting from the moment your character wakes up in the morning to the time they go to sleep at night, and document hour by hour how they spend a typical day, being as detailed and as specific as possible. You can do this in smaller time increments, but try not to use time increments longer than an hour. *Create both weekday and weekend schedules*, noting the differences between them. What time does your character wake up on a weekday versus on the weekend? What activities occupy their weekends that they don't have the time to do during the week?

3. As you work on their daily schedule, try to answer such questions as
   - What time do they wake up?
   - Do they get out of bed right away or linger for a while?
   - What do they eat and drink for breakfast?
   - How do they get ready for work/their day?

- Do they work from home? If not, what time do they leave? How do they get there? How long does it take? What do they do during the commute?
- Do they typically arrive early or late?
- If they are unemployed, then how do they spend their day?
- When do they take a lunch break? Do they bring lunch or eat out? With whom?
- What are their daily/weekly/monthly tasks at work?
- What time do they go home?
- How do they spend their evenings?
- When and where (and with whom) do they have dinner? What are some typical meals?
- What do they do before sleep? Read (what?), watch TV (what?), exercise (where/how), surf online (what sites to they visit?)?
- What time do they get into bed? Do they have trouble falling asleep? Why?
- What habits, hobbies, activities, and obligations do they have?
- Who do they spend time with? Spouse? Lover? Children? Friends? Alone? When and how?

4. Try to account for every hour, adding in additional events and activities other than those listed in step 3. If they do certain things only on specific days of the week (e.g., attend a playwriting class on Tuesday evenings, 6:00–9:00 p.m.), then include it, even though they don't attend the class every day.

5. (Optional) After you've finished the exercise, write a scene that depicts your character(s) engaged in one of the activities listed. Look for moments, activities, relationships, or events that both escalate the play's conflict and your character's emotional state and contribute to the plot. For example, how does

your character decompress after a stressful workday? What would happen if their opportunity to do this is thwarted?

Notes: An alternative way of approaching this exercise was discovered by one of my Dramatist Guild Institute students, the playwright William Fowkes, who created a "beat sheet" for everything his characters did between each scene. This is an ingenious method to identify your characters' actions, activities, encounters, emotional states, and challenges during those moments they are not depicted in your play and informs their mood, behavior, actions, and objectives when they enter a scene.

EAVESDROPPED CONVERSATION

Gab Reisman

Category: Listening, observation, writing dialogue, crystalizing and/or theatricalizing daily life

Overview: In a time when so many of us are constantly on our devices, this exercise reminds us to look outside ourselves for inspiration, to listen to the cadence of other people's speech, and to notice the true weirdness and nuance of how we communicate. It will help you diversify and differentiate the voices of your characters and realize that characters do not always go after what they want directly.

Participants: Best done alone, in proximity to other people, but can be done in a group.
Time to complete: At least 20 minutes, though you could spend infinite time on this.
Planning time: No planning time required.
Planning requirements: Public places where people are engaged in conversation, a notebook and pencil or laptop, phone (optional).

Other needs or considerations:
- *In a group:* Spread out, and seek out separate conversations, or like a group painting a still life, record the same conversation and compare takes.
- *On your own:* None.

Instructions:
1. Bring a writing device—a notebook or computer—as well as a phone to record if need be.
2. Plant yourself in a public place where you are in earshot of conversations; similarly, listen for conversations as you move through your daily life. What strikes you as interesting? What grabs your attention? Observe how the salacious or the outrageous runs up against the mundane in these conversations.
3. Write down the conversation verbatim. Honor *ums* and *uhs*, pauses, filler words—include it all. If you feel like you can't write as fast as folks are speaking, record it on your phone and transcribe it later.
4. Once you have your eavesdropped conversation down in all its intricacies and eccentricates, theatricalize it. Add a greater point of conflict, or shift the setting to somewhere more dramatic. However, do this while keeping the voices you've recorded intact.

Notes: Is it ethical to record the conversations of strangers without their knowledge for the purpose of a writing exercise? It's a gray area. I would encourage you to delete any sound recording you make of these conversations as soon as you have transcribed them and to theatricalize them in a way that obscures the identify of those you've eavesdropped on. Have fun, be safe, and happy listening.

USELESS SUPERHERO POWER

Justin Maxwell

Category: Building plot, finding a McGuffin

Overview: In reading and watching plays, plots often appear to happen organically based on something that a protagonist wants. However in practice, plots are completely arbitrary devices. While a writer may come to a plot unconsciously, thinking through the challenges that await a protagonist can often let first drafts, freewrites, or outlines happen much more concisely. This is an informal exercise to explore building plots consciously with a low-stakes approach.

Participants: Individual or group.
Time to complete: Varies.
Planning time: None.
Planning requirements: None.
Other needs or considerations:
- *In a group:* Allow extra time to discuss steps 4 and 6.
- *On your own:* Skip steps 4 and 6, or spend some metacognitive time seeing if they produce anything epiphanic.

Instructions:
1. Imagine the amazing abilities of various superheroes, like X-ray vision, flight, invisibility, strength, and so on. They're generally useful skills that one can use to do good deeds (or villainous ones, for the supervillains).
2. Now imagine a useless superpower, something beyond the ability of a normal person but that can't be used for good (or villainous) purposes. For example, the ability to telepathically know the name and address of the dentists of everyone within five feet of you or the telekinetic ability to life an object

weighing six ounces or less that doesn't extend beyond arm's reach or the ability to look like any person in the world but only when nobody can see you.

3. Give that superpower to the one person in the world who would be overjoyed to have it. Who are they? Why are they so happy for this ability?

4. If done in a group, everyone exchange characters and their powers with someone else.

5. Now, write the moment where that person gets a chance to save the day. Maybe it's in a small way, maybe a big way. Maybe the person who can see what happened on that day at the spot where they're standing 2,500 years ago realizes that they'll make a really good archeologist! Maybe the person who can smell uncommon nickel-iron mixtures knows an asteroid is coming and saves the world!

6. If done in a group, take a little time to share the results of step 5.

7. Write a brief outline with the experience of step 5 as the start of a narrative. What happens next? Where does the character go from here?

8. Write a brief outline with the experience of step 5 as the climax of a plot. How is this moment the moment of maximum conflict or desire? Does it produce an epiphany for the character?

9. Write a brief outline with the experience of step 5 as the resolution of a plot. How does this moment represent the culmination of a personal journey for the main character?

Notes: From steps 7, 8, and 9, it's easy to move into writing a first draft. Simply flesh out the outline that feels the most compelling, the one you care about the most, and turn it from notes into dialogue! Let that epiphany be your McGuffin.

MAPPING THE STORY

Rachel Rubin Ladutke

Category: Plot, structure, characterization

Overview: This is an exercise for developing the plot and clarifying the characters' relationships for yourself as the writer, which in turn will make them more accessible to readers and audiences.

Participants: The playwright.
Time to complete: Varies (according to length of play and how detailed you will get).
Planning time: None—just dive in!
Planning requirements: Paper and pencil.
Other needs or considerations: None.

Instructions:
1. Make a list of your characters. Include a very brief description of who they are (you will use this later). Don't be surprised if you add to it as the play goes along. Someone else may walk in the door.
2. Beginning with the first scene, write out a very rough outline of what happens in the scene. Don't worry about every entrance and exit—do this in broad strokes. Here's an example: "Act I, Scene 1. An afternoon in March. Liza returns home from a tour just as Marti's mother, Evelyn, shows up unexpectedly. The girls are less than thrilled because their friends are coming up for the weekend, and they are planning an important talk. Characters: Liza, Marti, Evelyn."
3. Continue this through each scene. You may find that the play has more scenes than you realized or that two scenes you thought were necessary can be combined.

4. At some point, you'll want to return to your character list. Draw a diagram to figure out each character's relationship to the other characters in the play. It doesn't necessarily have to only include characters who appear onstage together. For example, in *Hamlet*, the Queen is terrified when she hears that her son Hamlet has seen his father's ghost; she herself never sees the apparition, but of course she has strong emotions about him.

5. Resist the urge to write dialogue at this stage. Focusing on the big picture at the start will help the rest fall into place.

Notes: Whether you do your actual writing on a device or not, this should be done the old-fashioned way, with paper and pencil. I do this once I've got a rough idea of what story is being told and who will be a part of telling it. It has helped me bridge the gap between getting a germ of an idea and finding a way to tell the story. I find that this has been a very helpful process while writing my last three plays, which are all very different. The story and characters evolve naturally once the foundation is in place. At any point, you may find it helpful to repeat the process, this time with more detail. Dialogue may even begin to emerge—this is great (after the first go-round).

This can be an ongoing exercise or a one-time activity to get the play jump-started. There's really no way to misuse it. Also, upon repeating the process, it's fine to let dialogue flow. By then, you'll have a clearer idea of the story, and you can trust your instincts.

The best advice I can give: Don't argue with your characters; get out of the way and type what they say. You can always debate them later, but you want to establish a good relationship at the start so they will trust you with their stories.

Now, pick up that pencil (or, if you're feeling brave, pen!), and happy writing!

To help illustrate the process, see figure 2.1 for the character map from my play *The Way Home*.

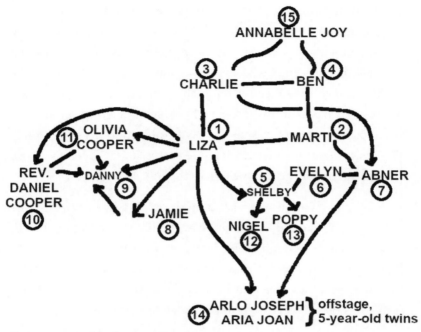

Character map for *The Way Home*

1. LIZA COOPER: Married to Marti. They have five-year-old twins. Charlie is her best friend. Shelby is her aunt. Evelyn is her mother-in-law. Danny is her brother. Jamie is Danny's teenager. Reverend Cooper and Olivia are her parents.

2. MARTI KAPLAN: Married to Liza. Mother of Arlo Joseph and Aria Joan (five-year-old twins; never appear onstage but often referred to). Ben is her best friend. She is currently a surrogate for Ben and Charlie's baby. Evelyn is her mother. Shelby is her business partner. Reverend Cooper and Olivia are her in-laws. Danny is her brother-in-law.

3. CHARLIE STUART-MORSE: Married to Ben. Liza's best friend since childhood. Charlie is the biological father of Liza and Marti's five-year-old twins, Arlo and Aria. Abner is his grandfather.

4. BENJAMIN STUART-MORSE: Married to Charlie. Marti is his best friend. Marti is the surrogate for Ben and Charlie's baby.

5. SHELBY COOPER: Liza's aunt. Danny is her nephew. Marti is her business partner in the inn. Evelyn is her best friend, and they are planning to open a coffeehouse together. Reverend Cooper is her brother.

6. EVELYN KAPLAN: Marti's mother. Liza is her daughter-in-law. Shelby is her best friend, and they are planning to open a coffeehouse together. Evelyn and Abner are in a relationship. Grandmother of Arlo and Aria.

7. ABNER MORSE: Charlie's grandfather. He's recovering from a double hip replacement and turning eighty-five. He was widowed many years ago. He and Evelyn are in a relationship.

8. JAMIE COOPER: Fifteen-year-old child of Liza's brother Danny. They recently came out as nonbinary, which has driven a wedge between them and their father. Liza and Marti are Jamie's aunts. Arlo and Aria are their cousins. Reverend Cooper and Olivia are their grandparents.

9. DANNY COOPER: Liza's older brother. Jamie is his middle child (of five) and his most beloved. Reverend Cooper and Olivia are his parents. Shelby is his aunt.

10. REVEREND DANIEL COOPER: Married to Olivia; Liza and Danny's father; grandfather of Arlo, Aria, Jamie, and Jamie's four siblings. Shelby is his sister.

11. OLIVIA COOPER: Married to Reverend Cooper; Liza and Danny's mother; grandmother of Arlo, Aria, Jamie, and Jamie's four siblings. Shelby is her sister-in-law.

This exercise is best done on your own. I do engage in it during my Zoom writing sessions, but each of us is writing independently and then periodically checking in, so it's still not a group.

BACKGROUND TIMELINE

Duncan Pflaster

Category: Making up research

Overview: In this exercise, you will make a year-by-year background timeline for your characters to help you think more deeply about the background/backstory of your characters.

Participants: Individual.
Time to complete: 5 minutes to as long as you want.
Planning time: 5 minutes.
Planning requirements: A spreadsheet program you like.
Other needs or considerations: None.

Instructions:
1. Decide what year your play is set in. (Unless I'm doing a period piece, I like to set my plays a year or two ahead of my present date because who knows how long a production might take.)
2. Make a spreadsheet in Excel or Google Sheets with that year at the top, and do a −1 formula going down the column.
3. In the next column, take a character and how old they are (or estimate a number). Drag that down with a −1 formula, as well, so you can see how old a character would have been in certain years.
4. Consider if any of those years overlap with . . . a war they might have been drafted for or avoided. The year same-sex marriage was legalized nationwide. The year Lunchables were invented. The three years your favorite TV show ran. Who was president when they were born? Who was president when they were first able to vote?
5. Check Wikipedia by year (or an encyclopedia or more granular reference book) to see what important world events might

have occurred during years that would be significant for your characters. Add anything you find interesting to the spreadsheet, and see if the knowledge of their past might spark anything new.

6. If you do this on the same spreadsheet for all your characters, then you can also decide how old all of them were the year a significant personal event happened for more than one of them, such as that game of spin the bottle that changed their lives, when a parent died, when their brother was born, and so on.

Notes: This is especially helpful for a period piece, but I've found it useful for most plays. This can also be helpful for a piece set in a fantasy universe to keep track of your own personal timeline of space wars, wizard events, and so on to give a sense of continuity. Table 2.1 is a sample I made while creating my play *Harmony Hall*. The play was inspired by the movie *Boom!* so I set it in 1968, when that movie premiered. *Boom!* is an adaptation of the play *The Milk Train Doesn't Stop Here Anymore* from five years earlier, so I put that on the list, as well.

In my play, Brother Linus, a monk, was sent to an island chapel called Harmony Hall around twenty years prior to the beginning of the play, so 1948. He's been cut off from most human contact since then. I looked for movies around the time he'd been sent away to see what he might have been watching and settled on *The Harvey Girls* as the last movie he'd seen; that led to the character's obsession with Judy Garland (so her big films before 1948 are on the chart). Knowing that World War II was still going on, Linus could have been worried about being drafted as a teen, and his mother would have had a victory garden.

The other character, Christian, washes up on the island where Linus lives during a storm. He ran away from an institution after

Year	Christian	Linus	Personal	World
1968	19	42		Summer of Love, *Boom!* with Elizabeth Taylor premieres
1967	18	41	Christian joins Merchant Marines	*Valley of the Dolls* with Patty Duke premieres
1966	17	40	Christian gets electroshock therapy	
1965	16	39		
1964	15	38		*The Judy Garland Show* ends run
1963	14	37		Beatlemania, Kennedy shot, Tennessee Williams's *The Milk Train Doesn't Stop Here Anymore* premieres on Broadway
1962	13	36		
1961	12	35		*Gunsmoke* ends run
1960	11	34		
1959	10	33		
1958	9	32		
1957	8	31		Allen Ginsberg's *Howl* published
1956	7	30		
1955	6	29		
1954	5	28		
1953	4	27		
1952	3	26		
1951	2	25		
1950	1	24		
1949	0	23		
1948		22	Linus is sent to Harmony Hall	
1947		21		*The Harvey Girls* with Judy Garland premieres
1946		20	Linus enters priesthood	World War II ends, Jack Kerouac and William S. Burroughs's *And the Hippos Were Boiled in Their Tanks* published
1945		19	Linus caught with Paul	*Meet Me in St. Louis* with Judy Garland premieres
1944		18		Ayn Rand's *The Fountainhead* published
1943		17		
1942		16		
1941		15		
1940		14		World War II begins, *The Wizard of Oz* with Judy Garland premieres
1939		13		
1938		12		
1937		11		*Love on the Run* with Clark Gable premieres
1936		10		

his parents gave him electroshock therapy when they discovered he was gay. He has an obsession with beat poetry, and it's implied he studied with Allen Ginsberg once he arrived in New York City. I read *And the Hippos Were Boiled in Their Tanks*, a fictionalized account of the David Kammerer murder, also fictionalized in the film *Kill Your Darlings*, which was written by beat-generation writers Kerouac and Burroughs and which gave me the idea that Christian could have easily joined the Merchant Marines. Christian also has information for Linus about Judy Garland's goings-on since 1948. He knows she had a television show (which he didn't watch often because he preferred *Gunsmoke*), that she was supposed to have been in *Valley of the Dolls*, and so on. I was looking for movie stars whom Linus could have emulated when dating girls and seized on Clark Gable—Linus could have seen *Love on the Run* when he was ten years old.

MOMENT MAPPING

j.chavez

Category: Structure, emotion tracking, moment work

Overview: In this exercise, you will visualize your play as moments and patch together a sequence of events. This exercise works for all forms of plays (linear, nonlinear, cyclical, etc.).

Participants: Individual.
Time to complete: As long as needed.
Planning time: None.
Planning requirements: Index cards, strips of paper, sticky notes, something to write with, and the basic understanding of your work in progress.
Other needs or considerations: None.

Instructions:

1. Using the index cards, write as many moments you have planned for your play. These can be large-scale scenes or very specific stage moments:
   a. Scene with Mom and Dad
   b. Halloween party at Brad's
   c. Big monologue from Lucille
   d. Dream dance sequence of Brad's murder
   e. The dragon and Lucille fly away
2. Think of the emotions at the beginning and end of each scene. How do you want the audience to feel? How do you want the characters to feel?
   a. Joyous → lonely
   b. Overwhelming → reassuring
   c. Scared → full of life
   d. Mysterious → laughing
   e. Fantastical → sad
3. Lay out the order of events, linking together how you want your narrative to go and the emotional journey you want to take the audience on.
4. When you finally feel as though you have it all laid out, write. You might change along the way, and that's okay. Let your characters live through these moments.

Notes: You can think of each moment as a ten-minute scene when you first write them down so that you can begin to visualize the potential length of your piece.

Don't be afraid to overwrite ideas. It's better to have too much and need to trim than try to stretch a couple moments longer than they need to be.

Thinking of stage pictures helps me formulate what emotions the audience feels. What does the lighting look like? What does the actor look like onstage? Is there music playing? How do these elements make the audience feel? What can you write to convey this?

What is required to get from one emotion to the next?

Is your play nonlinear? Try using the emotions within the scenes to track the audience's feelings toward the events rather than just the emotional arc of the characters. Sometimes they go hand in hand, but other times they don't.

Thematically, how do the moments fit together? Do you end one scene with the image of a murder and begin the next scene with a moment of birth? Play with the symbolism you've created, and try spacing out those moments to keep the theme in mind throughout the piece.

THE WHY OF WHERE AND WHEN

Justin Maxwell

Category: Set, setting

Overview: This exercise is designed to make the most of the set and the setting by thinking about where and when a play happens and how that serves us as artists.

The set and the setting are often the first thing we encounter in reading and watching a play, but these two elements are often over-looked because they appear so intrinsic to the show. But they can change the show wildly.

Participants: Individual or in a group.
Time to complete: Varies.
Planning time: Varies.
Planning requirements: Looking at a few masterworks could really help.

Other needs or considerations:

- *In a group:* Discuss your answers to the questions in the following thought exercise. This discussion can lead to some powerful epiphanies about all the ways the set and setting manifest our artwork before characters and dialogue even happen.

Instructions: Start with this thought exercise:

1. You've been commissioned to write a serious drama set in a Ford assembly plant on the night of Obama's first election. The lights come up on opening night. The characters haven't entered yet. What's on the stage?
2. Same as step 1, but this time it's a comedy instead of a drama. What's on the stage now?
3. Same as step 1, but now it's a nonrepresentational nightmare. What's on the stage now?

Then try this pragmatic exercise:

1. Go back to your own play, and think about what happens if it moves two hundred miles in any direction.
2. What happens if it moves twenty years through time?
3. Try it with progressively smaller units of distance and time.
4. If moving the play lessens the drama or the stakes or kills its viability, then the script is probably in the right place and time. If moving it doesn't affect those things, then this device is probably being underused.

If you're working in a nonrepresentational mode and the place is something outside of time or reality, then the place still serves you well. As someone who doesn't write realism, I use this a lot. My dark comedy *Your Lithopedion* simply happens on a couch in a spot of light. The audience sees a couch and the two characters when the show opens. Because of the conventions of contemporary theatre, they assume it's a stylized living room. As the play goes on and the nightmare world of the characters unfolds, the audience slowly realizes just how brutally nonreal the world they're experiencing is.

Conversely, my one-person show about Vincent Van Gogh, *Exhausted Paint*, always happens in an immediate now, on the night of the show the audience is watching. The script is built to accommodate that immediacy and frequently breaks the fourth wall. We have infinite freedom of selection when untethered from realism. This gives us many more choices and much more pressure.

Notes: Audiences tend to subconsciously wonder when and where they are, but as writers it behooves us to ask, "Why are we here and now?" Where and when a play happens often seems organic, thus not a conscious element of construction. We can set a play anywhere from a specific time and place, like *Cabaret* by Joe Masteroff, to something completely subjective, like most of Richard Foreman's oeuvre.

The set and the setting are often the first thing we encounter in reading and watching a play, but these two elements are often overlooked because they appear so intrinsic to the show. But they can change the show wildly.

How does your favorite play change if it's moved two hundred miles through space or twenty years through time? If *Hamlet* moves twenty years through time or space, there's no play. Twenty years earlier, Hamlet's dad is still alive, so there's no inciting incident, no conflict. Twenty years later, his uncle/stepdad has probably died of natural causes, and Hamlet becomes king automatically. Heck, move the play thirty days through time, and the inciting incident hasn't happened, or the players have already passed through, and Hamlet missed his chance to learn the truth. Move the play two hundred miles east, and we're not in Denmark anymore. Move the play two miles and we're not in the castle, which makes political machinations difficult.

When picking a place and a time, be sure to avoid the haunted-house cliché. Think of a haunted house–style ghost story. A family buys a house, moves in, and then discovers it's haunted. Why not just leave? They need to stay for a good reason. The film *Poltergeist* works because Carol Anne, the protagonist's five-year-old kid, is trapped in the netherworld, and they can only get her out from inside the house. How often have you watched a cheap horror movie and rolled your eyes when the teen's car doesn't start? It's disappointing because the set and the setting don't contribute, and the script resorts to clichés. Conversely, treat yourself to watching (or rewatching) the famous *Twilight Zone* episode "Eye of the Beholder." It's a masterpiece of setting.

3

DRAFTING

Exercises in this chapter:

"The Procrastination Technique for Completing a Play (a.k.a. Surrender)" by Rhiana Yazzie.
Embracing procrastination, fear, or panic to get writing started.   *99*

"Pass Along/Out of the Hat" by j.chavez.
Working in a group to overcome writer's block.   *103*

"The Bad Play" by Liz Duffy Adams.
Disrupting writer's block by disrupting your bad habits.   *106*

"Describe the Elephant" by Sam Hamashima.
Using questions and stream of consciousness to overcome writer's block.   *108*

"The Most Boring Play in the World" by Sara Farrington.
Embracing clichés to help the writing happen.   *110*

"The Worst Play (a.k.a. Get Out of Your Own Way)" by Rachel Lynett.
Making an impossible play to unlearn hindering rules.   *114*

"Writing Something You'd Never Want Anyone Else to See in a Million Years" by Young Jean Lee.
Using the personal to make a fast start or get unstuck.   *118*

"New Monologue Perspectives" by Franky D. Gonzalez
Using empathy to generate monologues   *119*

"List of Twenty" by Lindsay Carpenter.
Asking questions and making lists to get unstuck.   *120*

"List It Out" by Kaela Mei-Shing Garvin.
Listing scenes to increase the draft's potential.   *122*

"Miniscenes" by Aaron Ricciardi.
Getting scenes written.   *124*

"Character and Language" by Deborah Yarchun.
Using dialogue to build characters and scenes.   *127*

"Major Dramatic Question" by Reginald Edmund.
Creating strong conflict.   *129*

"Said and Unsaid" by L M Feldman.
Discovering dialogue by looking at what we don't discuss.   *130*

"Eavesdropping" by Adam Szymkowicz.
Working in a group to generate better dialogue.   *132*

**"Toolbox for the Theatrical Lyricist: Our Language"
by Carmin Wong.**
Using monologues to develop a character's voice.   *134*

**"Where Are We? Keeping the Audience Unlost"
by Justin Maxwell.**
Using dialogue to establish setting.   *140*

"The Big Winston" by Justin Maxwell.
Moving emotions into the subtext for more powerful
dialogue.   *141*

**"A Surprise Entrance: Dabbling with Dramatic Irony"
by Lavinia Roberts.** Using dramatic irony to make evocative
scenes.   *144*

"Expanding the Matter of Your Play" by Lisa D'Amour.
Using the "stuff" in a script to expand the draft.   *146*

THE PROCRASTINATION TECHNIQUE FOR COMPLETING A PLAY (A.K.A. SURRENDER)

Rhiana Yazzie

Category: Getting unstuck, getting started, immobilizing fear and panic

Overview: Well, my friends, chances are you've thumbed through this toolbox looking for help to get your play completed and have landed here because only a miracle is going get your damn play done.

Whether you've never written a play or are starting your fiftieth master opus, you're likely experiencing the same personal inquiry: "How the hell do I start?" While the more experienced playwright may be asking, "How the %*$@ did I do this the last time?!" I want to give you much needed comfort: This is completely normal, most of the time.

What you're looking for is a midwife of sorts to assure you that the pain you're experiencing is real and excruciating and to help get your labor started by giving you a few pointers on how to stay healthy and emotionally regulated while your baby play slowly makes its way into the world—whether that be this evening, two days from now, next week, in a couple of months, or on your deathbed.

The satisfaction of a newly written play is well worth the few moments of pride you'll feel before the regional theatre work- shop process slowly kills your soul, which then suddenly becomes renewed again when your beautiful new piece of literature enters the mouths of licensed actors, who will just end up paraphrasing the damn thing on opening night anyway.

Participants: Solo + optional consenting cat.
Time to complete: All your time, until it hurts more not to write than to write.

Planning time: Planning? Ha! Planning means nothing in procrastination land.

Planning requirements: A looming deadline is helpful for this exercise. A play commission or independent project are ideal.

Other needs or considerations:

- *In a group:* Don't bring your loved ones or colleagues into this, please.
- *On your own:* You'll need a lot of time on your hands, preferably time that doesn't belong to you.

Instructions:

1. Surrender. I'm not saying give up, but I am saying let go. Chances are you've already decided to start cleaning your apartment. You have a house? Well, you obviously took a loved one's advice and went into another field and have become an aerospace engineer; unfortunately, the pain of the hobbyist playwright is not real, so just cosplay this chapter, too. Feel that soap in that dirty sink of dishes. Squeeze that bubbly sponge between your fingers. Watch the soap turn pink in the tomato sauce from last night's unfinished pasta. Rinse any uneaten noodles out and let them dry on the windowsill. You can then reboil and attempt to eat again if you're not gonna get paid until you turn in that first draft. Really take a moment to enjoy this dirty diversion from that computer screen. Please note that this exercise can be done in other areas of your home, cleaning the bathroom, sweeping the kitchen, or actually cleaning your bedroom. The key to all these exercises is to surrender completely to the task at hand. Don't go into the future, and don't go into the past.

2. Time. They say time in physics terms is a relative concept. Depending on how close you are to your deadline, you'll have experienced this natural phenomenon yourself. The closer

to a large force of gravity, like a black hole or persistent literary manager, the quicker time passes—or is it further away? Again, I became a playwright, not an astrophysicist, like my father suggested. The further away, life seems like an endless dream of social media postings that you're excited about your new commission with XX regional theatre and can't wait to work with them, and the closer you are to a deadline, the volume of emails about fake illnesses of nonexistent family members rises.

3. It's time to surrender now to the forces of time and its wisdom in this exercise. No matter how much time is left on that deadline, self-imposed or otherwise, and you are still simply not ready to write, give this a go.

4. You'll need a cat. Please be sure the cat has agreed and continues to show its buy-in for the duration of this exercise, otherwise I and the publishers of this book cannot be held responsible for your results nor personal claims of cat-on-human injury. Remember, in Germany, a housecat is called a *Stubentiger*, literally a "living room tiger," so be alert.

5. Pick up the cat. Hold it close to your heart, careful not to squish. If you can get the cat to purr, that is ideal. Next, go to your bed, set the cat down quickly but not so quickly as to alarm the cat, and curl up next to the cat. If the cat needs help, place it on its side with paws facing you. Next stretch out your right arm as they lie on their right side while gently pulling it closer.

6. You will notice you're successful when the cat is so close to you that it can lay its fluffy little head on your arm like a pillow. Next, bring the cat slightly closer, if it is amenable to the idea, and wrap your left arm on the outer edge of the cat's spine. Now gently smoosh so that the cat is boxed in by your arms while laying comfortably with its adorable head rested on your

arm, face to face, human-to-earth representative. Blink slowly at the cat. The cat will blink slowly back. You will feel a connection of bliss and calm if your regional theatre past hasn't killed your soul yet. If your soul is dead, just repeat once a day, and your soul will slowly return to its natural state.

7. Lucky playwrights with consenting and relaxed cats will get a jolt of natural oxytocin release, which will then help the playwright to regulate nervous system and eventually finish the play.

8. Again, time is relative. The cat may remain here for hours, or the cat may bolt up at any moment, so you must stay in the present moment to enjoy the gentle connection with their comforting feline friend for as long as the cat wants.

9. Please note, this exercise can be done with any number of animals; a rabbit, a small dog, or a similar animal, might be cute, but I would advise against any hooved, finned, or fanged animals until you have more confidence in your ability to execute this exercise.

Notes: Now that you've tried both exercises, it's important for you to milk your time in either activity by staying in the present moment. Again, do not go into the future, and do not go into the past. And if you must go into the future or past, then don't go further than three minutes either way.

Something strange might happen as you give in and surrender to these exercises. Because you've placed yourself in the present here and now, that illusive play idea, plot point, or character trait may gently land in your head or sometimes your body. It's important for you to catch those tiny moments with observation and nothing more. Note the ideas, the dialogue, the plots that drift into the space, and say, "Thank you," every time an idea or clarity of story shows itself.

I suggest, after noting each idea mentally, that you, without any sudden movements or funny business, gently jot down the idea. Write that moment and nothing more. Eventually these little moments will cobble together an arc for the story and your characters. When you can mentally see how the play might end or might begin, it's time to bid adieu to procrastination and the gift it gave you to get out of the past and future so that you can come back home to yourself to be that stenographer of the trial of a play you're writing. Ugh, well, I was on a metaphor streak, but what can you do? I'll revise it later.

PASS ALONG/OUT OF THE HAT

j.chavez

Category: Writing containers, new ideas, group exercise

Overview: "Pass Along" is great when you have writer's block and can't bring yourself to conjure up the characters, setting, and other accoutrements in a scene.

Participants: The more the better, but it can be done solo.
Time to complete: 0–2 hours.
Planning time: 5–10 minutes.
Planning requirements: None.
Other needs or considerations:
- *In a group:* Stand or sit in a circle with a piece of paper and something to write with.
- *On your own:* Sit at a desk or wherever comfortable with strips of paper or note cards and a hat or container for jumbling up.

Instructions:
In a group:
1. Stand in a circle.

2. Each participant writes a specific location on the top of the paper and folds the top down to hide what they wrote. Example: A five-hundred-acre maple farm in Vermont.
3. Pass the paper around in either direction any number of times so that no one has the same paper they did before. Do not unfold the paper. The anonymity is fun.
4. Underneath the folded portion, each participant writes two to five named characters with a trait for each and then folds it down again. Example: Steve, collects table; Mariah, collects chairs; Thalia, collects rugs.
5. Repeat step 3.
6. Each participant writes a prop that is present and then folds the paper down again. Example: a carbon monoxide detector that is low on batteries.
7. Repeat step 3.
8. Each participant writes a secret within the scene and then folds the paper down again. Example: Person A thinks person B is cheating, or the walls are really thin.
9. Repeat step 3.
10. Each participant writes a line that must be said and then folds the paper down again. Example: I told you that my mother was visiting.
11. Repeat step 3 one last time.
12. Now open your paper and look at the amalgamation you have. Try your best to bring this to life as a ten-minute play or something bigger!

On your own:

1. Using cut-up pieces of paper or notecards, allocate into five different piles: setting, characters, props, secrets, dialogue.

2. In pile 1, write down as many specific settings as you can. Example: the dumpster behind an Arby's; a run-down Toys "R" Us; or the penthouse of a Ritz-Carlton, 1988.

3. In pile 2, write down as many named characters with traits, either individually or in groups. Example: Tanya and Sinai, two lesbians who ride BMX, or Sean, who has never voted.

4. In pile 3, write down various props. Example: a birthday card that needs to be signed.

5. In pile 4, write down secrets for characters to have. Example: Person A is a cheetah in a wig, or person A just saw person B cheating.

6. In pile 5, write down as many individual lines of dialogue. Example: Tom doesn't love you like I love you, or This onion is my *son*; you are *nothing*.

7. From each pile, randomly select one piece of paper. Draw as many characters cards as you feel necessary.

8. Now, try your best to bring this to life as a ten-minute play or something bigger!

Notes: Be as wild as you feel necessary. Just look around the room and let that spark. You might not end up with these, and it gives a fun challenge to your peers.

You can also do the "On Your Own" version in a large group. Have everyone write a couple of each category down and then draw them out of a hat.

The writing can be done on your own time; I like to lead this one toward the end of a class so that students can use it after class. For the extra challenge, see how much you can write in an hour.

THE BAD PLAY

Liz Duffy Adams (with apologies/hat tip to Mac Wellman)

Category: Liberation, disruption of habits at any point in the process

Overview: This exercise can (1) disrupt the paralysis that happens when you want something to be good so badly you can write nothing and (2) explode your usual habits, leading you to surprise yourself and ultimately the audience. I use it all the time. For example, toward the end of one play, I had a planned set piece, a play within the play that the characters and I had been building up to. I didn't know anything about it, but I felt it needed to be *amazing*. So when I got up to that point in the play, I became paralyzed to the point where I had to jump over it and "finish" the play with a gaping hole in it. At that point, I went back and deployed badness to such good effect that the bad version was the final one—and many people's favorite part of the play. In another example, before I wrote what I consider now my best work, I couldn't bring myself to begin. The idea of the play was for me so intimidating, I didn't think I could live up to it. Finally, I gave myself permission to write a bad version, and it shot out like a cannon.

Participants: Alone or in a group.
Time to complete: Elastic. It can take a couple of hours in a group or be the work of the moment alone.
Planning time: Zero.
Planning requirements: None.
Other needs or considerations:
- *In a group:* You need a leader and for the other participants not to know what the exercise is about until the challenge.
- *On your own:* Just the idea and a deep breath.

Instructions:

In a group:

1. Have a brief discussion of what the participants consider to be a bad play, everyone offering at least one thing they consider bad (horrible, indefensible) playwriting.

2. (Optional, recommended for beginning writers) Give a basic prompt as a jumping-off place. For example, write down a name; that's character A. Write down something character A wants very badly. Write down another name; that's character B. Write down a way in which character B is an obstacle to character A getting what they want. Or share street photographs with at least two people in them for members to choose from as a starting place for character and situation.

3. The challenge: Select an amount of time (perhaps forty-five minutes or an hour) to write a bad play. Do not settle for mediocrity. Aim for outrageously, radically, aggressively terrible. Go wherever it takes you. Don't feel obliged to stick with badness if you get interested, but if you get bored or stuck, go back to wild, untrammeled, disgraceful badness.

4. Read the plays out loud and discuss. They are often uproariously funny and always interesting, containing germs of excitement and expansiveness, full of the unexpected.

On your own:

1. Follow the previous steps on your own whenever you have trouble starting something or find yourself grinding to a halt during the process or writing in a way you are finding boring, predictable, or safe. Challenge yourself to write it badly. It will get you going again, and you may find your bad writing is exactly what the play needed.

Notes: None.

DESCRIBE THE ELEPHANT

Sam Hamashima

Category: Creative investigation, intention, tone, and objective

Overview: When writer's block hits, I find that this exercise based in creation with an emphasis on stream of consciousness can help quiet the inner critic and encourage me to follow my instincts.

Inspired by John Godfrey Saxe and Paul Galdone's parable *The Blind Men and the Elephant* (New York: Whittlesey House, 1963), you will describe what you feel and see in your work, as well as what you want in your work.

Participants: Individually but can be done alongside other individuals.

Time to complete: Time-flexible, with a minimum of 5 minutes.

Planning time: Limited planning time. Writers are encouraged to begin with a 2-minute meditation to clear their minds and subvert their expectations.

Planning requirements: Writers are encouraged to look at what's already written or anything connected to said piece. An already-written draft is not needed, but I always believe having something to reference is important.

Other needs or considerations: Word processor on a device is preferred. Writing utensils and paper are fine.

Instructions: "Of course they could not see him with their eyes; but they thought that by touching him they could learn just what kind of animal he was." In the parable *The Blind Men and the Elephant*, six blind men are given the task of learning about an elephant just through touch. Each blind man touches a different part of the elephant. One touches the side and draws a conclusion that an elephant is like a wall. Another touches the tusk and concludes that an elephant is similar to a spear. The other blind men touch different parts. The trunk? A snake. The leg? A tree trunk. Unable to see the possibility of the elephant being all their conclusions, the blind men quarrel well after the elephant has left. The men were not willing to see the potential for multiple truths and, because of this, failed to see the elephant in its truest form.

You, the writer, are the blind men. Your piece: the elephant. In a stream-of-consciousness fashion, you must write down anything that comes to mind about the piece and the story you're trying to tell. Once the stream-of-consciousness freewrite is finished, observe what is repeated and given natural emphasis.

Step 1: Freewrite about your piece. Your writing can be in complete sentences, fragments, strings of words, or all of the above. The important part is to avoid editing and questioning the work. *It is important to not question if you have written something already.* Be careful not to label your piece as tragedy or comedy or to make large assumptions that could limit your piece's breadth. Questions to consider during this freewrite:

- What colors do you associate with your piece?
- What phrases do you feel capture the piece?
- What words resonate? Themes?
- How do you want your audience to feel?
- What do you want your audience to say after they experience the script?
- What objects, animals, or things do you associate with this piece?

Step 2: After you've finished your freewrite, read it back. Anything said more than once should be bolded. After this, go word by word and omit things that are not of use. This can be a painstaking process! After this, you should be left with core phrases, words, and sentences. Let's call these your creative discoveries.

Step 3: Incorporate your creative discoveries into your piece. What was repeated throughout your freewrite? Perhaps the color pink kept coming up in your freewrite? Where can you put pink in your piece? Perhaps it is in the costumes or the lighting design. Perhaps the favorite color of a primary character of yours is pink. Perhaps the word *sharp* and its synonyms came up: *pointy, jagged, harsh*. All these words can be associated with each other. How can you put *sharp* in your piece? An idea for this could be making a character's diction short and blunt.

Continue to sew your creative discoveries into your piece using the tools at your disposal: dialogue, symbolism, allegory, action, and more!

Notes: Sewing in your creative discoveries does not have to happen all at once. For me, it is a long process drawn out over several edits and rewrites. What I like to do is print out my creative discoveries and keep them close by my writing desk so they are easy to reference.

THE MOST BORING PLAY IN THE WORLD

Sara Farrington

Category: Gimmicks

Overview: The purpose of this exercise is to avoid cleverness, action, gimmicks, devices, and clichés in an effort to write an innovative and original four-act play in an hour.

Frequent theatre gimmicks include "I'm pregnant," "I have _____ disease," "I have a dark past," and so on—or what director Anne Bogart calls "you, me, our apartment, and our problems" plays. These kinds of plays make for *legitimately* boring and conventional theatre. Our goal with this exercise is to write an *intentionally* boring play, which quite often results in an innovative, nuanced, funny, and even moving piece. This exercise is a direct rip-off from an exercise invented by *mon capitaine* Mac Wellman, which he called "The Bad Play," which is essentially the same idea, only bad instead of boring.

Participants: Just the playwright.

Time to complete: As a writing exercise, this will take 1 hour to complete. As a full playwriting endeavor, much longer—I'd say 2–7 years of writing, rewriting, workshopping, rehearsals, and performances.

Planning time: You'll need 5 minutes to just sit and think, then 1 hour to write each act in 4 × 15-minute chunks. In my experience, this is a more exciting exercise to do by hand in a notebook, but typing is okay, too.

Planning requirements: Notebook and pencil or laptop.

Instructions: Prelim—Sit and think for five full minutes. Don't do anything else. Simply sit, stare, and think. This can be hard, especially for Americans, but try it. Your goal at the end of the thinking: Visualize the single most boring environment you can. Make it a place where nothing or very little is capable of happening. A petri dish? The DMV? The inside of a toaster? A jail cell? A skin cell? A padded room? The reptile house at the zoo? The room you're in right now? Keep it unexciting. It can be anything past, present, or future, something familiar to humans or something totally unfamiliar.

Step 1: Act I. Visualize character A and character B existing in this most boring environment you thought of. They *can* be human, but they don't have to be. (A playwright I went to graduate school with at Brooklyn College, Siobhan Antonioli, created a dialogue between two glints of sunlight off of Joan of Arc's sword, for example.) Get characters A and B talking to each other and probably moving, too (unless they can't move for some boring reason). Remember, you must write under the "boring" limitation. If you find yourself getting clever and witty, stop. Keep it totally uninteresting to the typical theatregoer. Maybe A and B don't know who they are and are trying to figure that out. Maybe they speak a made-up language. Maybe they just repeat the same two words over and over again. (A fourth-grade playwriting student of mine once completed this exercise just using the word *duh* for several pages. It was profound in its nihilism.) Write for fifteen minutes without stopping. Don't edit. Don't delete. Don't think at all really; just write. Skim the dialogue leaves off the top of the swimming pool of your consciousness.

Step 2: Act II. Fast-forward the action. Take characters A and B into the future by at least ten years. It could be more—it could be one thousand years—but no less than ten. Has anything about their boring lives changed? If it has, then make sure that change is boring. In this future world, they meet character C. Get A, B, and C talking and moving. Remember, cleverness, wit, and intellect are verboten. Just drone on and on with no meaning. Write for fifteen minutes.

Step 3: Act III. Freeze the action in your boring play, and write a monologue from the point of view of an inanimate object that has been viewing your boring play unfolding. (Is it a tin can? A pen on the desk of the DMV lady? A pinch of salt? A bit of bacteria? The glass windowpane?) One rule here: Give this inanimate object a strong opinion about what it's been seeing and hearing. Write for fifteen minutes. (Credit due to the brilliant playwright Erik Ehn for the inanimate-object-POV idea.)

Step 4: Act IV. Rewind. Take the action of your most boring play in the world back in time to at least ten years before act I. Obviously, you can go back further than ten years, maybe a million—doesn't matter. From this flashback, write the origin story of character C, either in dialogue, monologue, or stage directions. Why is character C this way? What boring reason made C like this? This act can certainly involve characters A and B and the inanimate object, but it needs to explain something really boring about character C that the audience didn't know. Write for fifteen minutes.

Step 5: Nice work! You have completed writing your most boring play! If you wrote your brand-new, boring, four-act play by hand, then type it out. Then, do one of three things, in whatever order you'd like:

1. Get super excited, dive in, and edit like mad. Expand it, deepen it, enrich it with even more excitingly boring elements and characters. Don't consider the play finished until you reach step 2.

2. Get some actors in a room to read this version aloud, alerting them all to the workshop nature of this first stab at your most boring play. After the reading is over, ask for feedback and initial thoughts and ideas and the inevitable "What if we . . . ?" statements from the actors. Tell them you don't have any money, but you'd really like to keep working on this piece with them. Watch them get excited. Tell the actors you're going to rewrite your boring play but this time informed by their feedback and circle back with another workshop reading, maybe this time on their feet. Keep doing this for two to seven years, until you have a full production of the most boring play in the world.

3. Realize you either don't like or understand your new four-act play and put it away for one to six months, during which time you should work on other projects, the day job, kids, and so on. Finally come back to your most boring four-act play only to realize that it is, in fact, completely brilliant, that you are, in fact, a genius. When this happens, revert to steps 1 and 2.

Notes: Make sure your most boring play is performed in some way. In my opinion, plays are not meant to be read or talked about; they are meant to be performed; they are scores for performance, like sheet music. There is no exception to this rule. So no matter what you do, no matter how little money you have, make sure you write your plays with some manifestation of live performance in mind. It's okay if you think your play sucks. All plays suck at first. The only way to make something good is to work through the suck phase via workshop, collaboration, and performance. Be brave enough to fail in front of an audience. Failure is more important to your growth as a playwright than a hit play and a glowing *New York Times* review.

THE WORST PLAY
(A.K.A. GET OUT OF YOUR OWN WAY)

Rachel Lynett

Category: Writing

Overview: Write the worst possible ten-minute play you can. Everything is on the table, but the play has to

1. include at least two characters,
2. include dialogue,
3. be *at least* eight minutes long and *at most* fifteen minutes long, and
4. be written in one sitting.

Everything else is up to you. What's the worst play you can write?

How does it help a writer make a play or get unstuck from one of the problems? It forces a writer to unlearn some of the rules we were taught that ultimately hold us back.

What skill does it build?

1. Trusting your voice.
2. Opening your mind to the possibilities of production (and in turn thinking about production as you craft a play).
3. Allowing the playwright to edit from a place of critical thinking instead of attachment.

Why would anyone do this? Well, for one thing, it's fun. It's a bit of relief to write an impossible play or make bad art just for the sake of bad art. The pressure of having to create something "good" can oftentimes lead to writer's block. We get stuck in our heads and don't want to make something "bad." This exercise *begs* you to make a mess, make something horrible, get out of your own way, and just put words to the page even if you think they suck because that's the point. It's supposed to suck. One element of this exercise is to just get you started.

In addition to that, a lot of playwrights conflate *bad* with *unproducible*. We've been told that a play that breaks all of the rules is bad because no one will want to produce it. To be frank, unless you've worked in tech, you don't know what can be produced. I worked for years as a stage manager and production manager and have a strong understanding of all the elements of theatrical design. And even still, I continue to be amazed with how designers approach and solve problems.

Finally, this exercise (as you will soon see) encourages playwrights to find the good in the bad. Even your worst writing has something you can use, something you can apply somewhere else, something you can learn from. You just have to lean into it instead of immediately dismissing it.

Participants: 1.
Time to complete: However long it takes you to write a ten-minute play + 2–4 hours a week later.
Planning time: None.
Planning requirements: None.
Other needs or considerations: None.

Instructions: Step 1: Think about all the rules you were taught when you were first learning about playwriting. Some rules that come to mind for me are the following:

- Limit direct addresses. This worked for Shakespeare but for some reason can't work now.
- The playwright's hand should never show. (I've always found this one to be a bit vague, but basically the playwright's opinions and beliefs should not outweigh the play.)
- Stick to one genre. Plays can't mix genres.
- All conflict needs to be resolved, or the audience will feel cheated.
- Plays should have a "what makes this night special" quality about them. Slice-of-life plays don't really stick the landing.

What rules come up for you? Write down five of them.

Step 2: Now that you have your rules, you're going to write a ten-minute play that breaks all of them. Have some fun with it. Let your imagination run wild. Does a deer run onstage? Does the playing space and watching space switch somehow? What if there was no defined playing space? Is the whole play a recording?

Really give yourself permission not just to break the rules but also to write *what you think* a bad play is. What kind of play would cause you to sigh out loud in a theatre? What does a bad play look and sound like?

Be sure to write this play in a single sitting. No stopping and starting, so carve out enough time to get it done.

Step 3: Finished? Great! Save it, hide it, run from it—either way, don't look at it for a week. Don't talk about it. Don't obsess about it. After you're done writing, put a reminder in your calendar to look at it in a week (or more!), and then forget about it. Don't try to fix it. Don't try to analyze why you've done this. Let it gooooo.

Step 4: Okay, now it's time to revisit it. Read it. Read it as if someone else wrote it. Read it as if you're a playwriting professor and your student has written it. Write down three things you like about it, three things you have questions about, and one thing you think of as a critical problem. You can describe *critical problem* however you like, but you only get one. This is not a moment to beat yourself up, so be gentle. If you wouldn't say it to a student or a friend, then don't say it to yourself.

Step 5: Look at the three things you really liked. Throw away everything else. What's the story there? Is this something you can build from the ground up or expand on? If your play is a city on fire, then what can you save, and what can you let go? How do you rebuild from here? You can't say, "There's nothing here." Yes, I promise you, there is. Look again.

Step 6: Rebuild. And let that mean whatever you want. The last time I did this exercise, I ended up writing a full-length play that later went on to win the Yale Prize. Trust that even at your worst, you can make something absolutely brilliant.

Notes: Every time I do this exercise, everyone tells me how much they hate it, how they don't think it'll work. And yet, every single person who took this exercise seriously ended up with a play (ten minutes or full length) that absolutely worked for them. Give yourself a chance to give this a real try. All the examples I give in step 1 are the rules I broke when writing *Apologies to Lorraine Hansberry (You Too August Wilson)*. All the examples I give in step 2 are from real plays that I adore and am a big champion for each of them. Sometimes, in an absolute mess, there's something forming that just needs a second look.

WRITING SOMETHING YOU'D NEVER WANT ANYONE ELSE TO SEE IN A MILLION YEARS

Young Jean Lee

Category: Improving your writing

Overview: This exercise helps to give you a sense of what it's like to write from a very grounded, personal, real, and risky place. It can also help to get you unstuck when you've lost interest in what you're writing.

Participants: Either individually or in a group.
Time to complete: 15 minutes.
Planning time: None.
Planning requirements: Something to write with and a timer.
Other needs or considerations: None.

Instructions:
1. Set a timer, and take five minutes to write something about yourself that is so personal that you wouldn't want anyone to see it.
2. Set a timer, and take ten minutes to turn what you wrote into something for a play. You should disguise what you wrote sufficiently so that the result is something you'd be willing to share with others. It's fine if you don't use a single word from what you originally wrote, as long as you feel that what you wrote is a transformation of the original.

Notes: The point of this exercise is not to demonstrate that all writing must come from a deeply personal place because I don't believe that to be the case. Writing from a personal place is just one powerful tool among many.

NEW MONOLOGUE PERSPECTIVES

Franky D. Gonzalez

Category: Monologue, writing outside your own POV, empathy

Overview: Playwrights have a tough job. We must write characters that don't represent our own viewpoints. We have to find qualities in people or things we may find unsavory for the sake of keeping the drama going. Playwrights by nature are empathetic people.

Our empathy is the way we write compelling villains and relatable heroes. Empathy gives us the ability to see other perspectives and turn them into the stuff of drama.

This exercise will allow you to tap into your natural empathy using your lived experience to shift your viewpoint.

Participants: Individually.
Time to complete: 30 minutes to a little more than an hour.
Planning time: No planning time needed outside of thinking of an incident.
Planning requirements: No planning requirements.
Other needs or considerations:
- *In a group*: N/A.
- *On your own*: Your lived experience.

Instructions:
1. Recall someone who you got into a disagreement or argument with. They can be anyone. Friend or family. Co-worker or boss. Teacher or neighbor. Anyone with whom you can remember coming to some kind of "butting of heads."
2. For 20–30 minutes, write down what you'd say to this person if you had a chance to say whatever it is you wanted to in this fight to prove you're right. Say everything you either said or wanted to say. Make every point. Be petty if you want. Be in

your feelings. Show them how right you are and lay out every single reason or rationale you can think of.

3. For 30–40 minutes, take your monologue and, from the point of view of the individual with whom you argued, draft a response that debunks each reason or point you made in your monologue. Take time to consider what would be a good response that would take the air out of your assertions. What could they say that would stop your argument in its tracks? Even if that wasn't their actual reason in the real disagreement, find the things they could say that would make you either concede or understand why they did the thing that angered you.

Notes: Please, keep this in the realm of a disagreement or argument, and not something like violence or abuse. Trying to empathize or find reason for anyone to have done any kind of harm to you is not at all what this exercise strives to accomplish. There are things that should not be empathized with, especially at the cost of your own well-being.

LIST OF TWENTY

Lindsay Carpenter

Category: Generating ideas, getting unstuck

Overview: The purpose of this exercise is for the writer to get out of their own way. Often when we need to make a decision (What should I write next? What should the protagonist's goal be? What should the title be? How should this end?), we get stuck trying to find the perfect or "right" answer. This exercise can help the writer instead come up with a number of possible solutions or ways forward so they don't get stuck on the seemingly impossible task of having to come up with the ideal one. It can be used at any stage of the writing process, from initial brainstorming to rewriting.

Participants: Individual.

Time to complete: 3–5 minutes.

Planning time: 1 minute.

Planning requirements: Grab a pen or pencil and paper or notebook. You should handwrite this exercise rather than using a laptop or phone.

Instructions:

1. Decide on what your question will be. Examples of questions:
   - What themes am I interested in that I could explore for my next writing project?
   - What does the protagonist want?
   - What should the title be?
   - What other ways can the main character die?
   - What can Sarah do to Joe to show him she hates him?
   - Where should their date be?
- Who stole Sarah's cake?
- Why is Joe's mom missing?
2. Set a timer for three minutes.
3. During those three minutes, write a list of twenty possible answers to your question. They don't need to be fully fleshed out ideas; a few words are plenty. They can contradict each other, build off each other, not make sense, and so on. The important thing is you don't think too hard about each of them and just keep writing.
4. Once you reach twenty or the time runs out, look them over and circle the ideas that interest you.

The possibilities are endless. You can vary the amount of time you set for yourself, but the trick is to keep it relatively short and keep the answers coming quickly.

Here's an example of how you might use this exercise. Imagine you have a draft of a play, but you know a specific element is wrong.

For instance, in the play, Sarah proposes, and Joe says yes. Something about Joe's yes feels off, but you're not sure why, and you can't figure out what to replace it with. You might write, "How should Joe respond to the proposal?" and do a list of twenty. The answers might include something as simple as "Joe says no" or "Joe breaks down crying happily" or something as wild as "Joe leaves the country and ghosts Sarah" or "Joe reveals he's an alien." Often the solution you end up with or decide to move forward with is a mix of the answers you've created.

Notes: The simplicity of the exercise is deceptive. Over the years, I've used it to address all types of problems. The amount of time you have to create the list of twenty is intentionally short so that you don't have time to think about it or come up with the "good" or "right" answers. The list should feel closer to a freewrite or stream of consciousness. Ideas will evolve from each other.

The exercise centers on the concept that you can't have twenty good ideas, especially if you're going quickly. It's too many ideas all at once. So you allow yourself to write down the stupid ideas or the opposite idea or something really weird. It gets you out of your own head.

LIST IT OUT

Kaela Mei-Shing Garvin

Category: Tone, writer's block, structure

Overview: This exercise can help unstick writers later in the process, providing options in a variety of tones. It can also help focus on what the play might be missing structurally. I'll do an exercise like this when I've got some idea of what my play is about but am not sure what to do next.

Participants: Individual or group.

Time to complete: At least 5 minutes; up to 30 minutes.

Planning time: None.

Planning requirements: You'll need a timer and writing tools—challenge yourself to use a different modality than usual. Are you a handwriter? Try a keyboard. A typist? Try pen and paper.

Other needs or considerations: None.

Instructions: Set a timer for five minutes and create a list of
- five scenes that should definitely be in your play,
- five scenes that could be in your play but would push its bounds, and
- five scenes that would never be in your play.

You now have a to-do list of scenes that you can create—or avoid!—and can develop thoughts on why these might (not) fit.

You can pause here or continue to the following steps: Set a timer for seven minutes. Choose one of your scenes from your list of fifteen options, and write it as badly as possible. Make the worst decisions possible with how your characters use language, the stage images, actions taken, and so on. This is about making decisions quickly, so try not to overthink it.

Set a timer for seven minutes. Choose one of your scenes from your list of fifteen options, and write it as if you're translating it from an old master. What writers inspire you? How might they go about the scene? How would they use language and character? How would they experiment with or forward the plot? Again, try to make strong language choices within your short writing period.

Set a timer for seven minutes, and attack another one from your list. Consider genre: What might your play have a relationship with, and what tropes might serve the scene? See how many hallmark moments of genre you can fit into a short span of writing.

Now you can reflect on which of these scenes, if any, might fit in your work—and where. Don't discount the scenes that would never appear in your play; investigate if there might be any useful take-aways about why they aren't suitable.

Notes: I find that physical movement before starting (stretching, a walk, yoga) can open things up!

MINISCENES

Aaron Ricciardi

Category: Scene generation

Overview: When playwrights begin a new play, the process is often set into motion by a lightning strike of inspiration. We're walking or shopping or talking with our partners or friends or children when we see suddenly, clearly, the makings of a new play. It may come to us in an image, character, situation, line, or concept; however it does, we understand that we have entered into another intense, life-long relationship with yet another play, which we will love and tend, alongside our myriad other creations. (In this way, all playwrights are polyamorous.)

Initial scenes often flow feverishly, almost involuntarily, thanks to strong intuition, and this phase is a thrill. It's not long after this honeymoon period, though, that writing loses its charm and starts to look, as it has every time before, like a chore. You love your idea, but after you've written, say, thirty pages of your first draft, the generation of plot daunts you. What, you wonder, should I have these characters do?

Writer's block seems like it comes from having nothing to write about, when in fact it's the opposite: you could have your characters do and say anything. After the instinctive flurry of your first pages, how should you pick where to go next now that your gut isn't as sure as it was earlier in the process? Furthermore, scenes in a final draft should be complete miniplays of their own that inform and affect each other, linked in a tight web, and this expectation, combined with your waning intuition, arrests you. But you can't worry about the expectations for your final draft as you generate the first; your focus should be on skipping like a kid through the wilderness of your unconscious as you forage for your perfect materials: your scenes.

This exercise is meant to trick your playwright monkey mind into having fun with the midlife-crisis stage of the first-draft-generation process. Instead of worrying about how to write well-crafted, complete scenes, in this exercise you will simply focus on writing bold, varied scenes or moments that are intentionally left unfinished. This exercise forces you to act instinctively, move fast, and above all *play*.

Participants: Individual or group.
Time to complete: ~1 hour minimum; ~2 hours maximum.
Planning time: None.
Planning requirements: The writer should have a sense of their play (characters, setting, general idea) and already have some pages generated.
Other needs or considerations: Paper and pen or pencil or a computer.

Instructions:
1. Make a list of scenes or events that could happen in your play.
2. Add to this list any character combinations you have yet to write in your play. Have you not seen two characters alone together or a certain combination of multiple characters? How about a scene with all the characters in your play?
3. Add to this list any scenes or events that could happen in the world in which the play takes place. Perhaps there are scenes or events that would be impossible to put onstage in the way you've imagined your play theatrically or scenes you

are convinced should remain offstage. No matter—include those as well. Also include any characters you see existing in your play's world but whom you wouldn't write into the play because, say, the character isn't significant or you wouldn't ask an actor to play them.

4. Now, write a series of small scenes, each a maximum of one page in length. If you're stuck with what scene to write next, then consult the list you drew up, and tackle a random scene from there. Write what seems most fun. Your aim should be childlike exploration, which calls for impulsivity and speed. Do not go back and revise these scenes as you go; write these in a mad-hot dash. Mess around; fingerpaint; play. Here are some possible strategies:

   a. Each jump from one scene to the next should be a major shift in tone, setting, and/or time.
   b. Introduce characters you've never written before.
   c. Play with form or structure. Maybe write a few scenes in non-realism if your play normally takes place in reality. Maybe write in harsh realism if your play is ordinarily whimsical.
   d. None of these scenes have to make it into your final draft. In fact, if that were the result, it would be fantastic.

5. Continue generating these short scenes until you have at least five of them, one page each.

Notes: This exercise could be the end of this process for you. If so, great! But, if you want more, consider these two additional steps:

1. If you handwrote your miniscenes, then type them up and revise them as you go. If you typed them, then print out what you have, retype them in a new document, and revise them as you go. Allow them to get longer, more concise, or clearer. Add more characters or events within each scene. As you did before, let your gut lead you.

2. Expand any or all of your miniscenes into bona fide, respectable, full-length scenes of their own. After completing the messy, playful early steps of this exercise, embark on this step with an eye toward the finished product. You allowed yourself to relax and to play earlier, which hopefully brought you the calm, focus, and assuredness you need to make usable content for your play.

CHARACTER AND LANGUAGE

Deborah Yarchun

Category: Character development, dialogue

Overview: This exercise is designed to build a writer's ability to craft characters with unique voices. It helps writers consider how a character's identity affects the way they speak, the metaphors they use, and their dialogue. It can be particularly useful for writers starting out but is also a great exercise at any point in one's experience or process—whether they're finding a character's voice or revising.

Participants: Individually or in a group.
Time to complete: 30–45 minutes.
Planning time: None.
Planning requirements: None.
Other needs or considerations: None.

Instructions:
1. Pick a subject you are familiar with that has a very specific lingo or language attached to it. This could be related to a culture; an activity (tennis, gardening, etc.); or perhaps a musical instrument. Ideally, this is something you are an expert in or can quickly research.

2. Spend ten minutes jotting down specific words and phrases associated with it. Feel free to use the internet to research, if that's useful.

3. Take a moment to pick a location that lends itself to using language related to this subject (e.g., an auto-body shop if the subject is automobiles). Write down descriptions of this place. Write down metaphors related to the subject. Think in colors, textures, and vivid imagery.

4. Quickly come up with a scenario involving two characters engaged in an activity at that location, ideally related to the subject. The setting should play a significant role in the scenario.

5. Start drafting dialogue between these characters. These are two characters who know each other well and are both familiar with the lingo of the subject. Because of their relationship and familiarity, they speak in shorthand and with subtext.

6. Consider similes or metaphors these characters might use that are specific to their activity or occupation.

7. Now go wild with it all, and write a scene. Ideally this scene will build to a climax, and something should change by the end of the scene.

8. After about twenty minutes of writing, stop.

9. Take a few minutes and review your work. Are there more opportunities to integrate relevant language into your scene? Feel free to revise it.

10. If in a group, share a few examples, and discuss what felt particularly effective and why. If working alone, read your scene out loud.

Notes: Notice how people often speak through metaphors and similes connected to their occupations or interests. This is one way to build a character's voice. For more opportunities, I suggest filling out a full character profile and exploring other ways the characters' attributes and backgrounds might affect how they speak.

MAJOR DRAMATIC QUESTION

Reginald Edmund

Category: Dramatic stakes, character actions, the major dramatic question

Overview: An important formula to help you on your storytelling journey that all conventional stories follow to hit the major dramatic question is *goal + obstacle × lack of compromise = conflict.*

This exercise will help you create a strong and compelling plot that revolves around a central question that the audience wants to see answered. It will also allow you to explore your protagonist's motivations, emotions, and conflicts in depth, creating a complex and multidimensional character whom the audience can root for (or against).

Participants: Just you.
Time to complete: Variable.
Planning time: 0.
Planning requirements: None.
Other needs or considerations: None.

Instructions: All conventional stories follow the formula *goal + obstacle × lack of compromise = conflict.* Let's break that formula down to its core in this writing exercise.

1. Choose a character you'd like to write about. It could be a protagonist, an antagonist, or a supporting character.
2. Identify the major dramatic question. Think about what the character's primary goal or desire is in the play. What does the

character want more than anything else? This should be the major dramatic question that drives the plot of the play.

3. Write out the major dramatic question as a clear, concise sentence. For example, *Will Romeo and Juliet be able to overcome their family feud and be together?* or *Can Willy Loman achieve the American dream?* or even *Will Bruce Wayne save Gotham City?*

4. Identify the obstacles. Consider what challenges the character will face in trying to achieve their goal. What obstacles will stand in their way? These obstacles should be what drive the plot of the play.

5. Write a scene that puts the character in a situation where they face one of the obstacles you identified. This scene should highlight the conflict between the character and the obstacle and should raise the stakes for the character.

6. After writing the scene, reflect on how it relates to the major dramatic question. Did the scene bring the character closer to achieving their goal, or did it make things more difficult for them? How does this scene fit into the overall arc of the play?

7. Repeat steps 5 and 6 until you've completed your draft.

Write your revolution!

Notes: None.

SAID AND UNSAID

L M Feldman

Category: Verbal and nonverbal communication, when language fails, shining a light on what goes unlit

Overview: I think a lot about the *messiness* of communication: what we say, what we don't say, what we try hard to say, what we fail to say, what we almost say, what we accidentally say, what our bodies say, what nonhuman or inanimate things say, what does the talking . . .

Participants: Individual, pairs, or group—your call.

Time to complete: Approximately 30 minutes but feel free to shrink or expand it.

Planning time: None, silly.

Planning requirements: Just grab your favorite pen and notebook (or a laptop) and a snack to enjoy and/or to share with each other (cuz sometimes writing's more buoyant with a snack).

Other needs or considerations:

- *In a group:* Enjoy.
- *On your own:* Rock on.

Instructions: Warm-up: Lists (five to ten minutes). Feel free to write from your own perspective, experience, and voice or to write from your character's. Feel free, too, to respond within any context that interests you or your character (life, work, family, school, relationship, neighborhood, the world, human history, the current moment, a specific community you deeply know, etc.). Then jot down three to five things that

- you're totally comfortable talking about,
- in your opinion no one really talks about,
- you personally don't really talk about,
- you've said without meaning to,
- get communicated without being said,
- do the talking besides mouths, and
- do the talking besides humans.

Deep dive: Scene (twenty to twenty-five minutes). This is an invitation to write a new scene or to revise an existing scene. It can include characters you already know or ones you have yet to meet.

Write a scene about something that usually goes unsaid or untalked about. Explore the *effort* of communicating it, the *struggle* to communicate it. Avoid using the name of the thing itself, if it has a name (e.g., love, sex, cancer, racism, climate crisis). Feel free to play with language—fractured, repetition, stammer, do-overs, trail-offs, and so on. And feel free to use anything from your lists that draws you. For example,

- What if at some point something gets *said unintentionally*?
- What if at some point something is *communicated nonverbally*?
- What if at some point language *fails entirely*?
- What if at some point the scene becomes *purely physical or nonverbal*?

Capture every impulse. You can always edit later. Let yourself surprise yourself. And let the characters surprise you, too.

Notes: Anytime you feel an impulse, follow it. Screw the instructions.

EAVESDROPPING

Adam Szymkowicz

Category: Writing better dialogue

Overview: This is about getting into the practice of listening to how people actually talk and turning that into drama.

Participants: Group (or alone).
Time to complete: Depends on the number of students. 30 minutes? 60 minutes?
Planning time: Students need to bring in overheard conversations.
Planning requirements: Students have to write down a short conversation they hear out in the world.
Other needs or considerations: Something to write on or with.

Instructions: Part 1: If in a group setting, everyone sends in conversations they heard in the real world and have typed up. Make them all available to everybody. Read them all out loud together. The person who brought a conversation in can cast from the class or read it out loud themselves. Have students circle or highlight parts that they like or that stick with them.

My teacher in grad school, Kelly Stuart, got us in the habit of collecting found conversations and sharing them in class. Whenever I do this with a group, I always worry that students won't bring in interesting things, but without fail, they bring in fun stuff every time.

Part 2: Then everyone writes a scene using as much or as little of the conversations as they want. Anyone can use anyone else's fragments of found conversation. It's about making art from observations we make in the world. When we're in a group, it will be clear how everyone's art is different. We all just experienced these fragments together, but what we make with them, that's the filtering-it-through-ourselves part.

It's partially about paying attention to what interests us personally, and it's partially about what interests everybody. Sometimes I'll overhear a conversation out in the world that is riveting but wouldn't lead to characters I'm interested in or things I want to write about. And that's also an important thing to think about and realize. Are these characters I can write? Are these characters I want to write?

Notes: The purpose is to get in the habit of hearing the ways people actually speak and then figuring out how to edit and transform their language to make a scene. We all take from our lives and experiences to write, and this is part of that.

TOOLBOX FOR THE THEATRICAL LYRICIST: OUR LANGUAGE

Carmin Wong

Category: Using language to develop character(s) with attention to their voice—diction, prosody, rhythm, metaphor, and imagery; writing (and rewriting) monologues, finding the narrative arc, expelling the redundant tropes, building a lyric (as opposed to a lyrical) voice, deciphering an audience(s), and creating a personal intervention; the art of storytelling and the language we choose to tell our stories

Overview: I think writing a compelling story that you want people to read (not just witness onstage but actually experience while reading it) is about finding romance between text and subtext; that is, building an intentional relationship between the text you have written and what you have illustrated between those lines.

Many people I know, who are interested in writing a play or a poem but never do, often say they have never tried because they just don't know how. I have wondered, though, how much of genre writing is about knowing all the conventional strategies to use when writing versus using what we have access to in our daily lives to get a better understanding of how conventional techniques either work or don't work in our favor. The goal of the following exercise is to focus on what you *do* know. My first request and challenge for you to be open to what you don't know, to free yourself of any intimidations, fears, or insecurities that arise in the process of learning.

The following is a generative exercise. We will start small by writing a single monologue. It should encourage you to think intimately about a character's voice and their perspective against another character's viewpoint and against your own. Although we will focus on getting to know one character's voice, this activity can be repeated for numerous characters.

Participants: This exercise is for one or all.

Time to complete: This following exercise can take between 30 minutes to 1½ hours to complete. It can be condensed for shorter workshop periods or expanded for longer workshops. Writing is a process; take all your time.

Planning time: Planning can take between 15 and 60 minutes, depending on familiarity with the following terms and experience preparing a lesson plan.

Planning requirements: Become familiar with the following terms:

- *diction:* the style and choice of words a character uses
- *dramatic action:* what the protagonist wants to achieve overall and within each scene
- *imagery:* using sensory details (five senses) or figurative language to provide a visual description; the use of imagery in a monologue can turn an everyday sentence into an artful, poetic line worth remembering
- *lyric mode:* using a character's feelings, personal experiences, and state of mind to articulate their disposition, circumstances, and view of the world
- *metaphor:* comparison of two unrelated objects without using *like* or *as*; metaphors can also be understood as a symbolic representation of something else; the use of consistent metaphors through a play is one way to think about the relationship between text and subtext
- *persona:* when a speaker takes on the voice of someone or something (animate or inanimate) else and speaks through their assumed voice; persona poems and monologues offer a look into the hybridity of genre and genre conventions because both rely on the character's voice and diction
- *prosody:* patterns of rhythms and sounds (i.e., intonation, pacing, assonance) often used in poetry

- *protagonist:* a leading character with a dramatic action
- *rhythm:* an arrangement of repeated sounds (sonic or literary)
- *plot:* request of events as they unfold in a story

Instructions: First, world building:

1. Begin by considering the story you wish to write and its protagonist. Who is the protagonist? Consider your character's depth. Include a protagonist who has a tangible and intangible dramatic action. What is their dramatic action? For example, *Selah wants the lead role in the school musical* (tangible); *Selah wants to gain her mother's support for her dreams as an actor because it will help her develop more confidence in herself* (intangible).

2. Consider who and/or what is standing in the protagonist's way? Why? The why can be simple; however, if there is a person standing in the protagonist's way of achieving their goal, then you can repeat this same exercise for the opposing character and their point of view afterward. Remember that even if the audience does not see the others' backstories, the most rewarding and impactful plays have complex characters whose lives feel relatable and three-dimensional. Get to know all your characters. For example, *Auditions are at night, and Selah needs to convince her mom to let her go; the auditions are on the other side of town, and she needs a ride.*

3. Also consider the stakes in the play. What happens if the protagonist does not get what they want or if they do not get what they want on time? The bigger the stakes, the more invested audiences become. For example, *Selah misses the audition; she has no way to get home; her phone dies; her friends are worried; a storm is approaching; now her mother is sick.*

Next, character and voice:

1. Now that you have an imaginary protagonist and a situation in your mind, consider the intimate details of their life. How would they speak? How do they see the world? Why? How can the audience learn more about them from their diction and behavior?

2. Practice writing a monologue. Take the character out of this imagined scene you have created. Think of another, perhaps memorable moment of their life (e.g., a specific moment of loss, betrayal, disgust, frustration, surprise, or awe).

3. Let's try this: It's your protagonist's first day of school. They are twelve. Write three to four sentences in the voice of their twelve-year-old self. What would they say if they were excited about going to school? What would they say if they were nervous? Why would they be nervous?

   a. Write a sentence where they are saying one thing but notice something about their own body that tells them something different about how they are feeling. *This encourages you to think about imagery and diction. It also helps you to visualize how you might write your play; will it follow conventional ideas of form and structure?*

   b. Write a sentence where their thoughts are scattered across the page. *This encourages you to think about language clarity, lyric voice, and diction.*

   c. Write two to three sentences about their expectation(s) of their first day using only five words in each sentence. *This encourages you to think specifically about language selection, diction, rhythm, and pacing.*

   d. Write two to three sentences that begin with "If it were not for my." *This encourages your creativity. You should continue to think about lyric voice and the use of figurative language.*

4. Let's try this: Your protagonist is switching jobs. Today is their last day. They are twenty-five. Write three to four sentences in the voice of their twenty-four-year-old self. What would they say if they were excited about leaving or starting over? What would they say if they were nervous?

   a. Write two to three sentences from the perspective of their favorite coworker. *This encourages you to think about personas or perspective shifts.*

   b. Now write two to three sentences from the perspective of their least favorite coworker. *Again, this encourages you to think about personas or perspective shifts in the same scene. You might consider writing from the perspective of your protagonist's office desk or coffee mug.*

   c. Your protagonist says, "I am so glad I left before _____." Fill in the blank. In a few sentences, expose why they must leave their old job and reveal something new about them that audience did not know before. Make it something shocking! *This encourages you to think about stakes and intended audience. Another way to approach this prompt is to let the revealing fact also connect to the new job they will be starting. This will help you consider making decisions that move the story forward rather than making decisions for the sake of it.*

5. Let's try this: Your protagonist is experiencing one of the saddest moments of their adult life. How old are they? What is going on?

   a. Without telling us explicitly how they feel, what are their first words? *This encourages you to think about diction, timing, pacing, and lyric voice. This also forces you to consider their age across the two stages of their life, before and now. How might their language choice change or evolve?*

b. Write two to three sentences describing exactly where they are using imagery. *This encourages your creativity and use of descriptive and figurative language.*

c. If no one was listening, then what might your protagonist confess about themselves? Reveal something new about them that the audience did not know before. *This encourages you to think about stakes in the play, intended audience, and lyric voice. How might this connect to another part of their life?*

d. Something terrible has occurred. In only seven words, what is their reaction to someone nearby? *This encourages you to be dramatic and consider language and voice. Who is this someone else? How close are they to them? How would they talk to them?*

Notes: Continue to do these prompts with different characters in your story. This can help you develop a backstory, which can be woven into the central plot. Moreover, it should help you get a sense of each character's wants and desires and help you get to know them. Remember that writing is a series of rewriting.

More importantly, though, follow the prompts as you see fit. Constricting our writing to either a few words or sentences pushes you to pay closer attention to the language you use. For advanced writers, consider writing sentences that use alliteration, anaphora, first-person *I*, or reverse syntax. What would it sound like if every monologue was a poem? How would we (as the audience) know? What would happen if all the characters repeated the same line differently throughout the play? Or if something specifically being discussed was a metaphor for something larger about life? Begin with what you know about storytelling, and use that to your advantage.

WHERE ARE WE? KEEPING THE AUDIENCE UNLOST

Justin Maxwell

Category: Establishing context (surreptitiously telling the audience where and when we are)

Overview: One struggle that many new playwrights have is telling the audience where and when the play is happening without falling into exposition or metatheatre. While exposition can advance the plot and metatheatre can make compelling art, they need to be stylistic choices for the author, not the fallback approach of a creative shortcut. Similarly, relying on costume or set designers to nail it down deprives us of the opportunity to make a stronger script.

Participants: Just you.
Time to complete: Variable. However, setting an arbitrary time for step 3 will keep this endeavor from bogging down unnecessarily.
Planning time: None.
Planning requirements: This is best done after a first crude draft. Ideally, it will provide dialogue to cue the audience in to the time and place after you've decided where and when the show happens. Also, if you have an interesting place or a compelling time but no real characters or conflict, this process can be an interesting way to reverse engineer those important devices.
Other needs or considerations: None.

Instructions:
1. Before beginning, make sure you know where and when your show happens. That said, you can do this exercise several times if you're undecided about time and place.
2. Ask yourself, "How does the time and location tie to the play's conflict?"

3. Brainstorm or list all the ways that you can answer the question from step 2. It's wise to set a time limit for this step, as one can spend forever on it.

4. Reimagine one result of the brainstorming or one item from the list as a line of dialogue.

5. Reimagine another answer from step 3 as a line of dialogue. Repeat until you have three or four different lines of dialogue.

6. Keeping the lines in a separate file, return to the draft and look for points where the dialogue might fit naturally.

7. Insert the lines at those points. Such overt pasting will probably make a scene that feels clunky or sounds artificial, however this is an early draft. Much of it probably sounds that way. You can clean up dialogue in revision.

Notes: This exercise is a far more subtle task than it may seem. Remember, audiences don't necessarily need a spot on the map or a date on a calendar. Sometimes vague, abstract, or approximate times and places will serve your artwork best. Sartre's *No Exit* and Beckett's *Happy Day* are both masterworks built around a character or the audience asking some version of "Where are we?"

THE BIG WINSTON

Justin Maxwell

Category: Subtext, the telling detail

Overview: When a character declares an emotion, audiences are denied a surreptitious moment of discovery, and they (perhaps mildly) disengage from the material. However, when an emotion is declared in the subtext of the dialogue, that dialogue does a better job of holding the audience's attention. Consider the following exchange, often attributed to Winston Churchill and Lady Astor, though its veracity is murky:

Astor: If you were my husband, I'd give you poison to drink.
Churchill: If you were my wife, I'd drink it.

Whatever the original source, the emotions under the language are much more powerful than if the characters simply say their feelings. Notice how much less effective the dialogue is when the emotions are in the text instead of the subtext:

Astor: I despise you and resent our acquaintanceship.
Churchill: I would rather die than live with you.

The latter's text is directly expressed emotion and tends to move us toward silliness instead of malice. A more positive example:

Partner 1: I woke up next to you this morning and thought, "We need a puppy."
Partner 2: I'll buy a dog bed and leash on my way home from work.

Under the dialogue is love, commitment, partnership, bonding, and maybe a shared desire for a child.

Participants: Individual or in a group.
Time to complete: 18 minutes.
Planning time: None.
Planning requirements: None.
Other needs or considerations:
- *In a group:* Follow the instructions, but have each person in the group read their exchanges aloud after step 6. Then discuss a question along the lines of "What emotion did the author select in steps 2 and 5?"
- *On your own:* None.

Instructions:

1. List three emotional states that one person might feel toward another person. Keep the emotions simple (love, apathy, melancholy, etc.) (five minutes).
2. Pick one (thirty seconds).
3. Imagine the lights come up to reveal two people sitting at a table. The emotion picked in step 2 is how one person at the table feels about the second person (two minutes).
4. One character makes a concrete statement of facts that has the emotion selected in step 2 buried in the statement's subtext. Use no abstract language. Use no more than one sentence (five minutes).
5. Pick another emotion from the list (thirty seconds).
6. The second character responds in kind with a concrete sentence that has the emotion selected in step 5 as its subtext. Use no abstract language. Use no more than one sentence (five minutes).

Notes: The outcomes of this exercise can get strange because the emotions are often incongruous to one another. That said, strange can be a deeply productive place for a writer to go. Moreover, this can be a great exercise to return to, substituting different emotions in step 1.

A SURPRISE ENTRANCE: DABBLING WITH DRAMATIC IRONY

Lavinia Roberts

Category: Dramatic irony, literary devices, character creation, building tension, crafting strong endings

Overview: Dramatic irony is a literary device where the audience or reader knows something that a character onstage doesn't. Dramatic irony is woven into a work's structure. This literary device can be used to heighten tension in a drama. Examples from Shakespeare include Macbeth professing loyalty to Duncan even while plotting his murder and Romeo purchasing poison when the audience knows that Juliet is still alive. Dramatic irony can also heighten the humor in a comedy, such as the love triangle in *Twelfth Night* and the romance between Beatrice and Benedict in *Much Ado about Nothing*. Dramatic irony can be employed when developing the plot or can add an unexpected twist to the ending of a piece.

Participants: Individual or group.

Time to complete: 30 minutes individually or 1 hour as a group.

Planning time: 5 minutes.

Planning requirements: None are necessary. Optional: Ask the group to bring in an example of dramatic irony to share with the class before beginning the writing activity.

Other needs or considerations:

- *In a group:* Begin by having a collective discussion about what dramatic irony is and how this literary device can be used when writing a script. How is dramatic irony employed in different genres? How is dramatic irony different from verbal irony or situational irony?
- *On your own:* Reflect on dramatic irony from plays of different genres.

Instructions:

1. Individually or in pairs, write a short monologue or dialogue, about one to three minutes running time, or one to three pages in standard play format. This short piece should contain a clear major dramatic question and a protagonist with a clear goal. Writers should make the piece a drama or a comedy. Take ten to twenty minutes, depending on how much time is needed to write the piece. You also could have writers pull or write a short scene from an existing piece they are working on.

2. Next, take five to eight minutes to have the writers add a new character to the end of the piece. This new character knows nothing about what has just transpired during the piece. How can this new addition add to the tension of the piece in a drama? How can this character heighten the humor in a comedy? Can this character transform a dramatic piece into a comedy?

3. Have the pairs read the dialogues aloud for the group. Discuss the pieces. Which pieces resonated with the group and why? What did the audience know about the situation that the new characters didn't that created the tension or humor? The time needed for this portion of the activity varies depending on the number of participants and how long you take for discussion.

Notes: Explore playing with dramatic irony on an existing piece. Would adding a new character to the end of a short play create a twist or show that a cycle is beginning again? Can having another character enter a scene during a tense moment add to the tension or humor of the scene? Instead of having a character understand a situation in your script, could keeping them in the dark add to the tension of a scene?

EXPANDING THE MATTER OF YOUR PLAY

Lisa D'Amour

Category: Rewriting, getting unstuck

Overview: This exercise helps us mine the depths of the matter that makes up our play. Sometimes we set our play somewhere and don't fully activate that space. Or we place an object in a scene but don't realize its potential for action, conflict, or metaphor. This exercise helps us identify the "stuff" of our play and mine it to shape character, supercharge plot, clarify theme, and more.

Participants: Individual or group.
Time to complete: 20–60 minutes.
Planning time: None.
Planning requirements: Choose a draft of one of your plays, either a first draft or a draft in process.
Other needs or considerations:

- *In a group:* Nothing really, just a leader to read these instructions and make sure each group member has chosen a draft of one of their plays—either a first draft or a draft in process.
- *On your own:* None.

Instructions: Warm-up: Take a moment to take in the space where you are sitting. What is its shape? Color? How would you describe the tone of this room? What furniture is in it? What objects? Where are the windows or doors? When would you guess this space was built? How does this space make your body feel. Take a big breath in and out. Do you notice any smells? What is the quality of the air?

Part 1: Now, imagine one object you could bring into your space that would change the quality of the space completely. How does the object change the energy of the space?

Try this again with a different object. How does this new object change the energy of the space?

Now, choose a different object but imagine one hundred of that object filling the space. How does it fill it? Where are the objects? How do the objects change the energy of the space?

Now freewrite for five minutes. Is there an object(s) that needs to enter the space of your play to change or energize things?

Part 2: Come back to the space where you are writing, and take a moment to remember the things you noticed. Let's do a little time travel.

What was this space like ten years ago? Jot down what you discover. Then try fifty years ago, one hundred years ago, five hundred years ago, five thousand years ago. Note what fills your mind as you time travel? Is it the physical details of the space? Or what is outside the space? History, politics, people, weather, geology? Jot down ideas and images as you go.

Try the same thing with this room, flashing forward ten years, fifty years, one hundred years, five hundred years, five thousand years.

Now freewrite for five minutes. Is there anything about the history or future of the place of your play that can enter and energize your work through dialogue, flashback/flash-forward, a new character, props, revelation of space, and so on?

Part 3: Now that we have stretched space, objects, and time a bit, take a moment to list

- important spaces in your play,
- important objects in your play,
- the time period or periods in your play, and
- anything about how your play moves through time.

Look at these lists.

Each object, each setting, each space is probably more pliable and potent than you realize. How can you explore the ways they can stretch, break, reconfigure, transform? How can this matter work for you in ways that are playful, surprising, shocking, efficient, concise? The choices you made for this early draft came from intuition and impulse, which should be trusted. These choices hold secrets that can unlock your play. Go deeper.

Notes: None.

4

REVISION

Exercises in this chapter:

"Writing Isn't Writing; Writing Is Rewriting; or, Making It Look Like You Knew What You Were Doing All Along" by Timothy Braun.
Identifying what's important and shaping story, plot, and character.   *152*

"Revision through Writing a Dramatic Question and Mapping" by Erin Courtney. Returning to the inspiration to write.   *156*

"Map It" by Mashuq Mushtaq Deen.
Weaving a narrative texture.   *159*

"Seeing a Play in Two Dimensions, like Graffiti, Large Mural Art, a Good Landscape Painting . . ." by David Gow.
Using physical images to resee a draft.   *161*

"Shape Thinking" by Karinne Keithley Syers.
Using abstract shapes and perceptions of pattern to develop dramatic structure.   *165*

"The Organization Arc" by Becky Retz.
Graphing the writing process to strengthen the narrative.   *169*

"Problem as Point" by Rachel Jendrzejewski.
A meditative approach to clarifying theme.   *171*

"Using Theme for Revision" by Justin Maxwell.
Trimming and focusing a draft.   *174*

"Manipulative Bastards Are Fun" by Leanna Keyes.
Using emotional manipulation to build scenes.   *177*

"Five Becomes Three" by Gab Reisman.
Making dialogue urgent.   *180*

"Sensibility, Marginalization, and the Lingering Umami of Your Play World" by Ed Bok Lee.
Visually keeping characters vibrant as they advance the plot.   *181*

"Uniquely You" by Gary Garrison.
Developing character through dialogue.   *184*

"Targeted Revisions" by Justin Maxwell.
Methodically focusing on problems in the draft.   *186*

"Subtext as Relief" by Paige Goodwin.
Conscientiously using subtext overall.   *189*

"Questioning Reality" by Justin Maxwell.
Rebuilding questions for better subtext and emotional dialogue.   *192*

"The Typewriter" by Edward Einhorn.
Using transcription to organically tighten a manuscript.   *195*

"The Michelangelo" by Jon Elston.
A visual method for honing dialogue.   *196*

"Honing'in on Dialogue" by Matthew Paul Olmos.
Removing exposition while letting dialogue do the work.   *205*

"Language Made Sensuously Attractive" by Deborah Yarchun.
Including sensory details to improve dialogue.   *207*

"How to Fall Back in Love with Your Play"
by Sophie Sagan-Gutherz.
Stepping away from a draft to return refreshed and
inspired.   *209*

"Starry Night" by Liz Appel.
Reseeing a script to gain a new perspective on it.   *212*

"Predator and Prey: An Exercise in Tone and Pacing"
by Trista Baldwin.
Making the script more evocative.   *214*

"Inspirational Stage Directions" by Justin Maxwell.
Making evocative stage directions.   *216*

"Does It Have to End This Way?" by Charissa Menefee.
Exploring dynamic endings.   *219*

"Last Things First (Sort Of)" by Erik Abbott.
Envisioning endings for scenes and plays.   *221*

"Know What You Don't Know (Targeted Proofreading)"
by Justin Maxwell.
A systematic approach to strengthening idiosyncratic
weak spots.   *225*

"How to Process Feedback from Workshops, Readings,
and Discussions" by Saviana Stanescu.
Making the most of public discussions and feedback.   *228*

WRITING ISN'T WRITING; WRITING IS REWRITING; OR, MAKING IT LOOK LIKE YOU KNEW WHAT YOU WERE DOING ALL ALONG

Timothy Braun

Category: Revision, development

Overview: Neil Gaiman once said, and I am paraphrasing, that when writing a first draft, it is as if you are driving a car at night through the fog with one headlight out. It is the second draft where you need to make it look like you knew what you were doing all along. As the old phrase goes, writing isn't writing; writing is rewriting. Or writing isn't writing; writing is beating your head against the wall as you lose all confidence in your ability to tell a story.

If you are anything like me, I almost always ask, "What on earth am I supposed to do with this?" when I get to the end of the first draft. The rewriting process can be scary, annoying, stressful, and downright brutal, but if we focus on approach and mindset, then rewriting can be fun and inspiring. In this exercise, you will be looking at various techniques and ideas to help in the revision and development process of your play.

Participants: Individual or group.
Time to complete: Varies.
Planning time: None.
Planning requirements: Varies.
Other needs or considerations: None.

Instructions: The very first thing you need to do is duplicate your document, no matter what program you are using. If you dive into the original document and start cutting lines, characters, and whole scenes, then you might lose something you could come back to later. Perhaps you have a line you really want but don't need. You've probably heard the phrase "Kill your babies" or "Kill your darlings," implying that you need to be able to let go of those wonderful things that just don't work for the story at hand. My suggestion is to create the second document or third or fourth or where you are at in the revision process, so you are not killing anything but rather putting them in the back of your toy chest as you play with other characters, lines, and scenes to build the overall story.

Now, this leads to story, plot, and character development. Can you take the first draft of the story you have been working on and put what it is all about in a tweet? Now, I'm writing all of this as the social media site Twitter is under siege by a petty narcissist, but that is a story for another book. If you are reading this, which you clearly are, and if Twitter no longer exists, then consider taking your story and putting it into no more than 140 characters—not words—characters. For example, "Gloomy Danish prince seeks revenge for father's death" is basically *Hamlet*, and if you haven't read that play, then please put this book down and read it. I'll wait.

Ah, welcome back. I hope you enjoyed *Hamlet*. Now, can you take your play and put it into 140 characters? This is important because plays have strong moments and weak moments or softer moments, if you will, and if you are able to put the story in a short span of words, then you have something to anchor you as you get lost in your characters' wants and needs and the world they are in.

Oh, where are my manners? I've asked you to read a four-hundred-year-old play, and we aren't discussing the plot. Can you take a piece of paper and draw out the plot of *Hamlet*? When you do, what are the important elements that stick out, the important scenes we need to have to keep the characters moving forward? What's important is that you do this by memory. What you remember is the stuff that is most important to you. Every time I've done this with *Hamlet*, I always forget the gravedigger scene, which is odd, as it is one the most famous scenes of the play, but for some reason it is not important to me. I actually spend a great deal of time thinking about the one scene our gloomy prince has with Ophelia. For some reason, that scene means more to me than the rest of the play combined. For some reason, I feel like it is the most important section of the plot because it resonates with me. What resonates with you? Find those moments.

Now, from memory, without looking, can you draw the plotline of the play you have been working on? Make certain it is on a piece of paper where you don't have infinite room (most pieces of paper don't), so you have to make choices. Rewriting is about making choices. Once you do this, can you go through your first draft and see what lines up with your drawing and what you forgot? Whatever you have neglected, consider cutting, consider making that choice. If it is not important to you, then it isn't important to the story, and it won't be important to the audience. Find those strong moments, and amplify them.

And what is important to the audience? Character. Why do we have characters? So we can kill them—at least that is what I think William Shakespeare said when he wrote *Hamlet*. When looking at your characters, ask yourself what genre of this story is. Remember, the real title of the play I've been using as an example is *The Tragedy of Hamlet* not *The Romantic Comedy of Hamlet*. As you think about genre in your play, this may lead to your characters' wants and needs, and once wants and needs collide, this might help in sharpening your characters' motivations and the conflicts they confront. When I think of that scene between our prince and fair Ophelia, it is a scene filled with tension: "To be, or not to be, that is the question." What does Hamlet want at this moment versus what he needs? What Ophelia wants versus what she needs is yet another question. This famous scene has so many hard and soft moments for the audience to consume and ends with a fair amount of yelling while setting up more plot points to further the tragedy that this play is. Story, plot, and character don't work independently; they work together. Character choices inform plot, plotline informs the story, and story is all about the characters, which is to say, if you can figure all of that out as you develop your play with rewrites, then you might make it look like you knew what you were doing all along.

Notes: Here are a few more ideas on revision. Honesty trumps clever. Your brain lies all the time; that is where the clever stuff comes from. Listen to other body parts when you revise. The one between your lungs doesn't lie; the one you digest pizza and tacos in is another.

You need to keep in mind that what is fun for you may not work for the audience. Don't kill your babies; just leave them in other drafts.

Give yourself a working title. It can always change, but give your play a name.

A long time ago in a galaxy far, far away, I was in graduate school, and one of my professors, Anne Bogart, told me, "Go there," as I was workshopping a play about two boys planning a school shooting. This was in response to me saying, "I don't wanna go there," regarding the depths of where I need to go to make the characters as relatable as could be, and Bogart meant I had to confront what scared me, why was I writing this play, what the point of me diving into such a subject matter was, and I realized I want to forgive school shooters, that they weren't monsters but humans who needed help. It was easy for me to label these school shooters as evil, but to show their humanity, to show another side to them, was scary, and I don't mean boo. What scares you about the story you are trying to tell or the characters? What makes your play not easy to confront?

Coincidences to get characters into trouble are great; coincidences to get them out of it are too easy.

You need to know the difference between doing your best and fussing. Revision is testing, not refining.

Do I like *Hamlet*? Yeah, sure, a little long, but it ain't bad. Try dissecting plays you like (I like Annie Baker's *The Flick*), and see what sticks out to you, what resonates with you, and how that reflects on your revisions. I play a game called 5 × Why in this. What are five things I like about this but I can't repeat myself. Numbers 1 and 2 are often vague, but 3 and 4 dig deep, and by the time you get to 5, you're going down a rabbit hole. More importantly, what plays, what movies, what stories do you not like and why? *The Flick* takes place in a movie theatre. I can only imagine they show *Jurassic Park* movies, which I hate. I vivisect those movies and show myself what I don't want to do in a story. Among my favorite movies is *Star Wars: The Empire Strikes Back*. Watch it closely, and the fact that the *Millennium Falcon* is having issues with the hyperdrive is just a storytelling device for Han Solo to fly into an asteroid belt and hide so he and Princess Leia can fall in love, and it works.

Discount the first thing that comes to mind. Ask yourself what five things could or even couldn't happen next in your play. Surprise yourself.

And when in doubt, fill in these blanks to ground yourself in your rewriting process: Once upon a time there was _____. Every day, _____. One day, _____. Because of that, _____. Because of that, _____. Until finally, _____.

REVISION THROUGH WRITING A DRAMATIC QUESTION AND MAPPING

Erin Courtney

Category: Prompts to navigate the revision process

Overview: Sometimes the revision process can be filled with doubt and anxiety. After getting too much feedback, we can feel like we have lost our way. This exercise is designed to help you remember why you wanted to write this play in the first place, what matters to you about it, and how to revise based on an honest and focused dramatic question of your choosing.

Participants: You can do this individually or in a group.

Time to complete: 1 hour.

Planning time: None.

Planning requirements: Gather your supplies: the most recent draft of your play, a stack of 3 × 5 cards, and a timer.

Other needs or considerations:

- *In a group:* If you want to do this collectively, then pick someone to read out the prompts and someone to set the timer.
- *On your own:* Just follow the prompts.

Instructions:

1. Set a timer for ten minutes. Freewrite all the reasons you felt compelled to write this play in the first place. What emotion, question, or event inspired you to begin? What content are you exploring? What genre or tone are you employing? What scares you about the content? What delights you? What images, events, places, people, dreams, music have inspired the content? Remember, a freewrite is nonstop writing by hand, where you do not edit or judge your writing. Flow from thought to thought; allow your subconscious to drive the writing.

2. Read through your freewrite. Underline or circle sections that feel exciting and truthful.

3. Set a timer for ten minutes. Using your freewrite as inspiration, craft a central dramatic question that reflects the core of the play. For example, my play *I Will Be Gone* is about a group of people who are grieving, and I chose the question "How do the living connect with their dead?" Sometimes the dramatic question may need a revision. For an earlier draft of that play,

I organized my revision around the question "In what ways do people behave badly when they are trying to avoid grief?" Different drafts may require different organizing questions.

4. Using a separate 3 × 5 card for each scene, write down the essentials of each: location, time, characters, main event or action. Give a title to each scene. Lay out the cards on the floor or a table in the order they are currently in your play. If you have a lot of narrative strands, then you may want to color code.

5. Looking at your play stretched out in front of you, and reflect on the ways that each of these scenes shine a light on your central dramatic question. Are there any scenes you don't need? Who or what have you silenced or avoided? Examine the beginning, middle, and end. Could you begin somewhere else? End somewhere else? Consider which scenes to expand, rewrite, edit down, or reorder using that central dramatic question as a guide.

6. Now, on a separate piece of paper, map out the shape of your play. Is it linear, like an arrow, with the most dramatic moment toward the end? Is it circular? Is it a braided narrative? Your play could be a unique shape, a spiral, a spiderweb, a wave, a nesting doll, a leaf, a quilt. Once you have drawn a shape that in some way reflects the structure of your play, label the scene titles (from your 3 × 5 cards) onto the map or shape.

7. Take some time to question the shape you made. Is this the shape you want it to be? Could you change the shape in a way that better answers your central dramatic question?

Notes: You can do this exercise as many times as needed. This is an exploration, not a solution.

MAP IT

Mashuq Mushtaq Deen

Category: Symbols, associative connections, spatial and temporal relationships, weaving the whole

Overview: The purpose of this exercise is to see the texture of the whole work, which elements carry greater or lesser weight, and the way they all weave together across the time and space, which might not be immediately apparent if you only start with two characters talking to each other.

Participants: This is an individual exercise but could easily be adapted for use in groups.

Time to complete: The initial mapping should take about 30 minutes, but ideally, the writer keeps adding to the map over successive days. This is important because you want the unconscious mind to make associations that the conscious mind cannot.

Planning time: There's no preplanning for this, but get yourself a decently sized plain piece of paper to draw on. Large scrap pads, 8½ × 11 inches, white, sold in most office stores, work great.

Planning requirements: Writers should come with some kernel of an idea: a character, a theme, an image, anything like that. Then they should find a place of quiet inside themselves, find their feet on the floor, find their breath—basically get into their bodies and the present moment—before they begin.

Other needs or considerations:
- *In a group:* This could easily be adapted to a group setting, but any conversation should be open ended and full of curiosity.
- *On your own:* The writer needs space, quiet, some plain paper (no markings of any kind, no lines) to draw on, and ideally a window to look out of while waiting for more information to come to them.

Instructions: Ground yourself in the present moment. Feel your breath in your body and your feet on the floor. Turn the paper in the orientation you don't usually use—for most people this would be a landscape orientation (wider rather than taller). Call up your image, word, theme, or picture, and think about where on the page it wants to live and how big it wants to be. Write it down. What things, people, or places orbit this thing you've written down? Write those down in the ways they are spatially related. Are they close or far away, big or small, close to the center or close to the edge? What other elements are a part of this story? If you know how they are connected, then write them in and connect them with lines. If you don't know how they're connected, then start a list on one side of the paper, and place them there for now. If you can sense where they are spatially, then write them down in the space but don't but don't force a connection until an authentic one is revealed. Think about place. Think about symbols and objects. Think about characters. Are there areas of blank space, and you don't know what goes there? Are you unsure of what characters go where and how they're related? That's okay. Write as much as you know, connect what you can with lines, and allow the unknown to be unknown.

When you get stuck or get to a place where you're not sure, then stop and do nothing for a while. Don't switch tasks to something else; don't leave your desk. Just do nothing. Ideally, stare out a window. Allow your unconscious mind time to turn things over and get back to you. Then continue.

Even after about thirty minutes or when you feel you're done, you can stop, but understand that your unconscious mind is still working on it. You will likely have moments over the next couple days where another object or relationship will become clearer to you. You may even begin to see a scene play out or start to feel the trajectory of the piece. Or you may see a pastiche of scenes. This is all good.

Notes: Try not to drive the process. The best thing a writer can do is get out of the way. So do that and allow something else to emerge. Allow yourself to be surprised.

SEEING A PLAY IN TWO DIMENSIONS, LIKE GRAFFITI, LARGE MURAL ART, OR A GOOD LANDSCAPE PAINTING . . .

David M. Gow

Category: How to see a play in its entirety alone in a room, with colors, markers, and so on, which encourages one to enter the play's world and feel it at a glance

Overview: This exercise helps you to literally *see* what you are writing in a completely different way. Like looking at graffiti, this construct lets you see an expression of the play, its forms, and its intervals. By *seeing* the play as this exercise describes, you get another view of it, of how it *feels*, of what's in it and where it might need to go while constructing or reconstructing, of what it might be calling out for or trying to say. This is perhaps the equivalent to looking at an extremely detailed blueprint but has the feeling of looking at musical notation on a large scale or a grand work of graffiti or public art. It lets you into the piece you're working on, and that can help quite a bit and even inspire.

Working on two of my best-known plays, my third and fourth plays, *Cherry Docs* and *Bea's Niece*, I was looking to combine story and scene-to-scene structure into something more intertwined, dynamic, with a tensile strength and less-labored feeling. My previous play had taken ages to build, and while it worked, it felt to me at times a bit clockwork. I wanted a way to *look at* the play I was building, its structure and form, the contents to a degree, in a large, two-dimensional form with depth—both at a glance and more in depth, to be able to look at all of it in something other than scroll form prior to hearing it read aloud and to be invited into the work.

I wanted to see the work as a whole and examine the structure and intervals and what that might call for next. Once the play was further along, I wanted to see how often certain references came up, where each character appeared, and more. I wanted to be able to see the play, like a blueprint or design for a wooden boat of size. I wanted to see the ribs, the spine, the width, and the depth, so to speak. Because a play is not a boat, the structure is more varied, and I felt a real need to experience that prior to anyone else even hearing it or seeing it. So in a sense, as the constructor of the thing, I wanted to *see* what someone else might hear and see.

I developed early on the need to see a script as though a scroll rolling out left to right. This exercise increased that view, top to bottom, left to right, the whole damn thing, and it incorporated a view of intervals, which helped me to feel or experience what an audience or reader might in a visceral or visual way. For me, it is a powerful tool, as valuable as a blueprint in the rough, which one might examine and change before committing boards to the saw or, more specifically, actors to the stage. It's a way to create and shape *experience* and change a blueprint.

Participants: This is intended mostly for the writer but could include, upon review, a director or dramaturge in development or actors. It could also be used in collective creation as easily, but I describe it here for one writer, as that is how I have used it.

Time to complete: A half-day, 4 hours or so, should suffice. The ability to keep this on a wall for a week or more might be ideal. I keep mine up for the duration of writing and change it as the plays change, more than once, as I make corrections and alterations.

Planning time: Several minutes to 1 hour should do it.

Planning requirements: You will need access to a photocopier that reduces a full page to the size of very large playing card, say 3 × 5 inches; paper for the copying; paper glue or a lot of paper cellophane (sticky) tape; a box of highlighters of whatever colors you like to use; pens, including gold, silver, and so on; and a room with a high ceiling that you can spend a half-day or longer in.

Other needs or considerations:

- *In a group:* Same as above and below.
- *On your own:* Eyesight or extensive printing capacities with braille and something to mark the text with highlights.

Instructions: Run the whole play or draft portion (this can be done at any stage) that you have written though a photocopier that will give you reduced versions of the pages. These are representations of the pages—three inches by five inches (like large Tarot cards), or smaller (regular playing cards), if you are used to dealing with tiny text. Cut the reduced pages down to reduce to this size.

Now, glue or tape everything together, left to right and top to bottom. If your first scene is three pages long or twelve, that is your top row. If the second scene is nine or four pages, that is your second row, and so on. Gradually, you will find yourself constructing a wall hanging the size of a small to medium-sized carpet.

Doing this with my play *Cherry Docs* midway through writing it, I could see the structure very clearly. A one-page scene next to a one-page scene, followed by twelve pages; a one-page scene next to a one-page scene, followed by eleven pages; a one-page scene next to a one-page scene, followed by ten pages. I could *see* a mirroring and diminuendo, could *feel* how the play might feel to an audience. This helped me to think, not forcefully, but visually and intuitively, on what might follow or come next and even to try variations out, as I had open access to a copier and paper, which is ideal.

On the wall, or if you have a very large, clear floor, make tidy (or not-so-tidy) markings to help observe themes and subjects in the play. For example, you can mark all references to money in silver, love or sex in gold, threats or violence in red, pleading or hope in blue (or whatever colors and events, properties, or elements work for you). Each character entrance can be marked with a color or emoji of some kind, and you will gradually *see* what's in the play and where. You can even chart the height of drama or temperature of scenes.

Notes: It's good to take time with this process. It is not a forceful or mathematic process. If you have a writing room or space where you can leave the play up, then it will help to glance to it once in a while.

The exercise helped me build one play into a series of unexpected rhythms that seemed to dramatically embolden the play's impact via counterrhythms and counterexpectations in form. In another play, it helped me to *see* and go with a swirling, self-contradicting structure that seemed to pull a viewer into the experience of the central character. These were very different plays, but both benefited from the examination. I think this tool for looking at my work, as I am doing it, has had more impact than any other exercise or mode of measure beyond understanding a classical five-act structure.

I hope it helps or at least amuses you. I was kind of amazed at how shapes coming out of looking at the structure might mimic central motifs in a play. For example, with *Bea's Niece*, the play ended up resembling an upside-down hat, which is a central image in the play, but only after it revealed a dog, which was also an important motif. Have at it, and good roads to you.

SHAPE THINKING

Karinne Keithley Syers

Category: Midstage narrative development after a rough or raw draft has been written

Overview: Use this exercise to widen the sense of where your story can move, to summon a sense of narrative freedom, and to tune into the resources of other modes of compositional thinking. In this exercise, try to activate the kind of seeing that takes place in your mind's eye, where visual ideas turn into abstract shapes and perceptions of pattern in the world.

The priority here is to zoom out and perceive the large movements a play might make. It can be a way to discover new regions of the play. It can be a way to radically enlarge or radically compress the aperture of the play; that is, how much of the story it shows, how much detail or brevity is offered to each part of the story world that surfaces in the telling. We think here about large-scale relationships between internal durations (sections, stretches, passages, units) of the piece. The energy we're thinking about has to do with adjacency, juxtaposition, neighboring, sequence, and simultaneity. Call this relational energy.

The relational energy between sections has to do with both their meeting edges—the way one gives way to the other, as well as how an audience understands the things in sequence—and their internal content and relative proportions and how they relate in time. A tiny scene followed by a very long scene followed by a tiny scene will be understood differently than the same very long scene followed by the two tiny scenes. The very long scene compressed to its pith and the tiny scenes drawn out to longer breaths will likewise change the understanding of them, even if the basic information communicated in each remains the same.

Participants: This can be done either solo or in a group. A note on how to make this a group exercise follows the instructions.

Time to complete: 20–60 minutes.

Planning time: None or some. You can let your mind supply you with ideas improvisationally and follow the principals or take what comes, or you can spend some time gathering shape ideas in advance, say by taking a walk or browsing library books.

Instructions: You're going to make a projection of your play's possible shape. Think of this projection as a play in the form of a _____. You can borrow an existing form or image or use a generic one. What's the difference between a play in the form of a chess board and a play in the form of a donut? A play in the form of a mural or a play in the form of a triptych? A play in the form of a dormant volcano and a play in the form of an extinct volcano?

I suggest embracing a cross-disciplinary imagination here; get away from narrative shapes that hang out around playwriting (act I, act II, act III, or the triangle of stasis/crisis/resolution), and think in other terms. Do musical structures mean something to you (theme and variations, sonata form, concerto form)? What about plant structures (roots, trunk, crown; mother trees, rhizomatic root forms, blooms, petals in all their computational forms)? I've made plays in the form of gardens and telescopes and plays in the form of particular art-historical images (a life of the Buddha, with a large central image and a hundred small chronological scenelets). Gertrude Stein called her writing *portraits* and her plays *landscapes*. Understanding your play as having a secret affinity in its bones can give you freedom to let *it* surprise *you* with possibilities that don't fit the shape of a narrative form you already know. When you allow a new shape to offer itself to your play, it can teach you something about what is possible rather than careening toward the same old ending. But it can also teach you to behold your play from different perspectives, inviting you into considerations you may have overlooked otherwise.

Step 1: Find your shape. You can find your shape from inside or outside. From outside, go trawling for shapes. Look around you. Record a short list of interesting forms in your vicinity. For example, I'm looking at the outlet on the wall. I can take it locally as a shape: a rectangle with two identical regions that are both caves and faces, reaching back toward power. Or I cast to the structures it participates in, moving imaginatively through the wires that reach down to the fuse box and out to the utility grid or, in my mind's eye, plugging successive things into it. (Hmm, a play in the shape of the power moving in sequence through a lamp, a vacuum, and an electric pencil sharpener.) From inside, skim back through your existing draft and your raw material for visual images, and consider their forms. What already populates your play that could become a teacher of shape?

Step 2: Draw the shape you'll consider for the next ten or so minutes and label it. What are its *sections*? Where do its parts differentiate? If you drew a swan, then there's a beak; a head; a long, thin neck; two full, folded wings; and the lump of body with paddle feet below. Label the sections with a few key elements of your story, either thinking of elements as sequences of events or areas the story inhabits (areas considered geographically or perhaps mood areas). Allowing your imagination to supply you with an answer and following the principle of take what comes, ask yourself an *if* question. For example, "If the beak is when Susie meets Sally and the giant folded wing is the sermon that Bob is always quoting from, then what kind of pressure or process or event makes that S-curving neck that connects the two?" Or, "If I already have a story unfolding in three sections, then what would happen if I morphed their proportions so that they roughly aligned with the head; long S-curve neck;

and half-submerged body?" "If I have a story unfolding along a clear timeline, then what happens if I project it into the shape of a cloud?" "If I'm retelling my story in the form of an empty birdcage with an open door, then am I letting what I thought was the main action of my story escape and instead I'm going to tell the trace of what it left behind?"

Don't forget to play with the idea of aperture in both time and space. Might your story grow to encompass a section that tracks the resonance of the main action deep into the future? Might your story move geographically into a new region or, if you're working the kitchen sink of domestic narrative, go visit another house? Or a museum? Or the mall?

Finally, consider the potential relational energy of this projected shape—where you cut out and where you cut into each new section and how those edges create meaning.

Step 3: Digest what you learned. When you're done, write yourself a note about what you learned about the play's potentiality. Distill what you've learned into an aphorism, and keep that aphorism in view as you continue writing. Maybe leave your drawing of the shape on your desk, too, to occasionally remind yourself of the freedom to send your story somewhere new.

Notes: If you're doing this in a group, then let everyone contribute a shape to the table. Then everyone can choose a few shapes to use for projections. Because there's no right answer for how to read a swan for its narrative sections, it can be illuminating to see how other brains solve the riddle.

This exercise is an improvisation on an entertained question. You might need to repeat it a few times before you find a shape that is the right teacher for your play.

THE ORGANIZATION ARC

Becky Retz

Category: Structure, organization, pacing, script development

Overview: Starting a play is easy; finishing it is hard. This exercise helps the writer produce a fully fleshed-out piece by using a structural perspective to guide their creativity. It provides a simple visual that makes it easy to spot the holes in their script, pacing problems, and where scenes may need to be cut or expanded. It also can be used in the initial development of a script.

I remember when I was first asked to write a ten-minute play. I had read all about the two-act structure, character development, major dramatic questions, rising and falling action, climax. How was I going to fit all that into ten minutes? Having learned early in life that a big problem is easier to solve when it is broken up into a series of smaller problems, I came up with this idea.

Knowing that one script page generally translates to one minute of stage time, I drew an arc on a piece of paper. At one end of the arc, I wrote a *1*, and at the other end, a *10*. I made a note of my opening and ending at each of those numbers, respectively. I decided on a traditional structure for my play (because I was new at this, and I think it's a good idea to learn the basics before straying from them). So my climax needed to happen around page 6 or 7 in order to wrap things up by page 10. That told me I needed to introduce my initial conflict by page 2 so there would be time to further complicate matters on pages 3–5 or –6. This structure helped me create a series of smaller problems that were easier to solve and showed me a path to a finished product.

I've used this exercise ever since, both in the early stages of development and to figure out what my play needed next along the way. By the way, you could do this exercise with a straight line, but I find that the arc better represents the rising and falling energy I want the audience to experience. After all, who wants to see a flat play?

Participants: Individual or group.
Time to complete: Approximately 10 to 30 minutes, depending on the length of the script.
Planning time: None to 20 minutes, depending on script length and your desire.
Planning requirements: Blank paper and something to write with. It will save time to go through the script in advance and note page numbers where major plot points happen.
Other needs or considerations:
- *In a group:* Participants should work individually, focusing on their own work, until step 5.
- *On your own:* Rather than showing one's work to another group member in step 5, the writer should take time to make notes about what they gleaned from the finished arc. This will be the basis of their play's next to-do list.

Instructions:
1. Take a blank piece of paper, and draw a large arc.
2. On the underside of the arc, place numbers corresponding to script pages. For example, if you are writing a ten-minute play, place a *1* at the left end of the arc and a *10* at the right end. You don't have to write in all the numbers in between.
3. Write in major plot points at various points along the top edge of the arc based on where they happen in the play. Then write the scenes' page numbers underneath. The opening goes at the left endpoint of the arc, and the ending goes at the right endpoint. Be precise with your placement of the other plot points, based on where they appear in the script. For example, if you have an eighty-page script, and Margie and Robbie get into a big fight on page 40, then that goes at the top of the arc.

4. Now, take a look at what you've got. What does this picture tell you about your pacing? Is your initial conflict happening soon enough, or are you spending too much time introducing characters? Does your climax happen where you want it to? Are some scenes too long or too short? Is each scene building on the one before it? Do you need more rising action (increased conflict/problems) leading up to the climax?

5. If you are doing this as a group exercise, then switch your completed arc with a partner. Study each other's paper, and give an analysis. (Sometimes it's easier to see another person's work clearly than it is to see one's own.)

Notes: Consider keeping the arc as a sort of blueprint for your play. Perhaps update it as the script develops. Referring to it will help provide the structure produce a cohesive finished product.

PROBLEM AS POINT

Rachel Jendrzejewski

Category: Theme, writer's block

Overview: This exercise is designed to help surface and/or clarify theme. I think it's most useful when you're further along in a writing process, though it can be informative at different or multiple junctures along the way, including during moments of feeling stuck or uninspired.

Participants: Individual or group.
Time to complete: Variable, but I recommend setting aside at least 1 hour.
Planning time: none
Planning requirements: All you need is a piece in progress that you can think about and materials for writing.

Other needs or considerations:

- *In a group:* You could do this exercise with collaborators by having everyone do the exercise on their own and then discussing and comparing notes or by doing the exercise collectively, brainstorming responses aloud and perhaps having one person take written notes. If you go this latter route, I strongly suggest still making space for quiet thinking time at the top and ahead of making the first two lists so that everyone can tap into a focused headspace and gather their thoughts.
- *On your own:* None.

Instructions:

1. Take some time to transition into a quiet headspace. Maybe take a walk, light a candle, or drink some water.
2. Reflect on the play you are making. Sit with it in silence for at least five minutes (set a timer if need be).
3. Freewrite a list in response to the question "What is this play about?" Your answers may range from broad, single words like *family* or *mortality* to more specific phrases like *a queer person in rural Texas who's trying to figure out how to gather a chosen family* or *a postdramatic exploration of individual versus collective responsibility around climate change*. Write until you feel like there's nothing more to say, and then see if you can add ten more words or phrases to your list.
4. Now think about what's feeling stuck or incomplete or frustrating or confusing about your piece at this point in the process. Sit with it in silence for at least five minutes (set a timer if need be).
5. Freewrite in response to the question "What's the problem?" Your answers may range from single words like *flat* or *sprawling* to phrases like *We can't figure out how to end this thing* or *I don't like any of these characters* or *what happens next* or

As a group of collaborators, we're struggling to make decisions together or *I feel lost.* You can also write longer reflections if you like. Allow all your feelings and judgments to come out here. Write until you feel like there's nothing more to say, and then add ten more words or phrases to your list. (If that feels hard, then look at one of the more feeling- or judgment-oriented things from your list, and try to get as specific as possible about why you have that feeling or judgment. For example, in response to something like "I don't like any of these characters," see if you can unpack precisely why: "None of these characters are kind people. Most of them seem to be living in and acting out of fear.")

6. Now look over this problem list. Intuitively, without thinking too much, circle one to three items on the list that jump out to you the most, that feel like the crux of what you're struggling with and/or like the most surprising revelations.

7. Write a sentence rearticulating each item you picked with this starting phrase: "What if the whole play is actually about [item from list]?" You may want to rework the item a bit for this sentence. For example, building on "I don't like any of these characters," the sentence might be, "What if the whole play is actually about the fact that these characters are not very kind people?" or "What if the whole play is actually about people living in fear?" Or in the case of "As a group of collaborators, we're struggling to make decisions together," the sentence might be, "What if the whole play is actually about people trying to make decisions together, function as a society, or practice democracy?"

8. Now spend some time freewriting about how your play might change if you look at it through the lens of each new theme you've articulated in step 7. Write for at least ten minutes (set a timer if need be); if you have articulated more than one

possible new theme, spend at least ten minutes writing about each one. You may find that nothing contradicts your original "What is this play about?" list, but see if there's any clarification coming up, any more specific or nuanced understanding of the work's theme(s), any insight into a character's struggles or intentions, and so on. At the same time, be open to the possibility of a radical departure from what you thought the play was about. For example, maybe you thought you were writing about family, but what's really surfacing is someone's more personal, internal work of moving through trauma. Maybe you thought you were making a piece about climate change, but really what you're examining is how very different kinds of people move through this life together. What happens if you look at the piece with this new focus as a guiding light? How might it inform your revisions or what happens next?

Notes: This exercise was inspired by the dance duo HIJACK (Arwen Wilder and Kristin Van Loon) following the 2013 premiere of their performance *redundant, ready, reading, radish, Red Eye* at Walker Art Center, Minneapolis. In a postshow discussion, Arwen and Kristin talked about how they often embrace a challenge or stuck moment in their collaboration as the very point of the project—a practice that can lead their work in wholly unexpected directions.

USING THEME FOR REVISION

Justin Maxwell

Category: Revision, theme, focusing a draft

Overview: This exercise helps us think about your theme and how you can use it for revision. While academics may debate the idea of theme and plenty of writers eschew it completely, it can serve as a valuable tool to help us revise our texts. After all, if we take the idea that revision is "re-vision," seeing anew, then theme is the idea we're trying to show off. We can use theme to make tighter, more focused, and therefore more evocative drafts.

Participants: Just you.
Time to complete: Varies but probably at least 1 hour.
Planning time: 5 minutes or more.
Planning requirements: Take some time to do some metacognitive work. Ponder some questions: Why are we making this artwork? Is it a conscious reason? Are we just listening to the characters? If so, what are they trying to tell us and why? Why do we care enough to listen? Does each beat of the play tie back to the theme? If not, can it be revised into doing so? If it can't, is it really necessary? What happens if every line of dialogue that doesn't connect to the theme (however tangentially) gets cut? Try to apply those questions to a narrative masterpiece. Almost nothing can get cut without the play really losing something.
Other needs or considerations: None.

Instructions:

1. Write what your theme is. Be as detailed as possible. Remember, you're not writing this in stone. You may well want to change your theme later, or it may naturally evolve as the play develops. That's okay. This is just for you.
2. Go through the section of script you want to revise, and mark out each individual beat. A beat is a small unit of action within a scene. You can do this for as much of the play as you want to work on, the whole script, an act, or a scene.
3. Can you see how the beat ties to the theme? Is it overt? Covert? Subtle? Is it in action? Dialogue? Tone? Plot? Does the beat connect to your theme in some other way?

4. If you can't see how the beat connects to the theme, either revise that beat until it connects or cut that beat. If it connects, then jump to step 8.

5. If that beat doesn't connect, then there might be things in that beat that you'll want to keep. Perhaps an important piece of exposition or valuable moment of dialogue. If so, double-check, make sure your audience really needs those moments and you don't just want them because you want them.

6. If they need to stay, then find a new home for them somewhere else in the script or in a separate file to keep them for later.

7. If they don't connect, then cut them.

8. Once you know the beat fits the theme, it's time to dig down into the details. Does the place where and when the beat happens fit the theme? If not, change it until it does.

9. Does the dialogue fit the theme?

10. Do the actions fit?

11. Does the mise-en-scène fit?

12. Keep altering and cutting until everything fits.

13. Once you can positively answer "yes" to questions 8–11, that beat is probably doing important work for you.

Notes: This approach is often a good way to deal with scripts that feel slow or ponderous. Scripts that feel fun but empty can fall into this same issue, with characters talking wittily about nothing.

This process can feel like a lot of cutting, and that can be very scary, depending on the state of the draft and one's experience. Highlighters can help with that! To manage this process, one can simply take anything that affirmatively connects to the theme and highlight it. I like green for this. Take anything that doesn't yet tie to the theme but is doing something important (like exposition), and highlight it another color, maybe yellow. Anything that doesn't seem to connect to the theme gets highlighted a different color, red obviously. Then cut all the red or revise until you can color it green. Make sure the yellow points are so wrapped with green material that they don't stand out anymore, or revise them until you're inclined to change their color.

With only a little bit of imagination, this strenuous exercise could be applied to setting, tone, or characters, too.

MANIPULATIVE BASTARDS ARE FUN

Leanna Keyes

Category: Dialogue, character development, revision, contrast, conflict, subtext, tactics, structure

Overview: This exercise explores a character's ability and willingness to lie, to present half-truths, to withhold, and to disclose. Manipulation is commonly thought of as a morally bad tactic; this exercise attempts to complicate that and conceptualize manipulation as a tool without moral weight. By breaking down a scene's structure into a flowchart of possibilities, the writer can easily workshop and restructure beats and character moments. At the conclusion of the exercise, the writer emerges with a far more complex emotional landscape of character decisions and with multiple options for "levers" to pull for various effects on the characters and the audience.

Participants: Individual or group.
Time to complete: 30 minutes.
Planning time: 5 minutes.
Planning requirements:
- *Artistic suggestion:* Read or watch a scene with your favorite villain, and look for the emotional levers they pull.
- *Mechanical suggestion:* Gather some index cards, sticky notes, sketch pads, something that will let you draw or create a flowchart.

Other needs or considerations: Discuss some of your favorite fictional villains or fictional villains who "have a point." To make it easier to distance yourselves from the moral ick of deception, reach a mutual agreement that this exercise is about *characters and art* and not a personal statement about the moral fiber of any of the participants. Remember, *representation is not endorsement.*

Instructions:
1. Start by identifying a clear objective on the part of a character, the Negotiator, that requires an intentional decision or change on the part of a second character, the Target. This is the start point of your flowchart.
2. Identify the structural outcome of the scene in the larger context of your play. Often this can be the Target making the decision or change that the Negotiator wants, but not always. Manipulation is not always entirely successful, or something may interrupt the process. This is the end point of your flowchart.
3. From the starting point, create four next steps where the Negotiator can try four different tactics, such as the following (you might want to jot down ideas of how those specific tactics manifest, or you can just label the tactic):
   a. Tactic 1: A complete lie
   b. Tactic 2: A half-truth
   c. Tactic 3: A withholding of the truth
   d. Tactic: A disclosure of the truth
4. Consider how the Target would react to each of these tactics based on their own personality and relationship to the Negotiator or the perceived authority of the Negotiator. Would they
   a. believe the Negotiator?
   b. disbelieve them?
   c. seek clarity?
   d. try their own tactics to further their own objectives?

5. From your first set of next steps, create another section of your flowchart that has the Target's possible responses to each of the Negotiator's tactics. (If you know that your Negotiator can't or won't use a certain tactic, then you can choose to ignore that branch of the flowchart.)

6. Consider whether the Target's responses prompt the Negotiator to consider their goal achieved, to abandon their goal, or to try again with another tactic.

7. You can do further sets of next steps and responses until you feel that you can legitimately find a path through the flowchart that maintains emotional logic all the way from the start point to the end point.

8. Once you have a flowchart, consider the sum of the tactics and responses of the Negotiator and the Target. Look for patterns. Do the patterns tell the story you want to tell? Is it more interesting if the Negotiator never lies, always lies, or a mix? If the Target is proving resistant to manipulation, then what would it take to make them believe the Negotiator? Are there other paths through your flowchart that lead to the same end point but tell a more compelling story along the journey?

Notes: If you are doing this exercise in a group, how it manifests will depend on your collaborators. If you have other writers, then you might try doing a "writers' room," where different writers can pitch ideas to fill out the flowchart. If you have performers, then they might embody the Negotiator or the Target and try out different paths of the flowchart.

This exercise is particularly helpful in the revision process because, in the early drafts of a story or scene, characters can too easily disclose their true objectives and intentions (as the writer is figuring out what they want alongside the characters).

FIVE BECOMES THREE

Gab Reisman

Category: Editing, urgency, dialogue and scene sharpening

Overview: This exercise it to practice and sharpen our editing skills, learn when dialogue is extraneous rather than helpful, and (occasionally) kill our darlings; that is, a part of our play we love but that is no longer really serving us. By parsing down a scene from five pages to three (or generally culling it by two-fifths), we practice editing a thing to its essential parts, making room for more and deeper parts of a play and creating a narrative that moves more quickly.

Participants: Individually or in a group if writing collectively.
Time to complete: 15 minutes.
Planning time: 0 minutes.
Planning requirements: Come to this exercise with an existing scene from a longer play.
Other needs or considerations:
  - *In a group:* Select a scene written by the group that feels especially wordy or that feels written by many separate mouths.
  - *On your own:* Bring a scene that feels wordy or heavy, a scene where the pacing lags or there isn't enough forward motion.

Instructions:
  1. Read the scene from start to finish.
  2. Go through and cut words, phrases, and lines that feel unnecessary. Look particularly at places where characters may be repeating themselves or where the dialogue is slowing down the pace of the scene. This should get to a place where it feels difficult to cut anymore. Push past that place, and keep cutting.
  3. Now that you've trimmed down the scene, expand it—write past where you thought it ended. Let the characters keep talking but with a new and deeper urgency.

Notes: Save this culled scene as a separate draft, so if you feel like you miss something you cut, you can always go back and add it in again.

SENSIBILITY, MARGINALIZATION, AND THE LINGERING UMAMI OF YOUR PLAY WORLD

Ed Bok Lee

Category: Characters, plot

Overview: This method helps ensure your main characters, particularly marginalized human beings in your play world, are richer and more complex. Many, if not most, enduring works of drama throughout world history possess a poetic quality rooted typically in the characters' revelatory sensibilities. However, often in the process of creating a compelling story, our characters can begin to feel subservient to the engines of plot. If this happens, then the characters' sensibilities, what helps to make them unique and multidimensional, can sometimes inadvertently get pruned away for the sake of efficiency. This can result in a loss of richness, a loss of lingering theatrical umami, in relation to the play world and overall story. This exercise is designed to help forefront the richness of the human soul amid all the required dramatic mechanisms of a compelling plot.

Participants: The individual writer or writers.
Time to complete: 1–2 hours.
Planning requirements: A recent rough draft of a work in progress that is still wild with possibilities yet has some semblance of a functional plot and/or story arc. Two different colored highlight markers.
Planning time: None.
Other needs or considerations: None.

Instructions:

1. Go through your draft from the beginning, highlighting in, say, yellow all the lines and stage directions that depict each character's most singular, unique sensibilities in relation to the play world. Often their truest sensibilities will be congealed not only in what and why they say something but also in *how*. In the West, think Blanche DuBois's bruise-blue-purple musical exhortations or Hester Smith's linguistically blunt knife at work within the shadows of American history or Hamlet's refined moral verve. Far away once, I wrote a play, *History K*, about K, an aging Korean sex worker on her final night of work near a US military base camp town in South Korea. It felt important not to allow the plot that drives the story to overdetermine who she is as a human being. Specifically, I wanted the most compelling agency in the story to reside within her sensibilities and rich interior life and memories, not the physical encounter with one last john. Yet it was also important to me to be true to the character and her social standing and physical situation. Thus, as the physical action of one final evening in a love motel unfolds, so, too, does her inward-oriented lyricism in which memory and imagination and history blur. In short, my goal in this play was to see just how far and wide I could take her inmost lyrical mode of consciousness while remaining true to the very real external circumstances of her life. I did this to amplify her humanity and the profundity of who she is and what she's witnessed and experienced in her lifetime, which is as far away from the reality of her daily physical circumstances as common speech is from poetry.

2. Once you've gone through and highlighted all the lines (and directions) that make your characters' sensibilities most richly, uniquely true to who they most compellingly are (or

strive to be), then take your second, say, pink marker and highlight what you consider your characters' most necessary, plot-driving lines and stage directions.

Notes: Where your characters' speech and actions most approach the poetic is where their most singular sensibilities will typically reside. Of course, poetry can come in many forms: lyrical, surreal, minimalist, bluntly absurd, darkly depraved, and so on.

Look back at the ratio of yellow to pink highlighted regions. As a rule of thumb, I personally like it when the yellow highlights outnumber the pink regions by a factor of at least two. This is because actions speak louder than words, but words (and strong, vibrant sensibilities) still matter. Two to one is a good ratio to start with. You may wish it to be three to one or one to one. Most importantly, reflect and ask yourself if your plot presently *feels* subservient to your characters' most unique qualities and sensibilities, or is it the reverse?

This is not an exact science, but in particular, if you are creating historically marginalized characters relative to your play world and/ or the world in general, then consider the appropriate ratio between poetic sensibilities and plot that you wish to achieve in your final version, and revise with that in mind.

Again, each play world that you are developing will likely require a different ideal ratio of poetic sensibility to plot and will most likely only be arrived at slowly, intuitively over time. This method can be useful in accelerating the process by providing a rough, visual, ongoing reminder of the importance of the poetic sensibilities of your characters who are attempting to make their ways in an often punishing, two-dimensional world.

UNIQUELY YOU

Gary Garrison

Category: Character, dialogue

Overview: No two people speak alike. People speak similarly but not completely alike or identically (as is often the cases in the dialogue of our plays). The words we choose to express ourselves, the order of those words, and the omission of certain words or abbreviation of others are as individually unique to ourselves as our fingerprints. How you communicate in any situation is so uniquely you that your language takes on its own personality.

What influences our language? Does age shape how we speak? Does our level of education show up in our word choice? What about our health? The region of the country we live in or grew up in? Does religion influence our choice of words? Do we speak differently with our companion than we do our best friend, a casual friend, a new friend? Does our choice of career and what we do for a living find its way into our vernacular? These are all curious questions that, were we to answer them as they relate to the characters in our play, we might find that moments, scenes, acts, or whole plays become more resonant to the audience because they help define character in ways that action sometimes can't.

Participants: This exercise is best done during a writer's alone time, but there's something to be learned by all playwrights who share this with a room of writers.

Time to complete: For part 1, the exercise can be done in 5–10 minutes. For part 2, the exercise can be completed in 30 minutes to 1 hour.

Planning time: 5 minutes.

Planning requirements: If you're currently working on a script that has three or more characters, then use that script. If not, find your most recent script that has three or more characters.
Other needs or considerations: None.

Instructions: Part 1 is straightforward. Open to a scene of a play you're writing in which three or more characters are speaking. Copy two to three pages of your scene, and paste it in another file. In that pasted scene, while maintaining the spacing of the elements on the page, remove all the character names. What you should have remaining are pages of dialogue with the character names removed.

Now, hand those pages to another writer or a theatre-savvy friend or a director. Ask them this simple question: "How many people are speaking on these pages?" If you've written your characters with any kind of identifiers through language (age, health, religion, sexuality, etc.), then your reader should be able to identify the number of people speaking. In fact, they should be able to point to specific passages and say, "This is character A's dialogue—here, here, and here." But if you're like a lot of writers, all your characters sound the same.

Part 2 is also straightforward. If after part 1 you think you need to strengthen the language of your characters, then rewrite the scene, and strengthen each character's language by allowing it to be influenced by any number of the following:

1. Age
2. Gender
3. Race
4. Culture
5. Education
6. Religion
7. Sexuality
8. Politics
9. Values and beliefs

10. Physical health/attributes
11. Quirks
12. Friends and associates
13. Occupation
14. Region of the country

Simply said, a seven-year-old does not speak the same as a thirty-year-old. Interesting enough, a ten-year-old has different language than a thirteen-year-old. Someone who grew up in Boston does not sound like someone who grew up in Houston. How do you know the difference? Start listening, followed by writing. And practice. Play with your words. Remember: Playwriting is play at writing.

Notes: Keep a notebook of how you hear certain people speak. Make a resource library for yourself.

TARGETED REVISIONS

Justin Maxwell

Category: Focusing the revision process

Overview: There seems to be a natural impulse to revise by starting at the beginning of the play and working through to the end. After all, we read it in that order, and we probably write it in that order. However, this approach also means that we come to the same points in the play at the same time and miss the same shortcomings. There are two ways to do targeted revisions, and both approaches change how we see the text and break us away from our mental image of the material. The first way is to begin a conventional revision process by starting at different points in the manuscript. The second way is to pick something in the script that needs focused attention and go through the material focusing on that thing only.

For the first way, changing where we start reading a manuscript is a simple, effective way to see the play on the page and not the play in our head. When we start reading, we fall into the train of thought that leads us from scene to scene, beat to beat, and line to line. Following our own train of thought keeps us on the same mnemonic track, and we need our subconscious to derail. Simply starting a revision at a different point in the manuscript can be invaluable for this shift in perspective. Starting at point D in the manuscript, then E, F, and G, can show us things we missed when we start at point A with every revision. At the very least, this means that our minds get fatigued and our energy flags at a different point. If we start bright-eyed and eager at the beginning of the manuscript, our energy might be fading by scene 9, and we miss a flaw there because of fatigue. Starting a revision at scene 7 means we see the problem in scene 9 that we've been missing. Similarly, starting a revision with the last scene or even the last line and then working backwards can reveal the text on the page in an unexpectedly bright light.

For the second way, the revision targets a single device in the script. For example, someone writing a comedy might feel like their plot is solid, and their characters, round, so they then dedicate a draft to just working on each joke, making sure they are tight, smart, and funny. This means not worrying about anything else in the material, just looking at the humor. Someone writing a non-narrative, psycho-sexual horror performance might comb through the draft and just look at the tone. Almost anything we struggle with as writers can be targeted. Pace, symbols, and subtext are three I go to regularly. Really anything we struggle with probably deserves a few rounds of revision.

Participants: Just you.
Time to complete: Varies but . . . hours.
Planning time: Minutes.
Planning requirements: A script ready for some substantial revision.

Other needs or considerations: This could be modified for a group, with each participant bringing in a short excerpt, discussing what they want to target in a revision, doing that revision, and then discussing the outcomes.

Instructions:

1. Because there are two ways to go about this process, we need to pick one at the start. We can either look for a specific thing we want to revise, like making sure all our jokes are funny, or we can perform the conventional front-to-back revisions with a different starting point than the top of the show. If the target is a new starting point, then go to step 2; if it's a targeted device, then go to step 3.

2. Simply pick a new point in the manuscript to begin revising. I suggest starting with whatever part you think is weakest. However, simply starting in the middle or three-quarters through the text can be rather epiphanic. Give the work a normal read-through to the end, and then return to the beginning, until you get to where you started.

3. Select the device you want to revise. Maybe you want to focus on tone or stakes or theme or tension. Maybe just track a character as they change over the narrative. It doesn't really matter what you pick, but it can only be one thing. Trying to do two at once becomes overwhelming because this is an exercise in deep focus, and revising two things at once breaks that focus.

4. Once the device is selected, simply go through the manuscript, and just work at developing that device while doing your best to ignore everything else. As a side note: If you find you can't focus on one device, then the script may be in need of more holistic revisions instead of something this detailed.

5. If you had a few devices you wanted to focus on, then simply go through the manuscript again focusing on the new device.

Repeat this step for all the devices you want to focus on. With a little practice, this can be a fast, efficient way to shore up sagging elements of the script. That said, after a few targeted revisions, it's a good idea to go through and give a conventional, holistic revision to the text. I find that I can only do about three targeted revisions in a draft before I need to clean up the whole thing and make sure the changes are integrated smoothly.

Notes: There's a version of this exercise called "Know What You Don't (Targeted Proofreading)" later in the writing process that helps focus on more nuanced, detailed, or syntactical struggles.

Personally, I have exponentially more success doing this exercise with a paper manuscript and colored pens. I can assign a different color to each of the things I want to focus on and go through one issue at a time. Then I type up all my changes, and I'm ready to give the new draft a holistic read-through.

SUBTEXT AS RELIEF

Paige Goodwin

Category: Writing, revising

Overview: This exercise encourages you to consider subtext by adding it in layer by layer. What is subtext? Well, it's what grabs the audience in a scene, and it's what makes a play worth watching again because of the surprises. But more concisely, subtext is the meaning inscribed just below what a character is literally saying. For example, when a character pauses for a while before saying "I love you," there could be a lot of meaning there. Is it because this is the first time they're saying it and they're nervous? Or is it hard for them to say now that they've come to hate their spouse? All of this could be conveyed without ever having to outright tell your audience. We as people use subtext all the time ("No, that dress looks great on you," "I totally *forgot* to send that email," or any other time you know that you're not saying exactly what's on your mind). But as writers, early drafts of our writing often lack subtext because we're working out the details of a story. Subtext can be achieved in a lot of ways: It might be introduced visually (think a color, the way a character is dressed, a prop); through a gesture; through juxtaposed physical action (a character crying while saying something they ought to not be crying about); or through speech (references, pauses, or by saying the opposite of what one means). Personally, I learn best by knowing how something feels when its wrong and then adding in corrections, which is how this exercise is structured.

Participants: Individual.
Time to complete: 20–30 minutes.
Planning time: None.
Planning requirements: None.
Other needs or considerations: None.

Instructions:
1. Come up with two characters. The premise of the scene is that one of them has to tell the other bad news. Everything else is up to you.
2. Write the most horrifically backstory-ridden and subtext-free scene between them. Everyone says and does exactly what they're thinking, and they tell you all their history explicitly. The purpose here is to feel uncomfortable by how bad it is. Here are some example lines to get you started:
   - "Well Matt, since you're my brother who is two years older than me, I'm sure you remember how I was born with an extra finger."
   - "Wow, your newborn that you love very much is the ugliest baby I've ever seen."
   - "I cannot look at you because I actually hate you."

3. Read your scene out loud. Cringe a lot.

4. Focus on visual subtext. Are there any lines where, instead of the character speaking exactly what they mean, there's a prop or a visual component? For example, instead of having two characters talk about the fact that they're newlyweds, you could put in the stage directions that there's a recent wedding photo of the two in the background. It's the same information, but now we get to discover it in our own time as an audience. Revise a line (or a few) to include visual subtext.

5. Now focus on juxtaposed physical action. Are there any lines where, instead of the character speaking exactly what they mean, there's a physical gesture? For example, if character A says, "I'm concerned about you," to character B, character A could instead hand character B a coat before they walk out the door. It's the same sentiment, but now we get to infer the care. Revise a line (or a few) to include gestural subtext.

6. Now focus on juxtaposition. Are there any lines where, instead of the character speaking exactly what they mean, they are no longer telling the truth but doing something that shows us what they mean? For example, character A could say they're not mad, but they could be yelling it. Now the scene is interesting because we as an audience try to infer why character A won't speak their mind. Revise a line (or a few) to include juxtaposition.

7. Consider removing exposition in dialogue in a line. For example, if you want to convey that character A and character B are siblings, instead of someone saying this fact out loud, they might simply refer to "Mom and Dad." We as an audience can infer that because they aren't specifying "my Mom and Dad," the two share parents. Revise a line (or a few) to remove exposition.

8. Finally, find a line that might benefit from a pause before it. As noted in the overview, a pause can mean a lot of things. Why would someone wait to speak their mind? There are many reasons, including fear, displeasure, not wanting to hurt someone's feelings, and needing to think about something, but as an audience, if we hear someone pause rather than speaking the need to pause out loud, we're drawn in. Revise a line (or a few) to include a pause.

9. Reread the scene. Find relief in the subtext. Keep writing.

Notes: This exercise can be recreated using an existing scene in a play you're writing or revising. In that case, skip to step 3.

QUESTIONING REALITY

Justin Maxwell

Category: Stakes, tension, dialogue

Overview: This exercise helps make good questions, which sustain tension in dialogue. Well, that's a half-truth; it's sustained by a combination of the question and the answer, but we'll get to that.

The problem, I suspect, stems from an impulse toward mimesis and efficiency. While both are generally good things in a narrative play, our impulses toward them can cost the script emotionally. After all, an exchange that says, "Do you want to try the new Thai place for dinner?" "Yes." feels like real life and is very efficient. Unfortunately, it is too real and too efficient. Boring.

Participants: Just you.
Time to complete: Wildly variable, but it's hours, not minutes.
Planning time: None.
Planning requirements: Just a copy of a script that's fairly far along in revision—far enough that you know the scene is going to stay and

you know the beats of the scene are going to stay, so now it's time to polish language and dialogue.

Other needs or considerations: This is very much a solitary exercise, but it can be modified for a group. Each participant simply brings in their play (or a section of their play), and everyone does the exercise at the same time with their own manuscripts. In this iteration, it should be done for a predetermined amount of time because this endeavor can really eat up the clock. It can also be done for one or two questions instead of the whole text, but one should still watch the clock. After the time or number of questions has expired, each participant reads a few of their before and after drafts aloud. Usually, it's more impactful to hear the revised version first and then the raw material. If the people in the group can generally suss out the answer in step 5, then it's gone quite well.

Instructions:

1. Use a draft far enough along in the writing process that you're ready to polish up the dialogue. Go through and look at the questions—a literal text search for question marks is superefficient.

2. When you come to each question, ask, "Is the question direct or indirect?" "Do you love me?" is very different from "Where's your wedding ring?" One has more emotional energy than the other because the emotions are in the subtext.

3. Then ask, "Is the answer direct or indirect?" A direct question can have an indirect answer. "Do you love me?" "Yes." Doesn't have much energy. Answering "no" doesn't have much energy, either. However, "Do you love me?" answered by "I'm wearing the ring" or "Can't you see the wedding ring?" brings much more gravitas to the dialogue.

4. Questions and answers that are both indirect tend to be able to hold the most emotional energy. "Where's your wedding

ring?" "Probably still at the pawn shop" or "On your sister's nightstand" or "It was on my finger when I took out the trash" all have more tension because they expand the conversation outward instead of shutting it down with a "yes" or a "no."

5. At each question, ask, "What's the emotional need behind this question and this answer? Why are the characters saying it this way?"

6. By going through and looking at each question, we give it care and intentionality. Can it be made more powerful by moving the emotional need driving the question down to the subtext? Can it be asked in such a way that the character answering the question can't reasonably answer with a "yes" or "no," thus contracting the emotional energy of the moment. If the question gets a "yes" or "no" answer, is it powerful enough that the audience cares about that contraction of energy?

7. Revise the exchange to move their emotions and motivations into the subtext if it gives you better dialogue.

Notes: Obviously, there are times and moments when a simple, declarative answer to an emotional question is incredibly powerful. But that power should be wielded with care and with intention. The last line of my play *An Outopia for Pigeons* is "No," a direct, negative response to an implied question, which the audience has heard several times before. The "No" closes down a high-concept last scene of sadness and loss with a moment of simple rejection. The audience has a little gasp, and the lights go out. Then they clap, a lot, which I really like.

THE TYPEWRITER

Edward Einhorn

Category: Revision

Overview: This is a way to tighten a scene and get to its essence. Or maybe to find the places where the scene can be expanded. Or to simply rethink a scene that is not quite working.

Participants: Individual.

Time to complete: It depends on how many pages you are rewriting and how inspired you get, but generally, 30 minutes to 1 hour for a ten-page scene.

Planning time: 5–15 minutes.

Planning requirements: Print out the scene that you want to revise.

Other needs or considerations: Read through the scene that you want to revise on the paper like it is new before you start. Make notes of any thoughts about revision, in pencil or pen, on the physical page.

Instructions: Place the printout of your scene next to your computer. Treat it now like it is a typewritten document, and imagine that, in order to revise it, you have to type the scene in again, word by word. Open up a blank file, and do not reference the existing script in your computer. Transcribe the script into your new document. As you work, notice how the lines naturally rewrite themselves. Maybe a word or two gets changed, a moment gets tightened. Maybe some needed lines get added. The changes can be very minor, a few words or some punction. Or they can be major, and whole new character might enter the mix. What is the essence of the scene? Is every word necessary? Cut anything unnecessary out, and leave just the essentials. Use the printed version of the scene as a guide, but improve on it as you go.

Notes: This was, of course, the natural way writers revised their work, when they had to retype a scene anew in order to have a clean copy. My father was a luddite and refused to get a computer or word processor, so my brother and I used his manual typewriter that he himself had used a child. Finally, luxuriously, we got an electric. But my first stories were written and rewritten on those typewriters.

Now, like most people, I work on a computer, writing and rewriting without having to retype the whole document. But when I lost a file of a partially written play some years ago due to a computer meltdown, all I had was the printed version I had (fortunately) made for myself. At first, I was very unhappy to have to have the labor of typing in the same thing I had already spent so much time writing. But as I typed, I naturally revised my work, and I became aware of each word in a way I simply don't when I am scanning my existing computer document for revision. My eyes did not skip across the page, I thought about each word. And because I am essentially lazy, I found myself shortening lines of dialogue to make them more concise and direct. In the end, I had a much tighter play, better dialogue, and even a better sense of where my play was heading.

THE MICHELANGELO

Jon Elston

Category: Revision, cutting!

Overview: This exercise offers an offbeat solution to revision paralysis, specifically when one is struggling to cut dialogue. Few writers are eager to delete the dialogue that they (likely) worked so hard to compose. Many may feel uncertain about whether that sentence or phrase or clause or guttural monosyllabic interjection is in fact essential to the success of a specific dramatic moment and if they might come to regret deleting those precious few words or letters at some point in the rehearsal process. I myself have invested several minutes of my life (minimally) deleting, perseverating over, and then replacing certain crucial *ums* or *ahs* within my dialogue. "The Michelangelo" illuminates the myriad ways in which stripping away and streamlining words from any given page of dialogue might improve the concision, clarity, brevity, pace, drama, humor, or simple playability of a text, in a way that is slightly gentler and less intrusive than immediately and stridently spamming that "Backspace" or "Delete" key.

The great visual artist Michelangelo famously claimed that his sculptures were essentially complete and intact within each untouched block of marble—in other words, beneath the unbroken stone. All that was necessary to reveal their essential form was to chisel away every part of the block that was superfluous. Sounds so easy! Yet who wants to take a chisel to their beloved writing? Thus "The Michelangelo" exercise gives playwrights a low-impact method in which they can test-drive cuts and visualize the lithe, agile form that lays below each current block of text. If it looks a lot more like the dialogue you had in mind, then you can reach for that "Backspace" key and start chiselin'.

In brief, "The Michelangelo" involves highlighting sections of text that might be deleted and then setting the highlight color to black. Voila! You've created a preview of what a revised version of a line or passage might look like and can now read the revised text (around the black blocks) for clarity, cogency, and effect . . . without being reminded in real time of those specific words you've obscured. Is it just that simple? It is that simple, a tiny trick to momentarily make your brain focus on the good stuff that's still on the page rather than the stuff you've temporarily made invisible. If the remaining text still functions well—heck, if it functions better than the previous version—then there's nothing stopping you from saving a new file and then going right ahead and deleting those black blocks.

I stumbled on this technique back in high school, as I would pho-
tocopy vintage published versions of classic dramas (often translated
or adapted) and then go to work with my black sharpie, trying to figure out if I could strip away enough outré verbiage from a given text
so that the play might be turned into a suitable and playable one-act.
One of the first plays to which I applied this technique was Barrett
H. Clark's 1915 adaptation of Moliere's *Physician in Spite of Himself.*
In the following passage, Sganarelle is cornered by Lucas and Valere,
two thugs intent on securing confirmation of Sganarelle's medical
credentials. Sganarelle, an inveterate alcoholic and philanderer, has
no such credentials:

SGANARELLE: What is it then? Whom do you think I am?

VALERE: Just what you are: a great doctor.

SGANARELLE: Doctor yourself. I'm not one, never was, and never
hope to be.

VALERE: (Aside) Now he's got it! (To SGANARELLE) Don't pretend any longer, Monsieur, and please don't force us to take extreme
measures.

SGANARELLE: How's that?

VALERE: Oh, something we should not like to do.

SGANARELLE: Lord! Do whatever you like. I'm no doctor, and I
don't understand a word you are saying.

VALERE: Once more, Monsieur, I beg you to confess that you're a
doctor.

SGANARELLE: Why, I'm only a common woodman. Do you wish
to drive me crazy?

VALERE: Why do you persist in lying?

SGANARELLE: What's the use of my telling you a thousand times:
I am no doctor?

VALERE: You are not a doctor?

SGANARELLE: No, I tell you.

VALERE: So be it, then.

(They beat him severely.)

SGANARELLE: Stop, stop! Messieurs, I'll be anything you wish.

VALERE: That's better, now. But why did you force us to do this, Monsieur? I assure you I regret it very much.

SGANARELLE: What the devil? For Heaven's sake, are you joking, or are you both out of your heads? Do you say I am a—you're mad—a doctor?

VALERE: What! You don't admit it yet? You still deny that you're a doctor?

SGANARELLE: Plague take me if I am!

LUCAS: Ain't you a doctor, then?

SGANARELLE: No, I tell you. (They beat him again) Oh, oh! Well, since you will have it so, I am a doctor—an apothecary, too, if you wish it. I'll agree to anything rather than be beaten again.

VALERE: Very well, Monsieur, I'm pleased to see you so reasonable. I ask your pardon with all my heart and soul, Monsieur.

SGANARELLE: (Aside) Why, bless me, have I really become a doctor without knowing it?

VALERE: You shall have no cause to regret anything, Monsieur. You shall be satisfied.

SGANARELLE: But tell me, are you quite sure you're not mistaken? Are you sure I'm a real doctor?

LUCAS: Undoubtedly.

SGANARELLE: Really?

VALERE: Assuredly.

SGANARELLE: Deuce take me if I knew it!

VALERE: Why, you are the greatest doctor in the world.

SGANARELLE: Indeed!

LUCAS: A doctor who has done innumerable cures.

SGANARELLE: The devil!

VALERE: In short, Monsieur, you will be satisfied, and will be paid any fee you wish, if you will let us take you with us.

SGANARELLE: I shall receive any fees I wish?

VALERE: Yes.

SGANARELLE: Well, in that case, I certainly am a doctor. I must have forgotten it; but now I remember. Where do I go?

I read this passage and chuckled a bit, recognizing some appealing commonality with more contemporary texts like John Cleese's *Fawlty Towers*. But if I was going to actually produce this play (which eventually I did), I knew I'd need to cut all the classical formality to the bone and get right to the gags. So in the case of this passage, I applied "The Michelangelo" as follows:

SGANARELLE: ~~What is it then?~~ Whom do you think I am?

VALERE: ~~Just what you are:~~ a great doctor.

SGANARELLE: Doctor ~~yourself~~. I'm not ~~one~~, never was, ~~and never hope to be~~.

VALERE: ~~(Aside) Now he's got it!~~ (To SGANARELLE) Don't ~~pretend any longer, Monsieur, and please don't~~ force us to take extreme measures.

~~Sganarelle: How's that?~~

~~Valere: Oh, something we should not like to do.~~

SGANARELLE: Lord! Do whatever you like. I'm no doctor, ~~and I don't understand a word you are saying~~.

VALERE: ~~Once more,~~ Monsieur, I beg you to confess that you're a doctor.

SGANARELLE: ~~Why,~~ I'm only a common woodman. ~~Do you wish to drive me crazy?~~

VALERE: Why do you persist in lying?

SGANARELLE: ~~What's the use of my telling you~~ a thousand times: I am no doctor?

VALERE: You are not a doctor?

SGANARELLE: No, ~~I tell you~~.

VALERE: So be it, ~~then~~.

(They beat him severely.)

SGANARELLE: Stop, stop! Messieurs, I'll be anything you wish.

VALERE: That's better, ~~now~~. But why did you force us to do this, Monsieur? ~~I assure you~~ I regret it very much.

SGANARELLE: ~~What the devil? For Heaven's sake,~~ are you joking, or are you ~~both out of your heads? Do you say I am a—you're~~ mad—a doctor?

VALERE: What! ~~you don't admit it yet?~~ You still deny that you're a doctor?

~~Sganarelle: Plague take me if I am!~~

~~Lucas: Ain't you a doctor, then?~~

SGANARELLE: No, tell you. (They beat him again) Oh, oh! ~~well, since you will have it so,~~ I am a doctor—an apothecary, too~~, if you wish it. I'll agree to anything rather than be beaten again.~~

VALERE: ~~Very well,~~ Monsieur, I'm pleased to see you so reasonable. ~~I ask your pardon with all my heart and soul, Monsieur.~~

SGANARELLE: (Aside) ~~Why,~~ bless me, have I really become a doctor without knowing it?

~~Valere: You shall have no cause to regret anything, Monsieur. You shall be satisfied.~~

~~Sganarelle: But tell me,~~ are you quite sure you're not mistaken? Are you sure I'm a real doctor?

LUCAS: Undoubtedly.

SGANARELLE: Really?

~~Valere: Assuredly.~~

~~Sganarelle: Deuce take me if I knew it!~~

VALERE: ~~Why,~~ you are the greatest doctor in the world.

SGANARELLE: Indeed!

~~Lucas: A doctor who has done innumerable cures.~~

~~Sganarelle: The devil!~~

VALERE: ~~In short,~~ Monsieur, ~~you will be satisfied, and~~ will be paid any fee you wish, if you will let us take you with us.

SGANARELLE: I shall receive any fees I wish?
VALERE: Yes.

SGANARELLE: Well, in that case, I certainly am a doctor. ~~I must have forgotten it; but~~ now I remember. ~~Where do I go?~~

With all respect to Clark, and particularly to Moliere, I will not assert that my edits have unequivocally improved the passage in all possible regards. I would only maintain that these edits have made the passage (1) shorter and (2) punchier. As brevity and impact are often highly desirable qualities in a dramatic text, however, I submit that this technique is a useful means to reach those ends.

No playwright likes hearing unsolicited feedback like "You need to cut _____ pages from this scene." (I don't, anyway.) But when, in my new-play-development career, a playwright has come to me and solicited my input on possible cuts, I offer them a "Michelangelo." Think of it, if you will, as providing fellow playwrights with an alternative perspective on a heretofore unseen version of their work. They are welcome to reject that perspective or perhaps embrace it.

Participants: "The Michelangelo" may work best as a partnered activity, as (naturally) if an individual playwright could automatically identify their optimal cuts, then they'd likely go ahead and perform those cuts. I have performed "The Michelangelo" on my own work, however, when I find myself in a place where I am somehow absolutely convinced that every word and syllable of a passage is essential and cannot possibly be touched. Momentarily obscuring some of those words and syllables can be surprising and liberating!
Time to complete: "The Michelangelo" can be performed in real time, as one reads a passage.
Planning time: Prep time will vary. Essentially this is a plug-and-play exercise that can be performed quickly and with little preparation.
Planning requirements: "The Michelangelo" is ideal for situations where the participant who is highlighting the text (when not the

playwright) is already familiar with the text: that's to say, they have read or seen a reading of the play previously. This will prevent the playwright's need for explication in defense of the text. ("You haven't read act II, so you don't know this, but that reference is crucial because . . .") If the playwright acknowledges that their highlighter has at least a functional understanding of the play, then they will be more likely to trust and take seriously the suggested edits. However, "The Michelangelo" can be performed with no prep time by a highlighter who's never read or seen the play, if all they are looking for are perceived redundancies in language.

Other needs or considerations:

- *In a group:* Trust. Kindness. An open mind.
- *On your own:* Humility. Guts. An open mind.

Instructions: Sit down somewhere quiet and discreet with a trusted friend or collaborator, or alone, if playwright and highlighter are one and the same. Order or otherwise prepare to enjoy a beverage. This might take several minutes or much longer.

The highlighter begins to review and selectively obscure a digital version of the text. Use the cursor in your document app, writing program, or whatever to highlight any words, sentences, or entire blocks of language that do not seem to contribute essentially to the text.

Try to perform "The Michelangelo" in real time as you read, highlighting and obscuring words, phrases, and more instinctively. Does a character say something twice or more than twice to no clear purpose? Does a tangential exchange seem to go nowhere? Is there chatty dialogue that appears irrelevant or unfunny or detrimental to rising tension? Obscure it.

Be a mercenary. When in doubt, reread the last few lines and confirm that they function more optimally in your new obscured version than they did previously. If you find you've obscured too much, then highlight it again and reveal it anew. No harm, no foul.

If you are the playwright and are having a partner perform "The Michelangelo," then read something, do other work, check email or social media, and/or generally just dissociate from the idea that someone else is rendering invisible parts of your writing.

Continue for the duration of text that the playwright has asked the highlighter to review. When finished, turn the device over to the playwright (or otherwise forward a copy of their file) for their perusal.

In optimal circumstances, the playwright may touch their chin, nod, sigh thoughtfully, and agree that they have seen a version of their text that they themselves had not previously imagined. Sometimes the playwright will respond to the highlighter's edits, suggesting that the highlighter has obscured too much vital text. In this event, the highlighter should raise their hands plaintively and offer a mild shrug. Nothing has been deleted, thus no grievous wound has been inflicted. Hopefully the playwright will walk away having gleaned something useful about possible future revisions.

Notes: Whenever possible, perform "The Michelangelo" digitally—not with a sharpie on a hard copy of a script, as I did to Moliere's play. Moliere is no longer with us, but your friend the playwright is alive, and it can be distressing to see one's words scribbled over in black ink. The digital method, as it is impermanent, is gentler.

Although this exercise is outstanding for cutting dialogue, it can also be applied to cutting stage directions. Eugene O'Neill could really have benefitted from this strategy. How many individual bottles do you need to describe behind that bar, Eugene? Just saying.

HONING'IN ON DIALOGUE

Matthew Paul Olmos

Category: Dialogue, hiding exposition

Overview: This exercise helps to activate and streamline your dialogue to be less expositional, more immediate for your characters, and more actively engaging for your audience.

Participants: Individually or as an exercise in a class.
Time to complete: Depends on how long the scene is you are working with.
Planning time: None.
Planning requirements: None.
Other needs or considerations:
- *In a group:* Prep basic characters or a situation for a new scene or have an existing scene ready to rewrite.
- *On your own:* Either be ready to freewrite a new scene or rewrite an existing one.

Instructions: Free'write a new scene, then rewrite with the following restrictions below, or rewrite an existing scene and rewrite with the following restrictions.

For the free'write, the idea is to write from your subconscious and not think, to just let whatever comes out. If it helps, think of two or more people you know well, think of an environment you know well, and see what happens if you just start letting them talk, putting no pressure to make the scene about anything specific or to create a story. Just see what comes out when you let them talk. This is about allowing ideas, dialogue, events, and characters to come from your instinctual side instead of your thinking side; allow yourself to stumble'upon the dialogue instead of trying to plan it or impose upon it.

For the existing scene, just pick a scene you've written that feels too expositional or too on the nose or maybe one that you've been having trouble with. Then, take your free'write or the existing scene, and begin rewriting/editing to implement the following restrictions:

- Characters are not allowed to ask questions in any form.
- Characters are not allowed to use such titles as Mom, Dear, Love, and so on, any that give away the relationship.
- Characters are not allowed to use any phrases, such as "I've loved you since the first night we met," "That's why I hired you," "That's not how I raised you," and "But we just met," any that give away the relationship.
- Characters are not allowed to express how they actually feel about anything; they can pretend to be nice, they can front, they can ignore, they can feign, and so on, but their true feelings cannot be directly expressed. Nobody can say such things as "I'm really upset at you," "I missed you," or "I want to be with you."
- No stage directions, no time or place, no "sarcastically," "deadpan," or any instruction on how a line should be delivered. You are going to let your audience *have* to figure out where we are, when we are, and what is happening through the dialogue only.

Notes: The goal with implementing these restrictions isn't to create the perfect scene but rather to see what you can get across through your dialogue without the crutches of exposition and to engage your audience in piecing together the characters, ideas, situation, or story instead of you, the writer, laying everything out for them, thus making them more passive.

This exercise is inspired by the idea that we as theatre artists create half the play onstage, but the other half is created by your audience in their imaginations. As such, we allow our audience to actively create and actively piece together our plays, we allow them to wonder what a relationship is and then look for hints, clues as to the complexities of the relationship, as opposed to the writer feeling the need to spell it out for them. We allow them to actively figure out what a character might be feeling or thinking, as opposed to a character just plainly stating it.

Lastly, these are not guidelines for good dialogue; rather they are just helpful tools to help manage your exposition or on-the-nose dialogue. To remind you as you're rewriting, your audience wants to be actively doing something, like trying to figure out what a particular relationship is or how it functions, like piecing together the puzzle of how a particular character might be feeling or what they are thinking, especially when their behavior or words might run contrary.

LANGUAGE MADE SENSUOUSLY ATTRACTIVE

Deborah Yarchun

Category: Sensory language, dialogue, and impactful writing

Overview: This exercise is designed to help writers integrate sensory language and create engaging dialogue. When discussing language in *The Poetics* Aristotle refers to it as "language which has been made sensuously attractive." He later clarifies, "[B]y language made 'sensuously attractive' I mean language that has rhythm and melody." Beyond rhythm and melody, sensorial language (particularly vivid language related to sight, touch, taste, sound, and the body) is also key for creating a visceral or physical experience for an audience, bringing them into the characters' world. This exercise can be particularly useful for revising an existing play that could use an additional dimension and can be applied to any point in the writing process (including from scratch), helping a writer to become unstuck.

Participants: Individual or group.
Time to complete: 25 minutes individually or 45 minutes in a group.
Planning time: 1–10 minutes.
Planning requirements: Writers should take a moment to notice their immediate sensorial experience. What do they see? Hear? Smell? Taste? What are they physically experiencing (e.g., the weight of their body on the chair)?
Other needs or considerations:

- *In a group:* This exercise is best started with the quote from Aristotle's *The Poetics*. If there's time leading up to the exercise, reading an example from a work that does this quite effectively is useful. I suggest an excerpt from *One Flea Spare* by Naomi Wallace or the short play *A Bone Close to My Brain* by Dan Dietz. This will add about ten minutes.
- *On your own:* Consider plays where the language has been particularly visceral or had an impact on you.

Instructions:

1. Think of a character. This can be one you've already come up from a play you're actively working on or an entirely new character who pops into your mind.
2. Now place them in a sensory-rich setting (e.g., a beach, a bench on a bustling street corner in a city, a fragrant garden, a hospital).
3. Consider what they're doing there and their emotional state (relaxing, meeting someone, panicking).
4. Set a timer for five minutes.
5. Taking only five minutes, list sensory details related to the setting or the character's experience. What would they hear? Smell? Taste? Physically feel? Be as vivid and descriptive as you can. Experiment with metaphors and similes to enrich the sensory language. Consider how your character's experience

and perspective might influence the sensory details they notice in their environment or how they'd describe it.

6. Set a timer for twenty minutes.

7. Over the next twenty minutes, write dialogue between your character and another character or a monologue that incorporates some of the sensory details you came up with. The character(s) could be discussing their surroundings, reacting to their environment, or sharing memories that are connected to the sensory details.

8. As you're writing, think rhythmically. How does the rhythm of the dialogue shift when something shifts in the scene?

9. Read through your scene, and revise as needed. Look for places to enhance the sensory language, making it more vivid, engaging, and immersive.

10. In a group setting, I suggest a sharing session at the end with an opportunity for writers to read their work out loud and receive feedback from their peers on which lines felt particularly effective. If alone, read your work out loud to yourself.

Notes: Setting a timer can be useful in helping writers not to overthink the exercise. It's useful to steer participants toward recognizing that the amount of sensorial language they integrate into their play will depend on the world of their play. For the quote, I used Gerald F. Else's translation of *The Poetics*.

HOW TO FALL BACK IN LOVE WITH YOUR PLAY

Sophie Sagan-Gutherz

Category: How to get unstuck

Overview: This exercise is for when you're working on a play, commission, thesis piece, or deadline of any sort and you've fallen out of love with your project or, in the broader sense, your craft in general. You might be asking yourself, "Why am I writing this? Why does this feel arduous? Didn't I choose this wacko career???"

For me, it wasn't so much a specific play but theatre in general. I was feeling my life begin to revolve around New York City theatre in an unhealthy way, in that I was giving it a lot of real estate in my mind in a work sense and was losing the joy of art. "Isn't this supposed to have an element of . . . fun?" I would ask myself.

Participants: Individual or group.
Time to complete: Varies.
Planning time: 15 minutes and then time carved out to experience the chosen art.
Planning requirements: Writing utensil and paper, timer. This is an opportunity to use writing materials you don't normally use in your writing practice—think colored construction paper, brightly colored thick markers, glitter pens, and so on. I wrote very, very big in Sharpie, in all caps, and used a deep, dark purple.
Other needs or considerations: None.

Instructions: Put a timer on for fifteen minutes, and make a list of all the kinds of ways art can be consumed that don't involve theatre—and think broadly (e.g., planting a flower; seeing a morning movie that you know nothing about in an empty theatre on a weekday; walking into a free, maybe terrible, maybe amazing stand-up comedy set). Let yourself write things that may be costly and things that won't cost anything. Because I am based in New York City, for me, this looked like a visit to the botanical gardens, finally going to the bar near me that plays live music every Saturday, or volunteering in my neighborhood's community garden.

Take a look at your list, and pick a few things that you feel most drawn to. Live music really stood out to me. It made me realize how important this art form is to me from a pure enjoyment level and the range I could engage with, from price to genre.

Schedule time in the next few days or weeks, depending on your timeline, to do these things. (And make sure they have nothing to do with your play!) I have made it an active practice that, if there is a musician whom I love and who is playing at a smaller-end Brooklyn venue, I will get a ticket. Usually concerts also go on sale a few months out, which allows me schedule-wise to ensure the event will happen and have something joyful to look forward to amid my writing practice.

Bring a journal with you when you do these things; this will allow you to jot down ideas for your work as they may come up; however, treat this as a jot down—this is not an excuse to keep writing! I brought the journal—and wrote two words down: *punk rock.*

Experience the art fully: off your phone, alone or with friends, somewhere you've never been before, somewhere you've always wanted to go. For some, one art excursion or artist date can be enough; for others, you might need a few to unlock the muddied, eager creativity in your mind. Allowing myself to seek out live music made me realize how inherently theatrical women absolutely screaming into the microphone and slamming on the guitar is—and how this . . . could be me! This led me to begin writing my first one-person show, reinvigorated my love for musical theatre, and expanded my brain even further into what musical theatre can look like and be.

Once you feel creatively satiated outside of your theatrical process or theatrical spaces, return to the play! Return to the art (always)!

Notes: None.

STARRY NIGHT

Liz Appel

Category: This is a revision exercise used to gain perspective when working with a large chunk of text. It defamiliarizes language and creates distance, allowing the writer to encounter their own work in new ways.

Overview: The purpose of this exercise is to circumvent the conscious mind by turning a block of words into something more visual and spatial. The progressive stripping and replacing of words or parts of speech allows the writer to engage with their monologue in a more fluid way. It's about tuning into your own work on a different frequency to propel you forward in the revision process.

Participants: This exercise can be done individually or in the company of others.

Time to complete: 5–15 minutes, depending on how many iterations you do.

Planning time: A few minutes to choose the monologue and print it out or reformat it into a new document on-screen.

Planning requirements: Printer and paper, a pencil, an eraser, or a computer.

Other needs or considerations: A comfortable place to work.

Instructions: Identify a monologue. Print it out or cut and paste so it's by itself in a new document.

Do a pass, and take out every instance of a specific aspect of language. For instance, remove all personal pronouns. If working onscreen, leave a blank space where you erased the word. If working on paper, draw a box around the word, and color it in with pencil. You want to be able to see the blank spaces/dark boxes. Do this for every pronoun.

You should now have a block of text that has several blank spaces/penciled-out boxes. First step: Just look at it. What hits you? Are there any words or phrases that catch your eye? Make a note. Then read it aloud. What do you notice? Has the meaning of the monologue shifted? If so, how? What takes on more weight? What starts to recede? How do these changes affect the themes and images running through your play as a whole?

Revert to the original by restoring the deleted words or erasing the penciled-in boxes. Repeat the process, only this time take out another aspect of language (e.g., nouns, adjectives). Go through the same set of questions.

With every layer, try to notice shifts in meaning, texture, sound, and sense. Ask yourself what need or desire or action is allowed to come through these gaps in the text.

You could also do this with thematically relevant words. Let's say rain is a key image in the play. Take out all the words related to rain, water, clouds, and weather. What happens? Replace with them with their opposites: sun/fire words. What happens?

The idea is that punching holes out of language or allowing for silences can let you see and hear what you're trying to say in a different way.

I think of the blank spaces like stars in the night sky. Change the constellation, and you change the orientation of yourself in the world (of your play).

Notes: Have fun, allow yourself to experiment and rip your piece to shreds. It will still be there.

PREDATOR AND PREY:
AN EXERCISE IN TONE AND PACING

Trista Baldwin

Category: Developing the style, pace, and overall energy of your play

Overview: To help you create the appropriate form to follow the function of your play. This exercise is best used when nearing a first draft *and* after a first draft, when it's time to revise. It develops skills in pacing, tone, style, and the energy of a script meant for live performance. It can also help you develop the key physical metaphor in your script and can assist you in outlining as you revise your script.

Participants: Individually or in a group.

Time to complete: 1–3 hours.

Planning time: 5–60 minutes.

Planning requirements: It is recommended that you spend a bit of time watching nature clips or otherwise research the hunting methods of animals that rely on meat and the evasion methods of prey.

Other needs or considerations:

- *In a group:* If you are leading a writing group in this exercise, then prepare some varying examples of hunting methods and evasion methods.

- *On your own:* Consider different hunting styles of predators in the wild, such as the stout (also known as a weasel), which mesmerizes prey with a dance. Compare the trapdoor spider to a garden spider, a cheetah to a lion, a pack of hyenas to a pack of wolves. Consider the boa constrictor and the electric eel. Alternatively, depending on your play, consider the methods of evasion used by prey, such as the zigzag patterns of a hartebeest, the mobbing techniques of crows, and the killdeer's faking of a broken wing. It can be helpful to watch nature reels on mute and then spend some time thinking about the energy of your play. What and when is the revelation? How does the story come at the audience? How does your main character(s) attack or evade? Some examples I've used from my own plays: *American Sexy* is a rattlesnake (predator), *Patty Red Pants* is a horse (prey), *Sand* is a weasel, mostly, with a shadow boa constrictor (predators).

Instructions:
1. Imagine your play as hunting the mind, the imagination of your audience. Imagine it then as an animal of prey. What kind of animal would it be, and why? Write freely for a minimum of ten minutes and maximum of thirty.
2. If your play cannot be found as a hunter but rather as an animal of prey, then why is that so? Is it running from your audience, evasive of its ultimate revelation? And if so, when is it captured, and how is it caught? Write for a minimum of five minutes.
3. Highlight the words in your dialogue that sound or feel like this animal.
4. Highlight any action that feels like this animal, and/or consider adding the movements of this animal directly into your play. Is there something that a main character can physically do that can resemble the hunting or evasive movement of this animal?
5. As you outline your play, note the length of beats and scenes. Could sections be longer or shorter to feel like the method of hunting/evasion?
6. Feel the current rhythm of your play, and consider how it can be shaped and sharpened to best feel like the movements of this hunter or evasive maneuvers of the prey. Know when revelation is captured. Know how that feels for your characters. Know how that will feel for your audience as witness.

Notes: I always recommend freewriting any exercises with pen and paper rather than on a blank screen to the distracting and formal click of a keyboard.

INSPIRATIONAL STAGE DIRECTIONS

Justin Maxwell

Category: Revising stage directions

Overview: It's easy to unconsciously treat actors as marionettes—especially for those of us who don't have any actor training. When I imagine the show I'm writing in my head, actors often look a certain way and do certain things. Those mental images too easily become the first draft of stage directions. I've learned over the years that faithfully copying these motions, whether grand or trivial, tends to be a disservice to the other artists making the performance, which is then a disservice to my play. Such direct transcription from imagination to page can help me generate a first draft, but after that, they easily get in the way. I'm not a man of deep faith, but if I have a creed, it's that scripts need to inspire all the other theatre artists who manifest them. Instead of programmatic orders, I try to write stage directions that are just as inspirational as plot or dialogue. They are just as important.

Participants: Single.
Time to complete: Hours.
Planning time: None.
Planning requirements: You should have a script somewhere in the revision process.
Other needs or considerations: None.

Instructions:
1. Get that first draft down on the page. Give it some revision until you feel like everything in the text is more or less valuable.

2. Go through and look at each stage direction.
3. At each one, ask the following questions:
   - How does this action serve the tone?
   - How does it serve the theme?
   - How does it reveal/conceal/develop characters?
   - How does it contribute to plot or tension?
4. The answers might be trivial and simple or wildly complex and particular. It might be something like "Character X needs to come onstage now for the next step of the plot to begin." Or it might be something like "The audience needs to realize that character X is lying, even though none of the characters realize this." Or something like "The tone poem I'm staging needs to shift from joyful to raucous at this moment." The important thing to know is *why* that action is happening at that moment. This question could take a lot or a very little amount of time.
5. Ask, "Is this direction prescriptive?"
6. If it is, must it be prescriptive? If so, go to point 7. If not, go to point 8.
7. Yes, it must be prescriptive. Sometimes very exact things need to happen. Sometimes simple things might be necessary, like a character entering or exiting. Sometimes wildly unexpected things must happen exactly, like in the Societas Raffaello Sanzio's *Tragedia Endogonidia, #M.10 Marseille*, wherein we get an alarming moment when a man washes a real black horse with real milk: "The milk that spills on the floor forms a perfect circle." That's a moment when things need to be exact. Conversely, sometimes the actor needs to behave in a way that's different from what their dialogue might indicate. For example, in the famous ending of Beckett's *Waiting for Godot*, Estagon says, "Well, shall we go?" Vladimir replies, "Yes, let's go." We need the prescriptive stage direction to give us the iconic ending: "They do not move." One should follow in the

footsteps of these demanding masterworks carefully. Conscientiously. Even an exact and necessary direction can do more work with a smartly placed verb. "Character A goes to character B" gains emotional energy if *goes to* changes to *sleazes over.*

8. No, it doesn't have to be an exact action to fulfill the bullet points in step 3. If it doesn't have to be an exact action, then rewrite the direction to inspire. Saying, "The stage fills with blue light" is unnecessarily prescriptive, perhaps even counterproductive. Saying, "It is night, and the room is cold," will get the whole creative team pointed in the right direction. Saying, "Everything here is hopeless," may well inspire masterful outcomes. For example, the best stage direction I ever wrote, in my play *Your Lithopedion*, is simply "She does the raunchiest thing possible that's still funny." Every actor takes that in their own way, and every time, it's been hilarious. If that stage direction was prescriptive, some variation of "She does thing X," then it would force the actor to pull off something specific and shoehorn it into their performance. Given the touchy relationship between vulgarity and humor, it's a moment that could crumble into revulsion quickly. That doesn't serve the script. Humor does. I wrote a lot of drafts with specific actions that got progressively more vulgar and made casting and performance progressively more difficult, without any increase in quality of the play. When I changed "thing X" to something abstract, I made space for the creative team to find their own humor in that moment. My script needed the audience to laugh while also being skeeved out a little. The stage direction "She does the raunchiest thing possible that's still funny" did it better than any prescriptive or didactic thing I could have demanded.

9. Double-check for terrible directions, like "Enters stage right" or "Stands downstage center." They're simple looking but so

didactic as to get in the way. There was a theatre I went to regularly that had a structural pole in the middle of the center aisle and a cinder-block wall stage right. Directions like "Enters stage right" meant the actor couldn't come onstage and would have delivered their lines to a post if they had. Instead, set the action in the world: "Enters from the kitchen" or "Materializes from the seventh dimension." Or in the theme/tone: "She thinks it's funny" or "He's way turned on by this."

Notes: The playwright Lisa D'Amour occasionally writes questions as stage directions. Her play *Detroit* is a wonderfully surreptitious model. Such an approach might sound strange, but it's worth a try. After all, questions are about as unprescriptive as one can get. Each artist can bring their answer to rehearsal, and everybody can come together to build a powerful answer onstage. I have lovingly copied D'Amour's approach several times and have always been happy with the results.

DOES IT HAVE TO END THIS WAY?

Charissa Menefee

Category: Finishing and revision

Overview: This exercise incorporates the power and potential of alternate possibilities, both in drafting and in revision.

Participants: Individual or small group.
Time to complete: 20–30 minutes or so.
Planning time: However long it takes you to write your initial scenario or draft, if at that stage.
Planning requirements: You'll need something to write with and on. I'm partial to doing this exercise by hand in a journal, but you can use a laptop or tablet. It's important, though, to have a fresh page! Don't work within your actual draft.

Other needs or considerations:

- *In a group:* The advantage of working collectively is that you can share your results and talk through them, with group members asking clarifying questions that can inform the process. Group members can also keep each other accountable by setting time and word limits.
- *On your own:* You'll likely want a timer so that you enforce time limits on yourself. I suggest rewards, too, like chocolates that are only accessible after the timer goes off. Actually, you might need another person around to guard the chocolates until they hear the timer go off!

Instructions:

1. Review your scenario (or rough draft, if you are farther along in the process).
2. Identify where and when the ending of your play begins.
3. Copy that line and/or action onto your new journal or document page, and then close the original.
4. Set a timer for five to ten minutes.
5. Starting with the beginning of the ending, quick-write a description of a new, different ending.
6. Then write another one.
7. And then write another one—and so on, until the timer goes off.
8. Set the timer again.
9. For each alternate ending, answer these questions: What is exciting about the new ending? How does it potentially change the play?
10. Set the timer again.
11. For each alternate ending, make a quick list: What two to three things would have to change earlier in the play for this ending to work?

12. If you're writing with a group, share your favorite alternate endings and invite questions.

Example of the first timed quick-write: In a first draft, the play ends with Doris packing a small suitcase with her grandmother's dishes and sneaking out the kitchen's screen door. During the first timed writing session of the exercise, the writer comes up with three alternate endings:

1. Play ends with Doris filling a small suitcase with her grandmother's dishes, pausing, and then gently putting them all back.
2. Play ends with Doris breaking her grandmother's dishes, then sobbing as she scrambles to pick up all the broken pieces.
3. Play ends with Doris calling an Uber, asking specifically for a car that can hold five suitcases.

Notes: Don't be afraid to brainstorm huge changes. I'm a big fan of exploding parts of your play to see what might happen. You can always go back to an earlier version if your experiments fail, but even then, the discoveries you make in radical revision experiments will likely make your play stronger and better. In playwriting classes, I often require students to change at least 25 percent of their plays for the final revision project, even if the play (temporarily, at least) gets worse!

LAST THINGS FIRST (SORT OF)

Erik Abbott

Category: Building play endings (and scenes) visually to enhance theatricality

Overview: The exercise helps fill in gaps at any point in the play (especially the end). The writer who is stuck can discover new paths forward and reimagine the play's scenes with a less-specific focus on dialogue. This exercise builds playwriting skills beyond the creation of dialogue, helping the playwright to think three dimensionally about how the plot unfolds and is revealed. Emphasizing a more visual approach to structuring scenes, it can get a playwright past a block and/or to reimagine moments in the piece where the writing does not flow.

For a play in progress, finding a way to write more visually helped me in key scenes to move from monologue-driven action to propel key plot points visually. A part of the story (a longish backstory) is described in visual terms, with minimal spoken narration. It is more efficient and promises a more interesting theatrical moment in performance.

Participants: It is probably best suited for individual work or in a small groups, with ample time to share.

Time to complete: About an hour, depending on the writer.

Planning time: Again, very dependent on the writer but probably about a half-hour.

Planning requirements: Know your own play in terms of what you are trying to convey, the ideas and themes of the piece, and so on. Knowing every single plot beat is *not* essential at this point. (The exercise *may* help you figure out some of this.)

Other needs or considerations:

- *In a group:* The exercise requires sufficient time for the participants to discuss their results.
- *On your own:* Give yourself enough time before starting the exercise to develop a clear idea of the problem being addressed—and of what you need to accomplish in the scene(s).

Instructions: This exercise is intended to help open up ideas to broaden and deepen what the play can be by focusing less on the words spoken by actors and more on the images, metaphors, and so on within the play world created by the author.

What theatrical elements can heighten a play, whether dialogue driven or not? How can we create visual, aural, and kinetic experiences, both for audiences and for theatre artists, whether a given piece is linear or realistic or literal?

1. Picture the end of (or another important scene in) your play—not the dialogue, although if you've already written some of it for this draft, no worries. This exercise *may* help you with revisions. *Picture* the end (or another scene). Imagine how it will *look*. Think beyond what the scenery will be—although some suggestion(s) for the eventual designer(s) is okay (an office, a city street, the living room of an old house, the surface of one of the moons of Jupiter, etc.). Write what you *see*.

2. Imagine what the characters look like in the space. How should they move? What do their garments suggest? What *should* they suggest? How do these garments move and flow with the actors?

3. Describe the scene (or scenes) *without* dialogue. What happens? What *needs* to happen? How does the action unfold without spoken words? What images will the actors present? How will they present them? Is that different if the stage is bare? Write what you *see*.

4. How does the scene sound? Not the words, the *sounds*. What is the aural sense of the scene? If the characters make sounds, what are they? Write what you *hear*.

5. What has happened in the story (if the play uses a story structure—and this is a good time to consider to whether, for now, it will or not). What symbolic/metaphorical messages does the scene *need* to convey—without spoken dialogue? Write what you *imagine*.

6. Read what you've written. Using it, weave it together and create with words on the page the visual, aural, symbolic, and metaphorical panorama that the actors will present and that the audience will experience. Be as detailed as possible. Consider all sounds, vocalized or not. Consider the lights, the shadows. Consider the set. Do these things change as the scene evolves? As the actors move through the scene in your play's world?

7. When you've done all you feel you can, consider whether dialogue is needed for this scene in this play, and if so, feel free to write it—mentally noting, if you can, how your approach to that dialogue may have been affected.

A completely hypothetical example: Suppose you are writing a play about a family facing various significant challenges over the course of the play. In scenes throughout the play, the family addresses and tries to solve their problems in meetings around the kitchen table. Suppose the solutions at which they arrive never fully pan out.

What if the table meetings have become destructive to the family's ability to solve its problems?

What if the final around-kitchen-table meeting involves no dialogue because the characters are no longer able to give words to their desperate frustrations?

What if, in this final table scene, the table comes to life as a monstrous being and attempts to devour them all?

What effect would that as an ending—and crucially writing the rest of the play *toward* it—have on the rest of the play?

Notes: This exercise evolved from the idea of writing the end of a play first and writing the rest to that ending. It also came from being stuck on a play in progress in which I needed to communicate a lengthy backstory without using an overly long monologue to do it.

The exercise need not be confined to writing ending(s). Any scene that is causing problems can be approached this way. Hopefully it will help open up ideas to broaden and deepen what the play can be by focusing less on the words spoken by the actors and more on the images, metaphors, and more within the play world in which those words are spoken.

KNOW WHAT YOU DON'T KNOW (TARGETED PROOFREADING)

Justin Maxwell

Category: Targeting weaknesses, embracing shortcomings

Overview: This exercise uses targeted revisions to help writers focus specifically on managing their particular weaknesses. We all have them. As our writing grows, we become more aware of them. By focusing this targeted revision on them, we can reduce or manage shortcomings. After all, it's easy to mislearn a rule or carry a bad habit or just have a quirk that impedes you.

I'll give you two quick, personal examples. I'm dyslexic. While this shapes my life, art, and personality in all kinds of ways, it also has a pragmatic influence on my writing. It means that I struggle to correctly perceive typos, errors, or numerical sequences. It also means that I'm stuck with this problem. Consequently, I know that I have to allot much more time for proofreading, and I have to be much more thorough about it. That's not something I can fix, but it is something I can manage by going back and specifically searching for mechanical stumbles.

I also deal with it by asking readers to mark typos as they see them. Conversely, I clearly missed whatever day in grade school we were taught comma splices. I had no idea. I got to college, and a philosophy professor returned one of my first-semester essays with a red *F* on the top and a note that said, "Fix the comma splices, and I'll give you your real grade." So I went to his office, and asked, "What's a comma splice?" He said, "Get a grammar handbook." I said, "What's a grammar handbook?" He said, "Get out." So I went to the library, and politely said, "I need a . . . grammar handbook?" The librarian handed me one, and I looked up comma splices. That jerk was right. My essay was filled with them. I memorized the rules. I went through and fixed the many, many comma splices, and resubmitted the essay. It fared much better.

The next essay I wrote was still a briar patch of comma splices because learning a rule is different from applying it. Now, I knew that I didn't know comma splices, so when all the ideas were on the page, and it seemed done, I went back through the essay and performed my first targeted revision. I looked at each comma. I looked to see if it was a comma splice, and it probably was. I meticulously fixed each one. With each subsequent essay, I wrote fewer and fewer of them. That problem went away. Eventually.

Keep in mind, willfully breaking rules can be a powerful choice, but it must be a choice. Sure, we can embrace happy accidents—who doesn't love Bob Ross?—and we should manipulate language to serve us artistically, but if we trust only in chance, then we're bad builders.

Participants: Just you.

Time to complete: Varies. Hours.

Planning time: A few minutes to a lifetime.

Planning requirements: You'll need a few things. A script that's rather far along in the writing process, far enough to know that the scenes, beats, and characters are all staying. A list of your shortcomings as a writer. Maybe it's just in your head. Maybe it's an actual list. Don't let your shortcomings make you crazy. They're normal. By acknowledging them, we can make better plays.

Other needs or considerations: None.

Instructions:

1. Pick one thing from your list. It could be anything but just one thing. Maybe you compulsively write puns, but your lyric performance-poem can't really sustain them, or you want to keep them out of the mouth of your very serious antagonist. Maybe you changed a character's name in the last draft and want to make sure you've fixed each version. Maybe you spelled *theatre* and *theater* interchangeably (pro tip: I change the spelling to accommodate the venue or publication I'm planning to send material to). Maybe you just need to make sure that your color-blind character isn't misusing adjectives. Maybe you want to make sure the setup and punchline of each joke are right next to each other.

2. Whenever possible, go to the end of play (or a section of the play), and start looking for the thing from your list. While you don't have to start at the end, going from back to front decreases the odds of you following the trail of the play in your head and missing individual trees while you walk through the gorgeous forest on the page.

3. Every time you come to the thing you're looking for, give it some attention. Revise it until it's working right.

4. Move onto the next one, and repeat the previous step.

5. Repeat until you've gone through the whole play or the section you're focusing on.

Notes: This list of shortcomings will grow and change over a lifetime. At least my list has. I've shed old struggles (like comma splices) and gained bad habits (I've gotten sloppy with *it's* and *its* somehow!). Frankly, if I've just graded twenty freshman papers, my grammar is far worse than it is after I've had a first cup of morning coffee.

HOW TO PROCESS FEEDBACK FROM
WORKSHOPS, READINGS, AND DISCUSSIONS

Saviana Stanescu

Category: Processing/incorporating feedback for a new play in development without taking constructive criticism personally. ☺

Overview: Processing and incorporating feedback is an essential skill that writers frequently use and continuously refine. Novice playwrights usually have a hard time accepting constructive criticism of their work. They tend to explain their plays or stories and elaborate on the characters' dramatic intentions and choices instead of carefully listening to the audience's feedback. Defending your new play in development is not an effective way to improve it. Experienced playwrights know that opportunities to get feedback on a work in progress are crucial and try to make the most of any workshop, reading, or discussion.

Participants: The creative team (playwright, actors, director, dramaturge, stage manager, etc.) and an audience composed of peers, theatre industry professionals, and random spectators.
Time to complete: 2–4 hours, depending on the length of the play's reading or workshop, followed by discussion.
Planning time: Depending on the number of rehearsal hours offered by the theatre and/or agreed on by the participants.
Planning requirements: A play in progress.
Other considerations: None.

Instructions: Off-Broadway theatre companies like New York Theatre Workshop, EST, Playwrights Horizons, and the LARK have often used Liz Lerman's critical-response process when discussing a new work after a reading or workshop. The adapted version I use in classes and playwriting workshops incorporate the following steps:

- Community agreements: how we talk and listen to each other
- Affirmations: what was meaningful, evocative, interesting, exciting, or memorable in the work people have just witnessed
- Questions for the playwright regarding specific elements of the play: plot points, characters' choices/agendas, dramatic journeys, conflict, tone, pace, language, world of the play, cultural references, artistic statements, and so on
- The playwright's questions: the time to see if the playwright's intentions when writing the script come across for the audience
- Suggestions for the playwright: if the playwright is interested in hearing suggestions

Notes: The feedback sessions need a facilitator who is *not* the playwright whose work was shared. A literary manager, dramaturge, or instructor (for playwriting classes/workshops) could be an efficient person to moderate the critical responses. It is important to start the feedback session with creating/establishing community agreements and guidelines for the group.

Notes for feedback givers:

- Be respectful, kind, polite, and nurturing. The reading of a new play is a vulnerable moment for the playwright.
- Share responsibility for including all voices in the conversation. If you tend to have a lot to say, then make sure you leave sufficient time to hear from others. If you tend to stay quiet in group discussions, then challenge yourself to contribute so others can learn from you.
- Listen respectfully. Don't interrupt, turn to technology, or engage in private conversations while others are speaking. Use attentive, courteous body language.
- Recognize how your own social status (e.g., race, class, gender, sexuality, ability, ethnicity, religion) informs your perspectives

and reactions to the play. Practice antiracism and a language of equity and inclusion.

- Don't impose your opinions on others. Use a balanced and calm tone. Use humor. Don't be too funny—you're not there to steal the show.

Notes for the playwright who shared their work in progress: Write down the feedback you receive, and read it again the day after the reading or workshop. Let the new ideas settle. Don't rush into making rewrites immediately after the feedback session. Revise your play after you reread and reconsider the critical responses patiently. Incorporate only the feedback that you fully resonate with and the questions and solutions that are still lingering in your brain and heart.

While a structured feedback process with knowledgeable respondents is extremely helpful for new-play development, revise your work based on what feels right to *you*. You are the creator, the "parent" of this "baby" play, and you are responsible for your creature's birth and upbringing. Let it be what it needs to be. You are the one deeply connected to the work, the one who needs to cut the "umbilical cord" when the time is right. The audiences might respond to your play in the way you envisioned, or they might not. You did your best. Don't put too much pressure on yourself. Love your work. Enjoy being a playwright.

Write. Revise. Listen. Think. Feel. Play.

Please, don't forget to *play*.

5

TECHNIQUES AND TACTICS

Exercises in this chapter:

"Painting the Voice" by Ruth Margraff.
Using multiple artworks to inspire your voice.   *232*

"The Cathexis Box" by Justin Maxwell.
Imbuing mundane things with emotional energy.   *236*

"Humor Workshop" by Justin Maxwell.
Consciously using humor.   *239*

"The Metaphor Is the Road to the Simile; or, Aren't We All Trying to Make Metaphor-Jazz Work?" by Timothy Braun.
An extended exploration of metaphor and how to increase meaning.   *242*

"The World's Longest Preshow Metadisclaimer" by Kristina Wong.
Making a monologue that is also a manifesto.   *248*

PAINTING THE VOICE

Ruth Margraff

Category: Character, voice development

Overview: This exercise addresses monologue and dialogue skills. It helps you to expand the way your characters speak into more distinctive voicing. It bumps up the poetry and musicality of your style and gets formless with form and playwriting as art.

Participants: Either in a group or on your own.

Time to complete: Totally modular: can take 5 minutes (insert into your practice however you need), 1 hour (as part of a workshop advised by a teacher guiding the process), 1 week (given as homework to bring back to the group) . . .

Planning time: Minimal. You can just respond intuitively to the prompts in the moment. You can also go back and read more or listen to Fred Ho's music for context if you'd like.

Planning requirements: Learn to learn. Be ready and open to move in any new direction, to be disoriented, to work outside your comfort zone. Soundtrack: Try to find the music of composer Fred Ho (1957–2014): Big Red Media, Saxophone Liberation Front, Fred Ho and the Afro-Asian Music Ensemble (e.g., "Darker than Blue," "Warrior Sisters," "Journey beyond the West," "Night Vision").

Other needs or considerations: Print blank polyptychs to write on as storyboards. Leave room to move around and make microcabarets listening to Fred Ho's music. Access internet for the art images.

Instructions: Print out at least three of the blank polyptychs in figure 5.1 to write in whenever you get stuck. Use a new blank printout each for three of your characters: A, B, and C. If you see a word you don't know below—look it up or make up a meaning.

 Storyboard prompt: Write at least three miniature polyptych stories in wayward calligraphy or as microcabarets from the following:

Sample polyptych, adapted from the Polyptych of St. Anthony by Piero della Francesca, ca. 1470. *Photograph courtesy Wikimedia Commons user Attilios*

- Blue: Go online and look at such blue Pablo Picasso paintings *Buste de femme* (1909), *Nu à la Serviette* (1907), *The Old Guitarist* (1904), and *Les Noces de Pierrette* (1905). Write the story of the painting as baroque/cubist, with sprawling details of (your favorite city) or (your favorite landscape) as an excavation reveals itself in Venetian light. Use the melancholy humors of gray-blue shadows.
- Yellow: Go online and look at the painting *Les Hasards Heureux de L'Escarpolette (The Swing*; 1767) by Jean-Honoré-Fragonard. Write one of the "spring pictures" of your memories. Use the sanguine humors of golden sunshine in

a long and lovely day from dawn to dusk. Write a portrait of (your antagonist) as a courtesan in a sudden swing as a symbol of an unlikely affair in a wild forest. Write about a slipper that goes flying in flirtation versus more solid footing in the midst of a grand tour with a bear leader. Describe a neoclassical scene with stages of rational, moral, and high-minded conflict taking on some frieze-like geometrical warrior poses. Use a severity of tone for your great bear nude with great clarity and restraint. And then tragedy in voice and face. Then an awkward pose due to extra, hidden vertebrae in a centerfold moment. Use line over color, then color without line. Setting: awe-inspiring, uncivilized, and unspoiled nature. Climax: a sublime vortex of discordance revealing another nude's inner world.

- Red: Go online and look at the painting *Mitate no Soga: Juro, Goro, and Yoshihide (benizuri-e)* (ca. 1748) by Torii Kiyonobu II. Have your characters argue, leaping up from red thrones built from tree sap, cinnabar, and lamp-black lacquer. Use the choleric humors of red rage, excitement, and violet passion to blushed embarrassment. Reveal a shocking, based-on-something-true event that, to you, would be worthy of Delacroix's bare-breasted liberty with unshaven armpits to memorialize as political or patriotic.

- Green: Go online and look at the painting *Saint Peter in Tears* (1585) by El Greco as inspiration for a mask or masks that you imagine or make to write your characters. Write dialogue as jadeite (bright emerald green carving into spring blossoms), and then use the yellow-green phlegmatic humors of jealousy, bitterness, and bile.

- Purple: Paint the story of a ukiyo "floating world" [e.g., from Hokusai's woodblock print *The Great Wave off Kanagawa* (1831)] as "all illusion" in pursuit of fleeting pleasure. Write your benizuri-e (purple-printed) memory with rose pink and green. Write your nishiki-e (brocaded pictures). Which of your characters could have bijin-gaa (or beautiful upper-body private moments)? Write a moment of silver uwaki fickleness, a flirtation that gets disheveled in disarray, using a cloisonné enamel sort of voice . . .

Notes: I think it is the poetics of adornment that bashes me up against the glass ceiling of American realism. Why are we so afraid of pretension in the art of pretending? What are we pretending not to pretend in the shackles of formulaic realism and stifling reality-programmed seasons pumping the same narrative into us over and over? That one story we dare not get tired of! Where the hero we choose to like (because he represents ourselves) wins capitalist success by eliminating everyone else.

I came upon the Sanskrit word *alamkara* when I was in Kolkata, India, working with theatres that are part of the Seagull Foundation. I was struck by a bolt of epiphanies. It means "enough making," or an ideal ornamentation, and comes from a Hindu belief that "unadorned is not enough." Any doorway or dress or margin of a manuscript has to be embellished to be truly pure because it is incomplete unless it overflows with florid decoration and metaphor. I thought about the film *Gypsies Are Found near Heaven* and how the trills of Romani music use all five fingers on the accordion working as hard as a hand can work in facets of tone between frets of melody.

The secrets of you, your face value . . . as beloved, are unfolding now.

More marabou, in a harlequin mask.

And I think we need our masks of music and infinity.

To nude our counterfeited blasts of heaven.

These notes are excerpted from Ruth Margraff's essay "Provoca-
tion" for *The Drama Review* 53, no. 3 (Fall 2009). Humors inspired
by a workshop with Paul Zimet's Talking Band and workshops with
Maria Irene Fornes. For further exploration, please read Severo
Sarduy's "The Baroque and the Neobaroque" (1972) and chapter 3
of *Art: From Cave Painting to Street Art: 40,000 Years of Creativity*,
edited by Stephen Farthing (2010).

THE CATHEXIS BOX

Justin Maxwell

Category: Character development, cathexis, symbols, allusions,
dialogue

Overview: This exercise strengthens a writer's ability to build
cathexis, how we imbue an object (or an idea or a character) with
emotional gravitas. Cathexis makes an audience care about a thing
that they might otherwise be indifferent to. It's an invaluable tool for
both storytellers and writers working outside narrative. Moreover,
conscientious application of cathexis lets writers supercharge their
symbols, metaphors, and allusions.

For example, a baseball bat is an object that carries little intrinsic
emotional weight; however, as soon as someone is robbing an old
man who tries to keep a seemingly valueless baseball bat, we have
a narrative play. There's conflict, and the audience wants to know
why the old man cares about the bat. Then when the audience learns
the bat hit the winning run in the Little League World Series, the
bat gains more emotional energy. When they find out the batter
died of leukemia, there are stronger emotions attached to the bat.
When they find out the batter was the old man's grandson, there's
even more. An object that the audience might have dismissed in the
mise-en-scène at the start of the show is suddenly worth fighting for,

and we care who wins the fight. This is a good exercise for anyone struggling with subtext, metaphor, or dialogue.

Participants: Individual or group.
Time to complete: ~20 minutes individually or ~45 minutes in a group.
Planning time: ~5 minutes.
Planning requirements: None.
Other needs or considerations:

- *In a group:* The exercise usually starts with a brief definition of *cathexis* and an anecdote to illustrate its power, like the bat illustration. That said, if a group can be led through the exercise without knowing the individual steps in advance, then they will have a stronger emotional reaction to the outcome. They'll be surprised at just how much emotional energy fits into an everyday object.
- *On your own:* Individual writers should take a little time to think about a mundane physical object that is dear to them. Then think about what an audience member would need to know about that object to be emotionally invested in it. Writers doing this exercise on their own should skip steps 3, 5, and 7; let step 9 become a mental exercise, something metacognitive.

Instructions:

1. Imagine the lights come up at the start of a play. A black cube is the only thing on an otherwise bare stage. A character enters. Of course, a different mundane object can be substituted for the cube, especially if a character is already developed or if there's a good prop close to hand. However, for this exercise, an object with strong symbolism is counterproductive; avoid things like prison uniforms, the Statue of Liberty, a picture of the Buddha, and so on.

2. The character says the first line of the play. It is one sentence long and makes the audience curious about the box or its contents. Write that line now.

3. Read the line aloud. This is not for discussion, just sharing.

4. The character says a second sentence; it makes the audience care about the character as a person.

5. Read the two lines aloud. This is not for discussion, just sharing.

6. The character says a third sentence that makes the audience care about their relationship with the box.

7. Read the three lines aloud. This is not for discussion, just sharing.

8. Now revise. Take those three sentences and boil them down to one sentence.

9. Read the revised sentence aloud. Discuss how the sentence affects an audience. How does it make an audience curious? How does it make an audience care? How did the audience's understanding of the box (or investment in the box) change with each sentence the character spoke? How did it change when three sentences were condensed into one?

Notes: Doing the steps faster can punch up the emotional energy of the exercise but can also lead to hasty construction. Conversely, going through this exercise too slowly can cause novice writers to fret themselves into writer's block. Individuals doing this exercise should work promptly—a timer can help. Conversely, if a large group is doing the exercise, then cutting steps 3, 5, and 7 can create more time for discussion at the end, and there is always a lot to discuss with this one.

HUMOR WORKSHOP

Justin Maxwell

Category: Humor

Overview: People often assume that humor is somehow organic or unlearnable. However, when writers look at basic structures, they're able to consciously build humor into their material. Thus, an unfunny writer can still generate funny characters, scenes, and plots. It's the same process, just at a progressively larger scale. After all, humor is a powerful tool. It can make an offputting idea more palatable; it can shift the level of tension in the building of dramatic tension; it can control the narrative pace; it can characterize.

At its heart, humor is about juxtaposition. One thing is set against something else. This is an exercise to help set up different things and look at the results. Broadly speaking, we have language, action, and context to use in juxtaposition, and when the contrast is surprising, the result is laughter. This is setup and punchline. We end up with nine possible combinations with which to juxtapose and surprise:

1. Language and language
2. Language and action
3. Language and context
4. Action and action
5. Action and context
6. Action and language
7. Context and context
8. Context and action
9. Context and language

There are uncountable examples of this simple formula. One of the classic versions is a performer setting up the audience and then delivering an unexpected response as in the old Henny Youngman joke: "When I read about the evils of drinking, I gave up reading."

This joke is the simple juxtaposition of language and language. If you think about something far more complex, such as Monty Python's "Ministry of Silly Walks" sketch, the juxtaposition is between the action of Cleese's manic-stick insect strutting and the context of the seriousness of a state ministry, which Cleese sets up by talking about budget problems and the other ministries, like Defense and Finance, which are held in absurd juxtaposition to Silly Walks. While this second example is a little more complex, it still follows the same basic formula being applied here.

Participants: Just you or in a group.
Time to complete: 10 minutes.
Planning time: None.
Planning requirements: None.
Other needs or considerations:
- *In a group:* Simply conclude by having each participant read their results after steps 4 and 5, then discuss. The variety of results and the different applications of the process can be very informative.
- *On your own:* Do the following . . .

Instructions:
1. Make a list of three or four things you find to be very serious. They can be ideas, events, actions, beliefs, or objects. If this is being done in a group, then making a collective list of five or six things can be beneficial.
2. Pick one thing from the list.
3. Take the thing selected and think about ways to reunderstand, undermine, or parody it. In the Youngman example, the serious thing is the "evils of drinking," and we're set up to expect more about the problems of alcohol; however, Youngman does the unexpected and supports drinking while opposing reading.

4. A character is alone on a stage. They say the thing on the list and then they say something that undermines our expectations of the thing. If this is being done in a group, then read everyone's one-liners aloud. What do we learn about the character telling the joke? What is revealed about them? What is implied about them? What do we know about this person that they would tell this joke in this way?

5. Now try with two characters. The first character says a line that reveals the thing they value. The second character says something that undermines our expected response. How is the experience of the joke different when it's said between two people? Does it create conflict? What is revealed to the audience about the two characters?

6. The first five steps worked to make a moment of humor onstage using only language, which is only one of nine possible combinations. Because much of what happens in the script is language, it's the natural place to start. Now pick a different combination and repeat the previous steps.

Notes: For easy use, this exercise is written for two characters. However, it is easy to increase the scale. Simply replace the characters in step 5 with events in a scene or replace them with a larger plot point.

Obviously, delivery greatly influences how an audience receives a joke. However, if you can write a joke that lands even when delivered by a bad actor, then you know you've got a moment of quality humor. Similarly, don't dismiss a mediocre moment of humor on the belief that a good actor will carry the moment. It is bad faith to put the work of the writer in the hands of the actor; they've got enough to do already!

THE METAPHOR IS THE ROAD TO THE SIMILE; OR, AREN'T WE ALL TRYING TO MAKE METAPHOR-JAZZ WORK?

Timothy Braun

Category: Metaphors, analogies, metonymy, and similitude

Overview: Tony Hoagland wrote, "Metaphor is the weapon for the person who would protect himself from too much reality, or from the wrong kind of reality—it creates a buffer zone of imaginative negotiability. And it protects his right to dream, which, like all freedoms, is dangerous" ("'Tis Backed like a Weasel': The Slipperiness of Metaphor," *Writer's Chronicle*, March/April 2001). *Metaphor* in Greek means "to carry something across" or "to transfer," I think; I'm still working on basic Spanish, let alone other languages I should have studied years ago, but I believe if you go down the road of a metaphor, then it can become more than a transfer. I believe a metaphor is subjectively personal, and sometimes things can be lost in that transfer.

If we are sticking with the ancient Greeks, Aristotle would say a metaphor is the "act of giving a thing a name that belongs to something else," but that guy is dead, and in fairness, much of what he wrote about doesn't pertain to modern playwriting. (Ah, yes, I descend upon *The Poetics*, sinking my vicious beak into its pages like a starved buzzard, picking the dead flesh from what remains.)

Perhaps a healthier way to look at metaphor is to start by asking why we wish to use it? Are you trying to enliven your world building or character development? How does it function with your plot? Are you attempting to create new and layered meaning to your story? Are you, well, just looking to have fun? If you aren't having fun writing your play, then it just isn't worth it. I mean, even Anton Chekhov had a little bit of fun, and he dropped some heavy metaphors on us.

Here are some ways to explore and develop metaphors in your writing, for your own purposes.

Participants: Individual.
Time to complete: Varies.
Planning time: None.
Planning requirements: Varies.
Other needs or considerations: None.

Instructions: Let's start by talking a little poetry. I introduce this section with a quote from Tony Hoagland, a wonderful poet who is well worth your time and who used metaphors and symbols to great lengths to open his arguments. After all, metaphor is an argument. In his poem "America," Hoagland describes America as a prison with walls made from "RadioShacks and Burger Kings, and MTV episodes," which helps describe the capitalism and prerogatives Hoagland saw in America.

Metaphor works heavily in absurdist plays, as well. In Eugène Ionesco's *Rhinoceros*, the people of a small French town slowly turn into gray horned animals, which in itself is a metaphor for fascism. Now, the play is a little more complicated than that, but the point is that Ionesco was reporting, if you will, on the world he saw around him, a mob mentality that consumes the world building of his play.

Try sitting down with a notebook and a good ol' fashioned pen (stay away from a computer, as when you stare at that blank screen, it can often stare back at you, and that's no good when you are brainstorming), and make a list of things you notice in the world around you. Set a timer for two minutes, and try to write continuously. At the end of the two minutes, ask yourself, "What is a thread, a unifying factor between these things?" If we look at Hoagland's "America," then one might ask what cheeseburgers, electronics, and TV shows all have in common, and to Hoagland, it was the importance of a hollow American way of life.

What does your list look like? What is the unifying thread between people, places, and things?

Let's stick with poetry for a moment. A long time ago, I met Mary Ruefle, and she showed me a technique where she finds paperbacks of all sorts at used bookstores and thrift shops. She would black out every third word and use only the remaining words to build the poems she was writing that day. This can lead to simple yet fantastical words slamming into one another, but what about this technique when you are constructing a play? You need drama.

Start by taking a book (I like romance novels), and black out anything that is not a noun (a person, place, or thing) in the first chapter. Then, in the second chapter, black out anything that is not a verb (something providing action). Chapter 3? How about anything that is not an adjective (a describer). Now, pick one or two of the leftover words, and see what metaphors you can make from them. Add connective tissue as you see fit. Does playing with words in this manner open doorways for you? If so, how and why, with an emphasis on why?

A colleague gave me Metaphor Dice for the holidays last year. This present was meant to be a fun game we could play during happy hours, but I started using them as a challenge for developing metaphors that lead to story. I rolled twelve six-sided dice, each with a different word on each side, and chose three to build from. In this I got

Home

is a

Bootleg

Sideshow

If I were to start constructing a story from this, I can only think of characters who never had a home, that the concept of home was a joke to them.

No, wait. I can only think of *a* character who never had a home, that home was a joke.

Perhaps I can only think of a character who never had a home, that home was a joke, and now needs to be in charge of a home in some respect, and if I keep playing this game, it is only a matter of time before I might have something close to *Uncle Vanya*, a play dripping with the symbols of deforestation and despair, a play about how life just goes. Metaphors need to be personal to the writer. They need to be specific to become universal to your audience.

What is specific to you? Think of a time or a place. Can you write down five unique reasons this is specific? In playing this game, I think of Coney Island for myself, as that little pocket of Brooklyn is

1. A place of warped dreams for me
2. A place to feel the sun on my nose and breeze in my hair
3. A place where the poor can feel free, as if they own the world
4. A place where I am young again
5. A time when I was innocent

Perhaps that is the trick. Coney Island is and always will be on the edge of the world for me, a prison of games and roller coasters somewhere between hot asphalt and the sea. A few of my plays take place there, a place where dreams come close but are never met. Coney Island is also a place with Russians and seagulls.

In Chekhov's *The Seagull*, the seagull itself represents freedom and, to one character, love. There are jokes in the play, but in the end, the seagull is killed in an act of symbolism and foreshadows, dare I say, "Chekhov's Gun" (I've been waiting to drop that joke since the overview) that sadly leads to the suicide of a character, which guides me back to *purpose*.

What is the function, the purpose of the metaphor you are playing with? Answer that question five times, not repeating yourself, and you might surprise yourself. Your first and second answers are usually obvious. The third and fourth and fifth answers are the root of your metaphor, what you are really getting at. Fascism as animals. Capitalism as prison. Broken dreams as innocence. Something universal just for others. Something fun that is just for you. Find your metaphor and ask yourself why five times, and see what road that metaphor takes you down.

Notes: Metaphors are hard, and it can feel like you are stuck between a rock and an even bigger rock when trying to come up with them. Metaphors and symbols can take time. Take yours. Let "Aren't We All Trying to Make Metaphor-Jazz Work?" be inspirational to you. Someday I will change the name of this entry to "The Metaphor Is the Road to the Simile; or, Home Is a Bootleg Sideshow" but not today. I'm still looking for the right transfer point.

Home, *Bootleg*, and *Sideshow* appeared in the dice, but I also chose them from nine other words. Was it a gut feeling or my subconscious playing around with me? What words have you chosen? But why you have chosen them is maybe the most important aspect in understanding the metaphor(s) you are playing with.

A long time ago, in a galaxy far away (the summer of 1998), I was studying with a playwright named Mac Wellman, who actually studied poetry. In this phase of my life, I was listening to a great deal of Bob Dylan and Van Morrison while obsessing over the New York theatre scene of the 1960s and 1970s. Wellman encouraged me to be here, in the now, in the moment, to listen to music and read authors who were my contemporaries. To look at art of the "now." The next day I bought the album *Mezzanine* by Massive Attack, and it helped me focus on where I was instead of where we have been. In that, I wrote a play about domestic terrorism after the Oklahoma City bombings and used Midway Airport in Chicago as a metaphor for hell on earth.

Read outside of the theatre. Read everything you can get your hands on. I've dropped a few names, and I will drop a few more in no specific order: Kelly Luce, Ada Limón, Selah Saterstrom, Hanif Abdurraqib, and John Koethe are all writers that make me think about the "now." Aristotle, Chekhov, and Hoagland are fine, but they are gone. We read and write stories because we are alive, and we will all die someday, and you can't take the stories with you. Take advantage of them now. What symbols, connections, and correlations are you making with them? Let me know who you are reading. I'm easy to find.

It is important to watch movies. I refused to watch the *John Wick* movies, although I heard good things, because his dog dies in the beginning, setting off a chain of events. I don't care if humans die in movies, as long as the dogs are okay, but then my own dog passed away, and on the day he died, I turned on my TV to distract myself from the pain, and *John Wick* started to play. Wick became thunder wrapped in skin for me, a conduit for my pain. He was my own private metaphor. Now that years have passed, I've studied and written about the *John Wick* universe, and it's a murder of metaphors. I don't mean to sound like a broken record, but remember, a metaphor needs to be personal to the writer for it to have connection to the audience.

See art. I was in residence in Red Wing, Minnesota, and struggling with writing a protagonist who was on the run from his past. I needed an antagonist to fuel the plot. I went for a walk in the sculpture garden at the Anderson Center and came across a cement whale titled *Moby Dick*, and he appeared to be sailing in the sky. I realized my hero was being hunted by a giant cement whale who eats all time and space, hope and memories, an undefeatable creature of his mind, and when I looked at the main character, I realized the story was about my own regrets and fear of losing those regrets someday. As Hoagland suggested, the metaphor created a buffer zone of imaginative negotiability for me. I also killed the whale with a cement mixer. Don't be afraid to kill your metaphors.

Moby Dick is a book drowning in metaphors about obsession and revenge. It is also drowning in boredom. If you really want to see a good story about obsession and revenge, watch *Star Trek II: The Wrath of Khan*. It is literally the same story and a lot more fun. In fact, it uses *Moby Dick* as a metaphor.

And one last thing . . .

(*an email correspondence on May 11, 2023*)

Timothy Braun: Hoping to have the metaphor section of the book for you by tomorrow. I'm still trying to make this metaphor jazz work.

Justin Maxwell: Aren't we all trying to make metaphor-jazz work?

(*Braun pauses for a moment in time and space, like a buzzard eyeing a dead Greek philosopher.*)

Timothy Braun: I think I have a new title for the metaphor section.

(*The sound of the ocean and seagulls can be heard in the background, as if the water is washing away all regrets, all memories of a life that never truly was. Taylor Swift's "Coney Island" begins to play. Black out.*)

The End

Or

El fin because I'm trying to learn Spanish.

THE WORLD'S LONGEST PRESHOW METADISCLAIMER

Kristina Wong

Category: Beginnings, context, and framing the narrative

Overview: None.
Participants: Individual.
Time to complete: Varies.
Planning time: None.

Planning requirements: Writing implement (optional).
Other needs or considerations: Can be done off the cuff or written down.

Instructions: Before the show begins but at its beginning, imagine that you enter the stage as the most real unscripted version of you—the creator of the show who hasn't started the show yet. It looks to be the kind of casual way an artist might introduce themselves at the beginning of the reading—explaining where they are at in the process and what has yet to be added, but this disclaimer actually goes on so long that it's clearly the first scene of the show.

In this "beginning which isn't the actual beginning of the show," you appear to prep the audience for the scripted stuff they are about to see. You offer them directions on how to watch it "correctly" and how to take care of themselves and you in the process. But what you are giving them is a playful way for them to meet you, the protagonist, and perhaps set up a framework of rules (that you might break) in the rest of the show.

What's this inspired by?

Early on in my career, I felt that audiences had a certain expectation of what it was that my show might look like as an Asian American artist whose online presence was largely comedic but my shows were more layered and serious. I found myself having uncomfortable postshow conversations with audience members who couldn't grasp that, while I was playing a character named "Kristina Wong" onstage, I actually wasn't totally her offstage. Some audiences had a hard time shaking that I wasn't an extension of other Asian artists they had witnessed. For example, some audiences were confused why I didn't give my mother a nonexistent accent. After watching other artists of marginalized identities play with metadisclaimers in their work, it does seem like one strategy to get to greater clarity in our work and more control over our narratives.

Why do this?

What's really revealed in this long disclaimer is you, our protagonist; your anxieties; your conflicts; the rules of this world that maybe you wish existed; and a metatheatrical frame for how we understand the rest of the show. It also adds another layer to how the audience understands that the you that you'll present in the show is a character who exists with only a fraction of the layers that the real you has. But it also might give you a flexibility to critique what can't always be captured in a show.

Questions to think about as you create the material for this "World's Longest Preshow Metadisclaimer":

1. Before you open your mouth, what do you think the audience thinks they are getting the moment you step onto the stage? What cues is the audience already taking from your press material, your body, your stature to assume what this is going to be about? How much of this is accurate to the story you are going to share?

2. How have artists in your demographic before you set a misleading bar about what you will provide onstage?

3. What are your greatest fears for how an audience might misread you?

4. In your dream of dreams, what do you wish the audience would leave with after having experienced your show? What do you wish you could promise them?

5. What do you need to protect yourself from in making this work? What kind of things do you need to protect yourself from emotionally, mentally, and physically in order to present yourself emotionally and physically.

Some things that this long preface can include:

1. Apologies for what you don't like about the setup of the space and details on why it does or does not actually frame the story you are going to be telling.
2. Addressing the expectations of what your audience has of this show of you, even if these are ideas they don't actually have of you.
3. What you had to cut out of this show that you insist, for some reason, this audience know about now.
4. A list of trigger warnings that go from standard trigger warnings, like "mentions of violence, gunshots," to eerily specific new ones, "mentions of White people finding themselves in a yoga retreat, tales of teenage fandom of Scott Baio, names of exes that have not been changed."
5. Stories that come up out of nowhere that are brought up by this preface.
6. Promises (perhaps unreasonable) of what the audience can expect to experience from this show.

How to deliver this preface:
1. Casually, see what comes out of you.
2. Read from notes if you have to, but this is supposed to appear unscripted, so just sharing off the cuff works.
3. Even if it meanders, maintain the premise that, as soon as you are done getting through the disclaimer, you will start the "actual show."

Notes: None.

APPENDIX

DRAMATIC FORMAT

This appendix provides a quick guide to conventional play formatting. For a writer unfamiliar with formatting a script, the process can look difficult. Knowing that poor formatting surreptitiously marks a script as unprofessional only serves to increase anxiety about it. Fortunately, the format is neither mysterious nor particularly tricky.

There are many excellent resources for proper play formatting on the internet; however, having one close at hand while getting started can be invaluable. A writer who wants a more substantial exploration of formatting should consult the Dramatists Guild's webpage: https://www.dramatistsguild.com/script-formats. Of course, software exists that will format a play automatically; it is effective and unnecessary.

To format a play, start with a blank document:

- Put a tab stop at a ½ inch in (or however far you want your parenthetical directions) and one on the center line.
- Single space throughout.
- Use a common font, like Courier or Times.
- Use 12-point font.
- Number pages in the upper right corner. It's not a bad idea to include your name and the title in the header. Personally, I like to keep track of my draft up in the header, too.

- Before sending out a script, it should have a cover page, with the title and author centered about a third of the way down the page and contact information in the lower right corner.

While writing, keep a few things in mind:

- Delineate when new scenes and acts start and end. Inserting a hard page break after each scene makes proofreading much easier.
- Parenthetical directions should be indented. If that first tab stop is in the right place for the parenthetical directions, then it's easy to hit "Tab" once and be in the right spot.
- Stage directions should be left justified to the center line of the page. If that second tab stop is there, then it's easy to hit "Tab" twice, and the direction pops over nicely. If it's going to be a long direction, then grab the left margin slider on the ruler bar and just slide it to the center.
- One space between the end of a line of dialogue or a stage direction and the next character name.
- Character names should be in all caps and centered.
- It's a good idea to memorize the hotkey that centers a line in your preferred word-processing software. In Microsoft Word, that's Ctrl + E (in Word for Mac it's Command + E), and in Google Docs it's Ctrl + Shift + E.

It should look like this:

Act I, Scene 1

> Stage directions sit against the center line, like this. If there's a tab stop there, one can just hit the "Tab" key, and the cursor will pop over. Of course, if the directions wrap onto the next line, then grab the slider bar on the

top ruler and slide it over. However, be sure there's a hard return
after the directions so the whole
document doesn't reformat.

CHARACTER ONE
Something particularly witty.

CHARACTER TWO
(a note)
Their witty rejoinder.

End of Scene.

ABOUT THE CONTRIBUTORS

Erik Abbott is a playwright, author, actor, director, and theatre scholar. A member of the Dramatists Guild and the Playwrights' Center (former Core Member), Erik's plays include *Second Zechariah* and *#WTF Happened? On the Phenomenon of Trump*. His works have received productions or staged readings at Actors Repertory Theatre Luxembourg, Escher Theater, the Playwrights' Center, Red Eye Theater, the University of Kansas, and the University of North Carolina at Greensboro (UNC-G). He has twice been long-listed for the Eugene O'Neill Theater Center's National Playwrights Conference and is a two-time Jerome Playwriting Fellowship finalist. He has led playwriting workshops in Luxembourg, taught playwriting at the Loft Literary Center (Minneapolis), and was an artist in residence with SteppingStone Theatre in the St. Paul school system. He worked as a theatre critic for the online English-language edition of *The Luxemburger Wort* (newspaper) and has published in the academic journals *Contemporary Theatre Review* and *European Stages*.

Erik's professional theatre career dates to 1977, and he has worked on more than one hundred productions. He has a BFA in acting from UNC-G, an MFA in creative writing from Hamline University, and a PhD in theatre studies from the City University of New York (CUNY) Graduate Center. For CUNY, he taught at Brooklyn College, Hunter College, the Borough of Manhattan and Bronx Community Colleges, and John Jay College of Criminal Justice.

Liz Duffy Adams's *Born with Teeth* premiered at the Alley Theater in 2022 and moved to the Guthrie Theater in 2023. Her play *Or* premiered off-Broadway at WP Theater and has been produced more than eighty times since, including at Magic Theater and Seattle Rep. She's a New Dramatists alumna; other honors include an Edgerton Foundation New Play Award, Lillian Hellman Award, New York Foundation for the Arts Fellowship, Massachusetts Cultural Council Fellowship, and Will Glickman Award for Best New Play (for *Dog Act*). She received her BFA at New York University and her MFA at the Yale School of Drama. Adams has dual Irish and American citizenship.

Liz Appel's play *Bells like Hooves* was featured in the 2022 Roundabout Underground Reading Series. She's a 2022 Ucross fellow, 2022 Tofte Lake artist resident, and a 2021–2022 5th Floor Groundbreaker Grant recipient with Lia Romeo. She's been a finalist for the Princess Grace Award, Leah Ryan FEWW Prize, PlayPenn, BAPF, and the Ashland New Plays Festival. She was a winner of the Henley Rose Playwright Competition for Women, and an honorable mention for the Annual Parity Commission (Parity Productions) and the Hearth Theater's Virtual Retreat.

Her short play *Snow* was produced at the Old Red Lion Theatre in London, and her play *Moonshine* received a staged reading at the Cherry Lane. Her play *Remember* was published in *Blackbird*. She received an MFA in playwriting from Hunter College, where she was awarded a Roberts Foundation Fellowship. Liz is a current member of New Georges the Jam and the BMI Lehman Engel Musical Theatre Workshop. She interviews playwrights and directors for *Vogue*.

Trista Baldwin is the award-winning author of more than twenty plays, including *The Rise and Fall of Holly Fudge*, *Fetal*, *Patty Red Pants*, *American Sexy*, *Sand*, and *Chicks with Dicks: Bad Girls on Bikes Doing Bad Things!* Her work has been produced off-Broadway and throughout the United States, as well as in Australia, Chile, and Japan. A Seattle Rep Writers Group and Playwrights' Center Core Member alum, Trista is the recipient of Jerome Fellowships and a McKnight Advancement Grant. Trista was a founding coproducer of the playwright-run Workhaus Collective, producing twenty-five plays over a decade in the Twin Cities. Her work is published by Heinemann, Spout Press, and Playscripts.

Timothy Braun is a writer living in Austin, Texas. He has been a fellow at the MacDowell Colony, Djerassi, Santa Fe Art Institute, Edward F. Albee Foundation, and Ucross. His plays and operas have been produced across North America, Europe, and Asia. The *New York Times*, *American Theatre Magazine*, the *Texas Standard*, and the *Austin Chronicle* have published his essays. He teaches creative writing at St. Edward's University and serves on the board of directors of Austin Bat Cave. More at www.timothybraun.com.

Sharon Bridgforth is a 2023 United States Artists fellow, 2022 winner of Yale's Windham Campbell Prize in Drama, a 2020–2023 Playwrights' Center Core Member, a 2022–2023 McKnight National Fellow, and a New Dramatists alumna. She has received support from the Doris Duke Performing Artist Award, Creative Capital, MAP Fund, and the National Performance Network. Her work is featured in the *Yale Review* 110, no. 4 (Winter 2022); *Teaching Black: The Craft of Teaching on Black Life and Literature*; *Mouths of Rain an Anthology of Black Lesbian Thought*; and *Feminist Studies* 48, no. 1 (2022), honoring forty years of *This Bridge Called My Back* and *But Some of Us Are Brave*. Sharon's new book, *bull-jean & dem/dey back* (53rd State Press 10, 2022), features two performance novels produced by Pillsbury House + Theatre in Minneapolis in 2022–2023. For more info, see https://sharonbridgforth.com.

Lindsay Carpenter is a writer and director based in New York City and Boston. Her play *Our Black Death: Plagues, Turnips, and Other Romantic Gestures* was produced by Taffety Punk and Unicorn Theatre. Her work has been produced and developed across the country, including at the Kennedy Center, Synchronicity Theatre, the Barrow Group, Women's Theatre Festival, Fresh Ink Theatre, and more. She graduated from New York University Tisch's Dramatic Writing MFA Program and is a cofounder of Ghost Ship Murder Mysteries, which combines interactive theatre with role-playing games. She was a staff writer on the Canadian Broadcasting Corporation's (CBC) award-winning web series *Amours d'occasion*.

j.chavez (they/them) is a Seattle-based playwright, educator, and all-around theatre maker. Through the power of Red Bulls, they earned a BA in theatre from Western Washington University, concentrating in directing, dramatic writing, and education. They were crowned the unofficial title of Lil' Miss Kennedy Center and Miss Kennedy Center Continental for their play *how to clean your room (and remember all your trauma)*, which was awarded the Kennedy Center's American College Theatre Festival's National Undergraduate Playwriting Award in 2020 and the David Mark Cohen National Award in 2021. *how to clean your room* is featured in the *Methuen Drama Book of Trans Plays*, a first-of-its-kind anthology of trans plays written by trans playwrights for trans people. It's been more than two decades, and j.chavez is still chasing the knowledge of how wind works. A freelance teaching artist and puppeteer, j.chavez aims to bring joy and community into everything they do and write. Find more info on their website https://www.jaychaveztheatre.com.

Erin Courtney is a playwright and visual artist. Her new play, *Ann, Fran, and Mary Ann*, was published by 53rd State Press. Her Obie Award–winning play *A Map of Virtue* was described as "one of the most terrifying plays of the last decade" by the *New York Times*. She cowrote a musical *The Tattooed Lady* with Max Vernon, which premiered at the Philadelphia Theatre Company in the fall of 2022. She taught playwriting at Brooklyn College's MFA program and now teaches in Northwestern University's MFA program Writing for the Stage and Screen. She was a member of 13P, New Dramatists, Playwrights' Center Core Writer Group, and Space on Ryder Farm's Working Farm Group. She serves on the board of Clubbed Thumb. She was awarded a Guggenheim Fellowship in 2013.

Lisa D'Amour is a playwright, educator, and interdisciplinary collaborator from New Orleans, Louisiana. She came up in a world of ritual, activism, group spectacle, and care, all of which continue to thrive in her work. Her theatre company PearlDamour makes interdisciplinary, often-site-specific works that range from the intimate to large scale. Recent work includes *Ocean Filibuster*, a genre-crashing human-ocean showdown premiering at A.R.T. Theater in 2022; *MILTON*, a performance and community-engagement experiment rooted in five US towns named Milton; and *How to Build a Forest*, an eight-hour performance installation created with visual artist Shawn Hall. Lisa's plays have produced by theatres across the country, including Manhattan Theater Club's Samuel J. Friedman Theater on Broadway; Steppenwolf Theater (Chicago); Children's Theater Company (Minneapolis); Woolly Mammoth Theater (Washington, DC); and Southern Rep Theater and ArtSpot Productions (both in New Orleans). Her play *Detroit* was a finalist for the 2011 Pulitzer Prize and the 2011 Susan Smith Blackburn Prize. She is the recipient of the 2008 Alpert Award for the Arts in theatre, the 2011 Steinberg Playwright Award, and a 2013 Doris Duke Performing Artist Award. She is a former Jerome fellow, a Core Alum of the Playwrights' Center, and an alumna of New Dramatists. In New Orleans, she is on the collaborative leadership team of the Black and Blue Story Project.

Mashuq Mushtaq Deen is an award-winning playwright whose works include *Draw The Circle*, *The Shaking Earth*, *The Betterment Society*, *Flood*, and *The Empty Place*. His work has been supported by the The Playwrights Center, Sundance, Ucross, MacDowell, The Wurlitzer Foundation, The Bogliasco Foundation, The Yaddo Foundation, the Siena Art Institute, Blue Mountain Center, and more. His is a published playwright and essayist.

Rinde Eckert is a composer, singer, actor, director, and writer whose music, music theatre, and dance theatre pieces have been performed throughout the United States and abroad. Rinde is a recipient of the Marc Blitzstein Memorial Award for lyricist/librettist given by the American Academy of Arts and Letters. He is also a recipient of the 2009 Alpert Award in the Arts, a Guggenheim Fellowship in composition, and a Grammy Award (*Lonely Motel*). His music/theatre piece *And God Created Great Whales* won an Obie Award in 2000. His *Orpheus X* was a finalist for the Pulitzer Prize in 2007. In 2012 he became one of twenty-one recipients of the first ever Doris Duke Performing Artist Award. In 2017, he was one of five singers asked to do solo concerts in Renée Fleming's *Voices* series at the Kennedy Center.

In addition to his professional career, he has taught workshops and classes at many institutions around the country, including Juilliard, New York University, Barnard, Emerson College, Cal Arts, Wesleyan, and the University of Iowa. He was a visiting lecturer at Princeton University from 2009 to 2015.

Reginald Edmund is cofounder and managing curating producer of Black Lives, Black Words International Project, a grassroots organization that amplifies contemporary Black writers' voices from the United States, Canada, and the United Kingdom, exploring the relevance of Black lives today. He has been honored with the 2022 Gard Foundation's Excellence in Leadership Award. As a playwright, he has garnered accolades, including being a runner-up for the Kennedy Center's Lorraine Hansberry and Rosa Parks National Playwriting Awards. Additionally, his play series *The City of the Bayou Collection* has been developed at esteemed theatres worldwide. Reginald is also a company member at Towne Street Theatre, further contributing to the performing arts community.

Edward Einhorn is a playwright, director, librettist, and children's book author. He is the artistic director of Untitled Theater Company No. 61 and also of the Rehearsal for Truth International Theatre Festival, honoring Vaclav Havel. Prominent shows include *The Marriage of Alice B. Toklas by Gertrude Stein* (HERE and the Jermyn Street Theatre in London), a critic's pick from the *New York Times*; *The Pig, or Vaclav Havel's Hunt for a Pig* (3LD and the New Ohio), critic's picks from the *New York Times* and the *Village Voice*; *The God Projekt* (La MaMa), which received four stars from *Time Out New York*; *Do Androids Dream of Electric Sheep* (3LD), a critic's pick from the *New York Times*, recipient of four stars from *Time Out New York*; and *The Last Cyclist* (La MaMa), broadcast on PBS-affiliate WNET's *Theater Close Up*. Books include the recent graphic novel/script hybrid of his adaptation of *Iphigenia in Aulis*, published by Image Comics.

Jon Elston is a career educator and the award-winning author of more than thirty plays and musicals produced in Buffalo; New York City; and Washington, DC, as well as online. In 2002, Elston cofounded Buffalo's Road Less Traveled Productions (RLTP), where he ran the Emanuel Fried New Play Workshop, and supported the development of hundreds of new plays and the production of nearly forty world premieres by western New York playwrights. For RLTP's American Theatre Masters series, Elston conducted long-form public interviews with theatre luminaries Stephen Adly Guirgis, Stephen McKinley Henderson, Pam McKinnon, Eric Bogosian, A. R. Gurney,

Donald Margulies, James Rebhorn, and the legendary Edward Albee (for nearly three riveting hours).

He has taught and directed at the University of Buffalo, Niagara University, the University of Omaha, and elsewhere, and in public schools as a theatre instructor and certified English teacher. Elston is most proud of his work with Alleyway Summer Theatre, a unique annual program (now in its eleventh year) that enables young artists (ages eleven to eighteen) to write or devise and then produce their own original short plays and musicals. He also serves as dramaturge for Queen City Playwrights.

Sara Farrington is a New York City– and New Jersey–based play-wright, screenwriter, and cofounder with Reid Farrington of Foxy Films. She received her MFA from Brooklyn College with Mac Wellman. She is author or *The Lost Conversation: Interviews with an Enduring Avant Garde* (53rd State Press/TCG 2022) and a forth-coming book. Sara's plays have been nominated for two Drama Desk Awards and have been critically acclaimed by the *New York Times*, the *New Yorker*, the *Wall Street Journal*, *American Theatre Magazine*, *El Diario*, the *Village Voice*, *Lighting and Sound in America*, and NY1. Her plays include *A Trojan Woman*, *(the world ended tonight)*, *CasablancaBox*, *Mendacity*, *Leisure Labor Lust*, *BrandoCapote*, *The Return*, *Honduras*, *Near Vicksburg*, *Mickey and Sage* (Broadway Play Publishing, Inc.), *The Rise and Fall of Miles and Milo*, *Cosmicomics*, and *Lucky Breaks*. Her film *Mendacity*, directed by Reid Farrington, featuring Foxy Films, was an official selection of the 2023 New York Indie Theater Film Festival and the New Ohio Theatre. Her residencies include the Mercury Store, HARP at HERE Arts, Now-In-Process at the New Ohio Theatre, All for One Solo Collective, and Dragon's Egg. She was comanager for Foxy Films' *Tyson vs. Ali*; *Gin and "It"*; *A Christmas Carol*; and *The Passion Project*. Her work, independently and with Foxy Films, include tours to Copenhagen;

Budapest; Vancouver; Columbus, Ohio; Lenox, Massachusetts; Omaha, Nebraska; Nyack, New York; and Athens, Georgia. She has received support from NYSCA, NJCOA, Venturous Fund, Axe-Houghton, Arch and Bruce Brown, and others. For more info, see www.ladyfarrington.com.

L M Feldman is a queer, feminist, gender-nonconforming playwright who writes theatrically audacious, physically kinetic, ensemble-driven plays that are both epic and intimate. So far, her plays include *hands feet hands*; *S P A C E*; *Thrive, or What You Will [An Epic]*; *Another Kind of Silence*; *Scribe, or The Sisters Milton, or Elegy for the Unwritten*; *The Egg-Layers*; *Grace, or The Art of Climbing*; *A People [A Mosaic Play]*; *Tropical Secrets, or All the Flutes in the Sea*; and seven full-length devised works. L's work has been nominated for the Venturous Award, Herb Alpert Award, Wasserstein Prize, Stavis Playwright Award, New York Innovative Theatre Award, Doric Wilson Independent Playwright Award, and twice for the Blackburn Prize. Her work was also a finalist for the Jane Chambers Award, Terrence McNally Award, FEWW Prize, and the Lambda Literary Award for LGBTQ Drama. She couldn't be more grateful for the validation each of these has offered.

L is also ongoingly thankful to have been a Shakespeare's New Contemporaries winner, an Orbiter 3 member, a Playwrights' Center core writer, and an alum of the Yale School of Drama and the New England Center for Circus Arts. As a circus artist, L performed duo trapeze at festivals around the world. She continues to teach and dramaturge for circus artists around the country. She's passionate about theatre that *moves* and circus that *delves*. L has lived in seven cities and is based in Philadelphia, where she writes, devises, dramaturges, advocates, teaches (all over the place), and handstands (also all over the place).

Matthew Freeman is a Brooklyn-based playwright. He is a Mac-Dowell Colony fellow and New Dramatists alum. He is a 2021 Kesselring Prize recipient from the National Arts Club. His work has played at various and sundry independent stages in New York, including the Brick Theater, St. Mark's Church, House of Yes, and the Access. His plays and monologues have been published by Samuel French, Playscripts, Applause, and Smith and Kraus. His plays include *Silver Spring, Why We Left Brooklyn, Brandywine Distillery Fire, The Listeners, That Which Isn't, When Is a Clock, Glee Club*, and *The Death of King Arthur*. Freeman's audio projects have been a part of the HearNow Festival, Atlanta Fringe Radio, and Active Listening at New Dramatists. Freeman's podcasts include *Back at the Start, Places I Have Heard Voices*, and *Predictions*. Freeman is a graduate of Emerson College. For more info, see http://matthewfreemanwriter .com.

Gary Garrison was the executive director of the Dramatists Guild of America, the national organization of playwrights, lyricists, and composers headed by our nation's most honored dramatists, from 2007 to 2017. Until the spring of 2020, he was also the director of the Dramatists Guild Institute, a premier educational institution dedicated to the continued education of dramatists throughout the country. Prior to his work at the guild, Garrison filled the posts of associate chair, artistic director and master teacher of playwriting in the Goldberg Department of Dramatic Writing at New York University's Tisch School of the Arts, where he produced more than forty-five festivals of new work, collaborating with hundreds of playwrights, directors, and actors.

His plays have been commissioned by or featured at the Kennedy Center for the Performing Arts, City Theatre of Miami, Boston Theatre Marathon, Primary Stages, the Directors Company, the Theresa Rebeck Writers Residency (through the Lark), Manhattan Theatre

Source, StageWorks, Open Door Theatre, Pulse Ensemble Theatre, Expanded Arts, and New York Rep. He is the author of the critically acclaimed *The Playwright's Survival Guide: Keeping the Drama in Your Work and Out of Your Life, Perfect Ten: Writing and Producing the Ten Minute Play, A More Perfect Ten*, and two volumes of *Monologues for Men by Men*. In April 2014, the Kennedy Center instituted the National Gary Garrison Ten-Minute Play Award given to the best ten-minute play written by a university dramatist, and in the spring of 2016, they awarded him the Milan Stitt Outstanding Teacher of Playwriting in the country. For more info, see www .garygarrison.com.

Kaela Mei-Shing Garvin (they/she) is a writer, performer, educator, and new work advocate. Their plays include *Call Out Culture* (2022 O'Neill National Playwrights Conference finalist, 2021 NADIA Amplified Currents Festival, 2019 Ars Nova's ANTFest); *Harpers Ferry 2019* (2022 Know Theatre of Cincinnati production, 2021 Kendeda Playwriting Award finalist); *Tiger Beat* (2021 Bay Area Playwrights Festival, 2021 Seven Devils Conference finalist); and *The Well-Tempered Clavier* (2020 BAPF finalist, 2019 Paul Stephen Lim Award). Kaela has received six Kennedy Center Awards and has developed work with Gingold Theatrical Group, Exquisite Corpse Company, the Alliance Theater, the Road's Under Construction Lab, the Coop's Clusterf*ck, Playground-NY, and Pipeline Theater Company's Playlab. Commissions include work with Breaking the Binary Theater Festival, EST/Sloan, Montana Repertory Theater, Luna Stage, and College of the Holy Cross. Garvin is the BAPF Season 45 play selection advisor; the Tank's 2022 and 2023 Pridefest curator; and a founding member of Undiscovered Countries, a Brooklyn-based incubator of new interdisciplinary art. Kaela has taught playwriting, theatre history, and essay writing at Cornish College of the Arts and Indiana University. They currently work as the programming associate for the Tank NYC, a playwriting instructor at Freehold Theatre in Seattle, and the Literary Manager for Luna Stage in New Jersey.

Franky D. Gonzalez is a Latino playwright based in Dallas. His work has appeared with the Lark, the Sundance Institute, the Ojai Playwrights Conference, NNPN, LTC Carnaval, Latinx Playwrights Circle, Great Plains Theatre Conference, Goodman Theatre, the New Harmony Project, LAByrinth Theater Company, Ars Nova, and Dallas Theater Center, among others. A staff writer on season 4 of *13 Reasons Why*, Franky most recently won the Judith Royer Award for Excellence in Playwriting and the Risk Theatre Modern Tragedy Competition Grand Prize. He was named the 4 Seasons resident playwright, a Playwrights' Center core writer, and the Bishop Arts Theatre Center playwright in residence.

Paige Goodwin has an MFA from University of California–Riverside (UCR) with a concentration in playwriting. She has a BA in English with an emphasis in contemporary American drama from the University of Maryland. Paige's plays have been featured in the Mid-America Theater Conference and performed for the Bechdel Group in New York City, UCR's Playworks, UCR's New Play Festival, and in Maryland by the Weekday Players and Anne Arundel Community College's Theater Program. She was a member of Arena Stage's 2019 Playwright's Arena development cohort. She has been a new play dramaturge for the UCR New Play Festival and the DC and Baltimore Fringe Festivals, as well as the Young Playwrights Theater (YPT) New Play Festival in Washington, DC. Paige teaches English and playwriting at the University of California, Riverside.

David Gow's plays have been seen across the United States, Canada, and abroad (and have been translated into thirteen languages internationally), including productions in London, New York City,

Berlin, Rome, São Paulo, Tel Aviv, Jerusalem, Kraków, Warsaw, Manchester, Boston, Philadelphia, Los Angeles, Topanga, San Francisco, Atlanta, New Orleans, Chicago, Memphis, Montreal, Toronto, Vancouver, Edmonton, Ottawa, and more. David has seen dozens of productions of his work. He has near to a hundred to date and has had a production via CBC Radio International. Gow's first feature film, *Steel Toes*, based on his hit play *Cherry Docs*, has won numerous awards in the United States and Canada, including Best Feature Film (Beverly Hills Film Festival) and Best Independent Feature in America (Cine Golden Eagle). Gow's adaptation of his own material to film has found a mass audience in English and in translation. David often attends rehearsals and is involved in his productions. His work has seen major awards from the Canada Council for the Arts, the Ontario Arts Council, and CALQ.

Katherine Gwynn (they/she) is a nonbinary woman, CODA, and Chicago playwright who writes at the intersections of violence and tenderness. Gwynn is the winner of the 2022 Ucross + the Blank Theatre—Future of Playwriting Prize and a 2023 Venturous Fellowship nominee. Gwynn also won the 2015 Jane Chambers Student Playwriting Award and second place for the EMOS Ecodrama Playwrights Festival 2022. Their work has been developed and produced by Flint Rep, Jackalope Theatre, the New Coordinates, the Great Plains Theatre Conference, the Terra Femina Collective, Commission Theatre, the Fishtank, and Rockhurst University.

Gwynn was a 2021 Eugene O'Neill National Playwrights Conference finalist and two-time semifinalist, 2021 Playwrights Realm Scratchpad Series finalist, a two-time Bay Area Playwrights Festival finalist and four-time semifinalist, a 2020 Parity Productions Commission finalist, a 2020 Story Theatre Resident Playwright semifinalist, a 2019 Princess Grace Playwriting Fellowship semifinalist, a 2019 Ashland Play Festival semifinalist, a two-time New Works Festival at

Kitchen Dog Theater finalist, a 2019 LezPlay finalist, and a two-time invited submission for the Humana Festival of New American Plays.

Sam Hamashima, described as "serious whimsy" in the *Washington Post*, creates theatre with an emphasis on spectacle, surprise, and design. Full-length plays include *American Spies* (Washington, DC, the Hub Theatre, Helen Hayes recommended, 2018 Kennedy Center Undergraduate Playwriting Award, and the University of Michigan Hopwood Award in Drama, Dennis McIntyre Prize, and Roy Cowden Fellowship); *Supposed Home* (TheatreWorks Silicon Valley, Bay Area Playwrights Festival, Seattle Public Theater); *Shoyu Tell* (Lexington Children's Theatre); and *Possessing the Resurrected* (San Francisco Playhouse). Hamashima's work has been presented and/or developed by the Kennedy Center, Stanford University, National Queer Theater, Lyric Stage Boston, the Workshop Theater, and the Japanese American Citizens League. They are the second recipient of Seattle Public Theater's $10,000 Emerald Prize and are currently under commission from Chicago Children's Theatre. Hamashima is a graduate of the University of Michigan's Musical Theater Program. They are represented by DGRW and United Talent. @samhamashima

Rachel Jendrzejewski (she/her) is an experimental playwright who frequently collaborates with choreographers, musicians, and visual artists to explore new interdisciplinary and performative vocabularies. Her work has been developed and/or presented by Playwrights' Center, Red Eye Theater, Walker Art Center, Hair+Nails Gallery, Weisman Art Museum, Joe's Pub at the Public Theater, MASS MoCA, and Tricklock Company, among others. Publications include *Meronymy* (53rd State Press), *Encyclopedia* (Spout Press), and *In Which _____ and Others Discover the End* (a collaboration with SuperGroup; Plays Inverse). Rachel is a coartistic director at Red Eye. She received her MFA in playwriting from Brown University.

Leanna Keyes is a multihyphenate theatre professional. Her most well-known play is *Doctor Voynich and Her Children*. This play was published in *The Methuen Drama Book of Trans Plays*, an anthology of plays by trans playwrights that she coedited. Other recent work includes a Shakespeare adaptation called *Two Ladies of Vermont*, a tennis play about sports legend Renée Richards, and a still-in-development prequel to *Voynich*. When she isn't a playwright, she works as the cofounder of Transcend Streaming in Brooklyn, where she lives with her partner in all things, Kyra; their cat, Azkat; and their snake, ASM.

Rachel Rubin Ladutke is a produced and published playwright and director who lives in New Jersey. Excerpts of her works have appeared in numerous anthologies. Throughout the pandemic, Rachel became deeply involved in Zoom theatre, and it ultimately revitalized and informed her work. She presented both cold readings and rehearsed readings of established plays. These virtual presentations have reinforced her desire to create Theatre for Change: she organized performances to raise funds for a local Amnesty International chapter and for a foundation aiding victims of gun violence, both near her home in New Jersey. Rachel is forever grateful for the skill and generosity of many actors she calls friends, who have made invaluable contributions to her new work over the past few years. In early 2021, she kicked off the States of Play virtual series, which presents cold readings of new plays several times each month. One of her goals is to provide opportunities for her fellow playwrights to gain some of the same benefits in virtual theatre that she has found. Rachel teaches theatre at the high school level. She is a member of the Dramatists Guild, the Playwrights' Center, New Play Exchange, and New York P.A.G.E.S. and serves on the board of the International Centre for Women Playwrights. She hopes that other writers find something useful in her process of "Mapping the Story."

Ed Bok Lee is the author of three books of poetry and prose, most recently *Mitochondrial Night*. Lee's poetry has been translated into French, Italian, Spanish, Korean, and Chinese. His plays have been published by Vintage/Random House, Pearson/Longman, Smith and Krauss, Duke University Press, Playscripts.com, and have been seen at major regional and national theatres, including the Guthrie Theater, New York Theatre Workshop, Joseph Papp Public Theatre, Theater Mu, Taipei Theatre, East West Players, Trinity Repertory Company, and the Walker Art Center Out There Series. Other honors include an American Book Award, an Asian American Literary Award (Members' Choice Award), a Minnesota Book Award, and a PEN/Open Book Award. He is a recipient of the forty-ninth Modern Korean Literature Translation Grand Prize in Poetry, and his literary translations have ranged from the Russian prose of science fiction writer Anatoli Kim (Kazakhstan) to, most recently, *Smiling in an Old Photograph: Poems by Kim Ki-taek* (OHM Editions) and *Hail, Che Guevara!* by Park Jeong Dae (Black Ocean, forthcoming). Lee attended kindergarten in Seoul, South Korea; studied Slavic languages and literatures at the University of California, Berkeley; and holds an MFA from Brown University. He teaches fine arts part time at Metro State University in Minneapolis/St. Paul, Minnesota.

Young Jean Lee is a playwright, director, and filmmaker who has been called the "most adventurous downtown playwright of her generation" by the *New York Times* and "one of the best experimental playwrights in America" by *Time Out New York*. She's the first Asian American female playwright to have had a play produced on Broadway. She has written and directed ten shows in New York with Young Jean Lee's Theater Company. Her plays have been performed in more than eighty cities around the world and have been published by Dramatists Play Service, Samuel French, and Theatre Communications Group. Her short films have been presented at the Locarno

International Film Festival, Sundance Film Festival, and BAMcinemaFest. Lee is the recipient of a Guggenheim Fellowship, two Obie Awards, a prize in literature from the American Academy of Arts and Letters, a PEN Literary Award, a United States Artists Fellowship, and the Windham-Campbell Prize.

Rachel Lynett (she/they) is a queer Afro-Latine playwright, producer, and teaching artist. Their plays have been featured at San Diego Rep, Magic Theatre, Mirrorbox Theatre, Laboratory Theatre of Florida, Barrington Stage Company, Theatre Lab, Theatre Prometheus, Florida Studio Theatre, Laughing Pig Theatre Company, Capital Repertory Theatre, Teatro Espejo, the Kennedy Center Page to Stage Festival, Theatresquared, Equity Library Theatre, Chicago, Talk Back Theatre, American Stage Theatre Company, Indiana University at Bloomington, Edgewood College, and Orlando Shakespeare Theatre. Their plays *Last Night* and *HE DID IT* made the 2020 Kilroy's List. Rachel Lynett is also the 2021 recipient of the Yale Drama Prize for their play *Apologies to Lorraine Hansberry (You Too August Wilson)*. Lynett was the 2021 recipient of the National Latinx Playwriting Award and the runner-up for the 2022 Miranda Family Voces Latinx Playwriting Competition for their play *Black Mexican*. Their play *White People by the Lake* was also a 2022 Blue Ink Award finalist. They have previously taught at the University of Arkansas, Fayetteville; the University of Wisconsin, Madison; and Alfred University. Lynett was recently a staff writer for *The Winchesters* and is working on an upcoming feature.

Ruth Margraff's plays sit in the edges of opera, poetry, and art. She's been called a leader in the American avant-garde, with productions in more than thirty countries and translated into more than twenty languages. She is critically acclaimed for her six martial arts operas with Fred Ho for the Apollo, Guggenheim Museum, LaMama, Brooklyn Academy of Music, and CAMI. Margraff's writing for SEVEN began touring the world in 2008, was introduced by Diane von Furstenberg, and was featured in 2010 by Hillary Clinton and Meryl Streep at the Broadway Hudson Theater. She has received awards from Rockefeller, McKnight, Jerome, NEA, TCG, TMUNY, NYSCA, IAC, MASS MoCA, Fulbright, and more. Her work has been published by Innova Records; Dramatists Play Service; *American Theatre*; *Theater Forum*; *Performing Arts Journal*; Playscripts, Inc.; Backstage Books; Autonomedia; New Village Press; and Lexington Books, among others. She's an alum of Theater without Borders, New Dramatists, Playwrights' Center, and Chicago Dramatists and a professor at the Art Institute of Chicago.

Justin Maxwell (he/him) is a professor in the Creative Writing Workshop at the University of New Orleans. He's currently working on an adaptation of the Tennessee Williams novel *Moise and the World of Reason* into a full-length play. In 2022, he was the conference respondent for the Voices of the Earth Theatre Festival in Bemidji, Minnesota. His play *Palimpsests of Agrippina Minor* received an ATLAS grant from the Louisiana Board of Regents. His play *An Outopia for Pigeons* is published through Original Works Publishing, his play *Your Lithopedion* is published through Next Stage Press, and his collection of short plays *A Blinded Horse Dreams of Hippocampi and other plays* is published through Alligator Pear Publishing. His prose has appeared in multiple journals, including *Theatre/Practice*, *Eleven Eleven*, the *Fourth River*, *Minnesota Playlist*, *Contemporary Theatre Review*, *Rain Taxi Review*, *American Theatre Magazine*, and others. His work can be found on NPX or at www.justinmaxwellplaywright.com.

Charissa Menefee is the founder and artistic director of the EcoTheatre Lab. A multigenre writer and theatre maker, her research focuses on the intersection and interplay of writing, performance, and environmental and social justice issues. She is the author of *When I*

Stopped Counting: Poems and coeditor, with Hillary Haft Bucs, of *Embodied Playwriting: Improv and Acting Exercises for Writing and Devising.* She has been an EST/Sloan Project Commission recipient, a Tennessee Williams scholar at the Sewanee Writers' Conference, and a writer in residence with the Utah Shakespeare Festival's New American Playwrights Project and Fairhope Center for the Writing Arts. She recently directed a tour of Climate Change Theatre Action, as well as an acting company for the New Play Lab at the William Inge Theatre Festival. She codirects the MFA program in creative writing and environment at Iowa State University.

Matthew Paul Olmos is a Mexican American playwright who focuses on the creation of space for marginalized, underrepresented communities and gives them poetics and theatricality. While his work is always personal, it is aimed at reaching across socio'political boundaries, showing the ridiculousness of how separate we are, and illuminating hope for future generations.

He is a three-time Sundance Institute Fellowship/Residency recipient, Echo Theater Company Resident Playwright, lifetime Ensemble Studio Theatre member and Sloan Commission recipient, New Dramatists Resident Playwright, Playwrights' Center Core Writer, two-time Venturous Playwright Fellowship nominee, previous Actors' Theatre of Louisville Humana Festival Commission, Arizona Theatre Company's National Latine Playwriting Awardee, Baryshnikov Arts Center Resident Artist, Brooklyn Arts Exchange resident artist, Center Theatre Group LA Playwright, Drama League nominee, Geffen Playhouse Writers Room member, Ingram New Works at Nashville Repertory, INTAR H.P.R.L., a proud Kilroys nominator, New York Theatre Workshop Fellow, Oregon Shakespeare Festival Black Swan Lab, two-time Ojai Playwrights Conference, inaugural Primary Stages Creative Development Grantee and Dorothy Strelsin New American Writers Group, Princess Grace Awardee in

Playwriting, and Repertorio Español Miranda Family Nuestra Voces Playwriting Awardee. He spent two years as a Mabou Mines/SUITE Resident Artist mentored by Ruth Maleczech, was chosen/mentored by Taylor Mac for Cherry Lane's Mentor Project, and was La MaMa e.t.c.'s Ellen Stewart Emerging Playwright Awardee as selected by Sam Shepard. He will world-premiere his newest play at Steppenwolf in 2023–2024, and his work has been presented nationally and internationally, taught in university, and is published by Concord Theatricals/Samuel French and NoPassport Press. For more info, see www.matthewpaulolmos.com.

Azure D. Osborne-Lee (he/they) is a multi-award-winning Black queer and trans theatre maker from south of the Mason-Dixon Line. He teaches at New York University and the New School. Azure holds an MA in advanced theatre practice (2011) from Royal Central School of Speech and Drama as well as an MA in women's and gender studies (2008) and a BA in English and Spanish from the University of Texas at Austin (2005). He is a still-standing artist in residence at StonehengeNYC, recipient of Waterwell New Works Lab's 2021 Commission, Kilroys List 2020 playwright, recipient of Parity Productions' 2018 Annual Commission, and winner of Downtown Urban Arts Festival's 2018 Best Play Award and the 2015 Mario Fratti-Fred Newman Political Play Contest. Azure's full-length play *Crooked Parts* was published in *The Methuen Drama Book of Trans Plays*. His full-length play *Mirrors* received its world premiere, produced by Parity Productions, at Next Door at New York Theatre Workshop in spring 2020. Unfortunately, this production closed early due to the COVID-19 pandemic. Azure's new play *Red Rainbow*, a National Playwrights Conference semifinalist, received a production at Mt. Holyoke College in spring 2022 and at Tufts University in spring 2023. He was a finalist for the 2023 Terrence McNally New Works Incubator, 2022 Dramatists Guild Fellowship, Theatre Viscera's 2022 and 2020 Queer Playwright's Contest, VanguardRep's 2019 summer production and semifinalist for the 2021 National Playwrights Conference, the 2021 Doric Wilson Award, and the 2019 Burman New Play Award. For more info, see www.azureosbornelee.com.

Duncan Pflaster is a multiaward-winning indie playwright and screenwriter from New York City. He is best known for his Beckettian romp *The Underpants Godot*, which has been produced in New York, San Francisco, and Arizona. His play *A Touch of Cinema* is published by Next Stage Press and is available through their website. Other plays include *Harmony Hall*, *Nothing but Thunder*, *Malvolio's Revenge*, *Messin' with the Kid*, *Fourteen Hundred and Sixty Sketches of Your Left Hand*, *The Empress of Sex*, *The Taint of Equality*, *Prince Trevor amongst the Elephants*, *The Thyme of the Season*, *The Starship Astrov*, *The Wastes of Time*, and many, many more. His action-comedy films *Strapped for Danger* and *Undercover Vice: Strapped for Danger II*, produced by Scorpio Film Releasing, are streaming on GayBingeTV, Amazon, and Tubi. For more info, see www.duncan pflaster.com.

Bella Poynton (she/her) is a playwright, director, and theatre scholar from Buffalo, New York. Her scholarly work has been published in *Theatre/Practice*, *Global Performance Studies*, *Journal of Dramatic Theory and Criticism*, *Texas Theatre Journal*, and *Comparative Drama*. Her creative work has been published with Concord Theatricals and can also be seen in *The Best Ten-Minute Plays of 2019*, *The Best American Short Plays 2018–2019*, *The Weirdest Plays of 2020*, and *WE-US: Monologues for Gender Minority Characters*. Poynton is a cochair of the Playwriting Symposium at the Mid-America Theatre Conference, the director of the Playwrights' Wing at First Look Buffalo Theatre Company, and an assistant professor of theatre and English at Medaille University, where she also serves as English program director.

Gab Reisman's plays explore the ways place writes itself on our bodies, examining the connections between geography, history, and identity. Inherently queer and keenly irreverent, her work looks at what it means to live on the precipice of chaos. Besides her own work, Gab builds immersive and devised performances in nontraditional spaces, most recently with utopia-based trio Bender/Mars/Reisman, and her own incubator, Brooklyn Yard. Gab has developed work with Clubbed Thumb, Page 73, Fusebox Festival, Sundance Theatre Lab, and the Playwrights' Center, among others. She's received commissions from the Humana Festival of New Plays, EST/Sloan Project, the NOLA Project, New Plays at Barnard, Clubbed Thumb, and ZACH Theatre. Gab is a MacDowell fellow, an Orchard Project, Ingram New Works, I-73, and New Victory Lab alum and a former NNPN playwright in residence. Her plays *Spindle Shuttle Needle* and *Catch the Wall* have appeared on multiple Kilroys Lists and won the Holland New Voices Award. Gab has taught playwriting and theatre-making at the University of California, Riverside; the University of New Orleans; New York University; and the University of Texas, Austin.

Becky Retz pursued an early acting career onstage and in television commercials, as well as working as a stand-up comic. Her later playwriting work has been accepted by such prestigious organizations as Southern Rep Theatre in New Orleans, the Mid-America Theatre Conference, and the International Women's Voices Day. She is the coauthor of *Globe Pequot's Insiders' Guide to New Orleans* and *Food Lovers' Guide to New Orleans*, as well as *The Cake Café Cookbook*, and is a contributor to *National Geographic Traveler: New Orleans*. She also spent two and a half decades working for a local daily newspaper, where she wrote stories on dining, education, health, and entertainment, as well as penning a weekly automotive column. Becky holds a master of fine arts degree in playwriting from the University of New Orleans Creative Writing Workshop, as well as undergraduate degrees in both English literature and history.

Aaron Ricciardi writes plays and musicals about people who are unable to communicate with each other successfully or healthily, and he often covers perception, delusion, cult behavior, abuse, and triangular relationships. His work is political but accessible and funny, and it often experiments with form. His plays and musicals include *The Star Killers*, *Only Child*, *A Bushel and a Peck*, *Nice Nails*, *The Travels*, and *Hanukkah Harriet*, which is published and licensed by Stage Partners. His work has been produced and developed by Clubbed Thumb, the Playwrights' Center, the New York Musical Festival, Jewish Theatre of Bloomington, Stages Bloomington, and the BMI Workshop. Awards and residencies include Clubbed Thumb Early-Career Writers' Group, Playwrights' Center Core Apprenticeship, BMI Advanced Musical Theatre Workshop, Roundabout Theatre Company's Space Jam, and the Clubbed Thumb Constitution Commission. Aaron graduated from the theatre program at Northwestern University, where he studied playwriting under Laura Schellhardt, and he received his MFA in playwriting from Indiana University, where he studied under Peter Gil-Sheridan. Aaron is on the faculty at the State University of New York, New Paltz, in their Creative Writing Program.

Molly Rice is a playwright, experience designer, and musician who creates big, aspirational community collaborations and small, strange musicals. Molly's plays have been developed/produced in NYC and nationally. Honors and awards include Brown University's Weston Prize, Women's International Theater Festival, Princess Grace Award (finalist), O'Neill National Playwrights Conference (two-time finalist), Heidemann Award (two-time finalist), PONY Award (finalist) and nominations for the New York IT Awards, Cherry Lane Mentor Project, the Carole R. Brown Award, the Kesselring Fellowship, and Global Pittsburgh's Organizational Diversity Champion Award (2020). Favorite residencies include the Orchard Project (2017, 2020, and 2021); artist residency with the Office for Public Art and Pittsburgh's refugee population (2017–2019); Yale/P73; Tofte Lake; and the Missoula Colony (2007, 2014, 2016). Her favorite productions include *The Birth of Paper* (2021), a humanitarian theatre work involving more than sixty pen pals, makers, artists, and volunteers in Pittsburgh and Beirut, Lebanon; *Khuraki*, created with Afghan refugees (nominated for 2019 Mayor's Award for Public Art); *Angelmakers: Songs for Female Serial Killers* (54 Below, developed by WP Theater); *Futurity* (book cowriter, additional text and story) at ART and Soho Rep/Ars Nova (Lucille Lortel Award, Best New Musical, 2016); *Canary and the Agee/Evans Project*, coconceived with director Rachel Chavkin (2019 Tony winner, *Hadestown*); and *The Saints Tour*, a site-specific play occurring across the country since 2009. With director Rusty Thelin, she is cofounder and co–artistic director of RealTime Interventions. She teaches in the Point Park University MFA Writing for Screen and Stage Program; her MFA is from Brown University.

Lavinia Roberts is an award-winning playwright and educator. She is published with Brooklyn Publishers, Eldridge Publishing, Heuer Publishing, *Plays: The Drama Magazine for Young People*, Pioneer Drama, Smith and Kraus, and others. She has received productions in all fifty states and internationally in Australia, Bermuda, Canada, Ireland, New Zealand, Singapore, South Africa, South Korea, Taiwan, Turkey, and the United Kingdom. She has an MA in theatre from New York University and an MFA in playwriting from Southern Illinois University. She is an assistant professor and Murphy fellow in theatre at Hendrix College in Conway, Arkansas.

Sophie Sagan-Gutherz (they/them) is a genderqueer, crippunk storyteller who schleps around New York City occasionally donning a butterfly-covered cane. Their recent work includes *marked green at birth, marked female at birth* (Faultline Theatre, writer/actor) and *t4t, c4c* (Easterseals Disability Film Challenge, writer/actor/EP). They are a member at Greenhouse Lab (Orchard Project). Other honors include artist in residence at Fresh Ground Pepper BRB Retreat and the Barn at Lee. They have been a finalist at Williamstown J. Michael Friedman Fellowship, Soho Rep Writer/Director Lab, the Civilians R&D Group, New Georges the Jam, the Public Emerging Writers Group, and EST Youngblood. They are a two-time semifinalist for NPC/the O'Neill. Select performer collaborations include the Lincoln Center, Ars Nova, TFANA, the Public, and Williamstown. Sophie is currently in preproduction for their next short film *Possum* (writer/actor/producer).

Saviana Stanescu is a Romanian-born award-winning playwright, poet, and ARTivist based in New York. Her US plays include *Aliens with extraordinary skills, Ants* (both published by Samuel French), *Useless, Toys, For a Barbarian Woman, Bechnya, Lenin's Shoe, Waxing West* (2007 New York Innovative Theatre Award), *Kilometer Zero—The Revolution Project, What Happens Next, Gun Hill, Lab Rats, Bee Trapped inside the Window, Zoom Birthday Party, e-Motion,* and *Zebra 2.0.*

Her honors include Fulbright, NYTW Usual Suspect, EST member, Indie Theater Hall of Fame, NYSCA playwright in residence—Women's Project, TCG New Leaders, Women International Leadership, writer in residence for Richard Schechner, Audrey residency—New Georges, director of International Exchange for the Lark, John Golden Award for playwriting, Goldberg Award, O'Neill finalist, Yale Drama Series runner-up, MacLaine artist in residence, KulturKontakt Vienna fellow, Marulic Prize for Best European Radio Drama, and Best Play of the Year UNITER Award.

Saviana holds an MA in performance studies and an MFA in dramatic writing from New York University, Tisch School of the Arts, as well as a PhD in theatre from the National University for Theatre and Film (UNATC), Bucharest, Romania. She has taught playwriting and contemporary theatre at New York University, Fordham, ESPA Primary Stages, Transylvania Playwriting Camp, and more. She is a tenured associate professor of playwriting at Ithaca College and visiting scholar with the Cornell Institute for European Studies. As the founder of Immigrant Artists and Scholars in New York (IASNY), Saviana curates/hosts such regular events as Liberty's Daughters: Immigrant Women's Monologues, Global Poetry Series, and New York with an Accent. For more info, see www.saviana.com and www.savianastanescu.com.

Caridad Svich is a playwright, screenwriter, poet, essayist, translator, lyricist, editor, educator, and artivist. She has received the 2023 Flora Roberts Award from the Dramatists Guild, 2018 Tanne Foundation Fellowship, 2018 Ellen Stewart Award from ATHE, 2013 Edgerton Foundation New Play Award, 2012 Obie for Lifetime Achievement, and more. Her plays include *12 Ophelias*, *Iphigenia Crash Land Falls . . .*, *Red Bike*, and *The House of the Spirits* (based on Isabel Allende's novel). Her books include *Toward a Future Theatre* (Methuen Drama), and *Mitchell and Trask's Hedwig and the Angry Inch* (Routledge). She is artistic director of new play development at the Lucille Lortel Theater, drama editor at *Asymptote* literary journal, and editor at *Contemporary Theatre Review*.

Karinne Keithley Syers is a teacher and artist whose work spans writing, performance making, sound, song, essay, animation, choreography, bookmaking, game making, and points in between. She founded 53rd State Press, maintains an A/V web treasury at https://www.fancystitchmachine.org, and teaches independently through the Pelagic School.

Adam Szymkowicz's plays have been produced throughout the United States and in twenty countries. His published plays include *Deflowering Waldo, Pretty Theft, Food for Fish, Hearts like Fists, Incendiary, Clown Bar, The Why Overhead, Adventures of Super Margaret, 7 Ways to Say I Love You, Rare Birds, Marian or the True Tale of Robin Hood, Kodachrome, Mercy, The Book Store, Old Fashioned Cold Fusion, The Parking Lot, Night Children, Clown Bar 2, Heart of Snow, When Jack Met Jill, Stockholm Syndrome, The Wooden Heart,* and *Nerve.* His plays are published by Dramatists Play Service, Concord/Samuel French, Playscripts, Broadway Play Publishing, Stage Partners, and Original Works Publishing and featured in numerous Smith and Kraus and Applause books. His monologue book *Small Explosions* came out from Applause in 2023. He holds graduate degrees from Columbia and Juilliard and has interviewed more than 1,100 playwrights on his blog.

Alice Tuan is a nationally acclaimed, internationally produced playwright, teacher, performer and dramaturge. She is a playwright associate at East West Players, where she facilitates their yearly Playwright Group. Her play *Last of the Suns* (Berkeley Rep, Ma-Yi Theater) had a bilingual Chinese-English version commissioned and performed by the Chinese International School in Hong Kong, where she was artist in residence in March 2019. Almasi Collaborative Arts also staged a reading of this play with an African cast in Harare, Zimbabwe, in July 2019. Tuan is best known for *Ajax (por nobody)* (Flea Theater, Salvage Vangard, Melbourne Fringe, Toronto SummerWorks Festival). *Ajax (por nobody),* along with four of Tuan's other plays, are archived in the Billy Rose Collection at the New York Public Library for the Performing Arts at Lincoln Center. Other works have been produced at Humana (*BATCH*); the Foundry (*The Roaring Girle*); East West/Taper Too (*Ikebana*); Edinburgh Fringe (*COASTLINE*); LATC (*Hit*); and the University of Massachusetts, Amherst (*Some*

Asians). Tuan has taught at the University of Southern California, the Playwright Center, the Michener Center, the Ojai Playwrights Conference, University of California at Los Angeles, Cal Arts, and East West Players. Her essay "Nowhere Is Now Here" sees our current moment through the eyes of seventeenth-century dynamo Moll Cutpurse (a.k.a. the Roaring Girle) and is published in the Foundry Theater's *A Moment on the Clock of the World* (Haymarket Books). Before she was a playwright, Tuan taught English as a second language (ESL) in Guangzhou, China, and Los Angeles.

Greg Vovos is a playwright, screenwriter, theatre director, and senior writer at American Greetings. He's a two-time winner of the Ohio Arts Council Individual Excellence Award in playwriting; a Cleveland Public Theatre Nord Playwriting fellow; a Dobama Theatre Playwrights Gym member; and a Dramatists Guild member. Greg was resident playwright for the Willoughby Fine Arts Association's Theatre for Healthy Living Program, for whom he's written fifteen plays about issues facing youth today. His work has been seen around the world, translated into several languages, and published by several outlets. He's taught playwriting at various theatres and universities, including the University of Nevada, Las Vegas (UNLV); Baldwin Wallace University; and Case Western Reserve University, where he teaches today. He earned his MFA in playwriting from UNLV and a BA in English from Ohio State University. He's married to his best friend, and together they have two amazing kids and a lot of pets.

Sheri Wilner is an award-winning playwright and respected playwriting teacher who has been working in the theatre for more than twenty-five years. Her plays include *Kingdom City, Relative Strangers, Bake Off, Father Joy, A Tall Order, The End, Joan of Arkansas,* and *Hunger* and have been presented at the La Jolla Playhouse, the Old Globe, Guthrie Theater, Actors Theatre of Louisville, Signature Theatre (Washington, DC), Williamstown Theatre Festival, the O'Neill Playwrights' Conference, Bucks County Playhouse, 24 Hour Plays, the Old Vic/New Voices, and many others. Her work has been widely anthologized and published by Dramatists Play Service, Dramatic Publishing Company, Samuel French, Smith and Kraus, and Playscripts.com, leading to more than four hundred productions of her plays worldwide. Her playwriting awards include a Bush Foundation Artist Fellowship, two Playwrights' Center Jerome Fellowships, and two Heideman Awards granted by the Actors Theatre of Louisville. An established playwriting teacher, she has taught at the Playwrights' Center, New York University's Tisch School of the Arts, Boston College, Vanderbilt University, Florida State University, PlayPenn, and the Dramatists Guild Institute. She serves as associate chair and head of the MFA Playwriting Program for the Actors Studio Drama School at Pace University.

Gary Winter was a member of Obie Award–winning 13P. His plays have been produced at the Actor's Theatre of Louisville (2015 Heideman Award), P.S. 122, the Brick, the Flea, the Chocolate Factory, Defunkt Theater, HERE, and the Cherry Lane Alternative. He has received support from Page 73 (2018 Interstate 73 Writers Group), the New Group, Playwrights Horizons, Puffin Foundation, Jewish Play Project, MacDowell, and YADDO. He wrote the scenario *Pi'ilani and Ko'olau* for composer Jonathan Newman, which was performed in fall 2019 by the Florida State University Wind Orchestra. Gary received a Spielberg Righteous Person's Fellowship to study Eastern European Jewry in Krakow, Poland. He has tutored incarcerated individuals taking college classes at the Queensboro Correctional Facility. Gary was the director and cocreator of *The Scott & Gary Show*, which was included in a recent exhibit at the Museum of the City of New York, New York, New Music. He received his MFA from New York University.

Kristina Wong is a Pulitzer Prize–nominated (2022) writer, comedian, performance artist, actor, activist, and elected representative in Koreatown, Los Angeles. Following its highly acclaimed premiere at New York Theater Workshop, *Kristina Wong: Sweatshop Overlord* was a *New York Times* critics pick. Wong was then named a Pulitzer Prize finalist in drama in 2022. *Sweatshop Overlord* also garnered a veritable awards sweep in 2023, including the Drama Desk Award, the Lucille Lortel Award, and the Outer Critics Circle Award. *Sweatshop Overlord* had its premiere at the La Jolla Playhouse, is running at Portland Center Stage, and will move on to the Kirk Douglas Theater at Center Theater Group in Los Angeles. Wong's other works have been presented across North America, the United Kingdom, Hong Kong, and Africa.

Wong has been a guest on late-night shows on Comedy Central, NBC, and FX. As a published writer, her work is included in Routledge's *Contemporary Plays by Women of Color*. Wong wrote the introduction for *The Auntie Sewing Squad Guide to Mask Making, Radical Care and Racial Justice*, published by University of California Press. She also had artist residencies at MacDowell, Hermitage, Montalvo, and Ojai Playwrights Festival. Wong's work has been awarded with grants from Creative Capital, the MAP Fund, Center for Cultural Innovation, National Performance Network, a COLA Master Artist Fellowship from the Los Angeles Department of Cultural Affairs, nine Los Angeles artist-in-residence awards, Center Theatre Group's Sherwood Award, and the Art Matters Foundation. She is developing a new work during her three-year artist in residence at Arizona State University, Gammage. Other major projects include *Wong Flew over the Cuckoo's Nest*, *Going Green the Wong Way*, *The Wong Street Journal*, and *Kristina Wong for Public Office*. Other career highlights include the Visionary Award from East West Players, Local Hero of the Year nominee from KCET/PBS, Asian Pacific honoree from Fuse TV, and the Best of Arts Los Angeles issue of *LA Weekly*.

Carmin Wong is a poet, playwright, educator, and student of the arts whose artistry and teaching invokes a tradition of Black feminist praxis. She is also a devoted aunt, sister, and daughter. Carmin was born in Georgetown, Guyana, and raised in Jamaica, Queens, New York. She earned a BA in English with a minor in playwriting from Howard University. She holds an MFA in poetry writing from the University of New Orleans, where she served as associate poetry editor of *Bayou Magazine*. Her poems and interviews have been broadcast on WRBH and WPSU Radio, and her writing is featured in several print and online publications. Carmin has competed in poetry slams, and her work has taken the stage at the John F. Kennedy Center for Performing Arts, Lincoln Center, the Nuyorican Poets Cafe, the Apollo, and more. She is the recipient of artist grants from *Poets and Writers Magazine*, Scholastic, Jeremy O. Harris, the Bushwick Starr, and more. She is the coauthor of *A Chorus within Her*, produced by Theater Alliance, and *Finding Home: Adeline Lawson Graham, Colored Citizen of Bellefonte*, performed in Centre County, Pennsylvania. Carmin is pursuing a dual-title PhD in English literature and African American and diaspora studies at the Pennsylvania State University, and she teaches poetry reading and writing at Centre County Correctional Facility. To learn more about her and her work, visit www.theCarminWong.com.

Deborah Yarchun's plays have been produced and/or developed at Ensemble Studio Theatre, Centenary Stage Company, the Civilians' R&D Group, Capital Rep, the New Harmony Project, Martha's Vineyard Playhouse, Alleyway Theatre, Amphibian Stage Productions, the Great Plains Theater Conference, Jewish Ensemble Theater, the Playwrights' Center, Rattlestick Playwrights Theatre, TheatreSquared's Arkansas New Play Festival, the William Inge Center for the Arts, Jewish Plays Project, the Minnesota Fringe, Minnesota Jewish Theatre Company, Northern Stage, the Philadelphia Fringe, the Samuel

French Off-Off Broadway Festival, Playwrights Horizons' Peter Jay Sharp Theater by Young Playwrights Inc., and Williams Street Rep and at theatres and universities across the United States and in Canada. Deborah's honors include two Jerome Fellowships at the Playwrights' Center, a Dramatists Guild Foundation Fellowship, an EST/Sloan Commission, Dartmouth's Neukom Literary Arts Award for playwriting, the Kennedy Center's Jean Kennedy Smith Playwriting Award, the Kernodle New Play Award, the Richard Maibaum Playwriting Award, and Women in the Arts and Media Coalition's Collaboration Award. Her play *Great White* was an honorable mention for the Relentless Award, and her play *Atlas, the Lonely Gibbon* was a finalist for the National Playwrights Conference. Deborah is a 2021–2024 Core Writer at the Playwrights' Center and a New Georges affiliated artist. She earned her MFA from the University of Iowa, where she was an Iowa Arts Fellow.

Rhiana Yazzie is a 2021 Lanford Wilson Award– and 2020 Steinberg Award–winning playwright; a director; a filmmaker; and the artistic director of New Native Theatre, which she started in 2009 as a response to the lack of connection and professional opportunities between Twin Cities theatres and the Native community. A Navajo Nation citizen (Ta'neeszahnii bashishchiin dóó Táchii'nii dashinalí), she's seen her plays on stages from Alaska to Mexico, including in Carnegie Hall's collaboration with American Indian Community House and Eagle Project. Some of her plays include *Like the Polar Bear Mom* (Long Wharf Theatre and Rattlestick Theater cocommission); *Nancy* (Mosaic Theater); *Queen Cleopatre and Princess Pocahontas* (Oregon Shakespeare Festival and Public Theater cocommission); *The Nut, the Hermit, the Monk and the Crow* (Yale Indigenous Performing Arts); and *Ady* (Pangea). In 2023, she directed the US premiere of *Missing*, a story about a missing and murdered Indigenous woman, at the Anchorage Opera, and directed her debut feature film, *A Winter Love* (Best Narrative Feature, 2023 Minnesota Film Festival; Achievement in Directing, LA Skins Festival), which has been in mainstream and Indigenous film festivals around the globe. She is a graduate of the University of Southern California's master's of professional writing, where she produced events featuring Stephen Hawking, Herbie Hancock, and Spalding Gray. Rhiana is writing plays for the Kennedy Center and Solas Nua and Fishamble Theaters and is also a writer on AMC's *Dark Winds*.